LIGHT RAIL
TRANSIT SYSTEMS

EUROPEAN CONFERENCE OF MINISTERS OF TRANSPORT
ORGANISATION FOR ECONOMIC CO-OPERATION AND DEVELOPMENT

THE EUROPEAN CONFERENCE
OF MINISTERS OF TRANSPORT (ECMT)

The European Conference of Ministers of Transport (ECMT) is an inter-governmental organisation established by a Protocol signed in Brussels on 17th October 1953. The Council of the Conference comprises the Ministers of Transport of 31 European countries.[1] The work of the Council of Ministers is prepared by a Committee of Deputies.

The purposes of the Conference are:

a) to take whatever measures may be necessary to achieve, at general or regional level, the most efficient use and rational development of European inland transport of international importance;

b) to co-ordinate and promote the activities of international organisations concerned with European inland transport, taking into account the work of supranational authorities in this field.

The matters generally studied by ECMT – and on which the Ministers take decisions – include: the general lines of transport policy; investment in the sector; infrastructural needs; specific aspects of the development of rail, road and inland waterways transport; combined transport issues; urban travel; road safety and traffic rules, signs and signals; access to transport for people with mobility problems. Other subjects now being examined in depth are: the future applications of new technologies, protection of the environment, and the integration of the Central and Eastern European countries in the European transport market. Statistical analyses of trends in traffic and investment are published each year, thus throwing light on the prevailing economic situation.

The ECMT organises Round Tables and Symposia. Their conclusions are considered by the competent organs of the Conference, under the authority of the Committee of Deputies, so that the latter may formulate proposals for policy decisions to be submitted to the Ministers.

The ECMT Documentation Centre maintains the TRANSDOC database, which can be accessed on-line via the telecommunications network.

For administrative purposes, the ECMT Secretariat is attached to the Secretariat of the Organisation for Economic Co-operation and Development (OECD).

1. Austria, Belgium, Bosnia-Herzegovina, Bulgaria, Croatia, the Czech Republic, Denmark, Estonia, Finland, France, Germany, Greece, Hungary, Ireland, Italy, Latvia, Lithuania, Luxembourg, Moldova, the Netherlands, Norway, Poland, Portugal, Romania, the Slovak Republic, Slovenia, Spain, Sweden, Switzerland, Turkey and the United Kingdom. (Associate Member countries: Australia, Canada, Japan, New Zealand, the Russian Federation and the United States. Observer countries: Albania, Morocco.)

Publié en français sous le titre :
LES SYSTÈMES DE MÉTROS LÉGERS

TABLE OF CONTENTS

Part one

Part Two

Part One

EXECUTIVE SUMMARY AND CONCLUSIONS

I. EXECUTIVE SUMMARY AND CONCLUSIONS

1.1 Introduction

In recent years there has been an upsurge of interest in the ECMT Member and Associated countries in building new urban Light Rail Transit Systems (LRT) and extensions to existing ones. Many urban areas that did not have the size and density for conventional heavy urban rail systems have considered light rail transit as an attractive alternative. LRT systems are less expensive than heavy metro systems but nevertheless entail substantial transportation investments for urban areas and the organisations that finance them.

National and local governments are, therefore, concerned about the appropriate role of light rail transit systems in providing transport in urban areas (as well as other concerns related to the environment and livability of these areas). They are interested in the economic performance of these systems and the factors and conditions which affect that performance.

In light of this current interest in and concern for LRT and the large amount of resources being dedicated to light rail systems, the Urban Transportation Coordinating Group carried out a study with the following objectives:

a)   to trace the development of LRT in ECMT participating countries;

b)   to review current trends in LRT;

c)   to identify current economic, financial and broader social policy issues and concerns in LRT; these broader social issues were to include environmental considerations as well as safety, congestion relief and urban structure and planning questions;

d)   to analyse the cost-effectiveness of light rail systems in the context of broader social policy issues and concerns;

e)   to determine the conditions that affect the economic performance of LRT and make LRT more successful.

Information for this study was obtained from six countries: France, Germany, the Netherlands, Switzerland, the United Kingdom and the United States. The participating countries represented a sample of ECMT countries in general. Each prepared overviews of their existing and proposed light rail systems. These were supplemented from other data sources, particularly the International Union of Public Transport (UITP), which joined the ECMT Coordinating Group as an active participant throughout the study. Moreover, each participating country undertook an analysis of one of its own new LRT systems. A consistent framework for the case studies covering data to be assembled and analyses to be performed was developed and agreed upon. The framework defined seven analytical

7

areas with issues and concerns to be addressed. A set of data items and performance ratios were developed to provide the basic tools for analysis of the issues. The analytical areas, issues, and data items defined a minimum foundation for analysis. Participating members were successful in applying this framework to these individual situations, thereby permitting the comparability of results and the synthesis of findings and conclusions.

Each of the case studies selected by the participating countries was evaluated across a wide range of performance measures including those that measure patronage, cost-effectiveness and cost-efficiency. It was not the purpose of this study to select the "best" of these LRT systems. Rather, the purpose was to ascertain from analysing these systems generally applicable conclusions that could be used in planning and implementing future LRT systems.

The results from all of these studies and analyses were synthesized to produce the conclusions and recommendations. In addition, discussions were held on the policy issues to identify those that were important and the implications of the analyses for these issues. The policy conclusions reflect the consensus of the national delegations participating in this study.

1.2 Recent developments in Light Rail Transit systems

In the six countries participating in this study, LRT systems have enjoyed strong support during the last fifteen years. Most large cities in the former West Germany never abandoned their tram systems and began during the 1960s to upgrade them to full LRT systems by building tunnels, buying large capacity vehicles, and integrating them with other travel modes. Trams have remained popular in the former East Germany, but have generally not been upgraded and will require substantial new investment.

Trams passed into virtual extinction in France and the United Kingdom in the early 1970s, but by the end of the decade LRT was receiving new attention. Since then, new French systems have been built in Grenoble, Nantes and Paris and a new British system has opened in Manchester. Additional urban LRT systems are planned or proposed in both countries. The British seek to route LRT on under utilised railroad rights of way and the French are designing their systems to be the focal points of downtown urban development.

After declining to seven systems in the 1970s, LRT in the United States enjoyed a resurgence during the 1980s. Old systems were reconstructed or extended and new lines were opened beginning with the San Diego Trolley in 1980. Between 1980 and 1992, the number of LRT systems in the United States doubled from seven to fourteen and additional service is planned.

Trams have continued to operate in several large cities in the Netherlands and since the late 1970s the Dutch government has regarded LRT as one solution to the transportation need of smaller "satellite" cities to connect the Central Business District with the suburbs. In Switzerland, trams remain in a number of large cities and electrically powered regional rail lines operate throughout the country. Many of the regional lines have been modernised with light rail vehicles and a completely new LRT system has recently opened in Lausanne.

1.3 Current innovations in Light Rail Transit systems

Technical and managerial innovations have emerged as means of improving the transit service provided to patrons while maintaining the cost and location advantages of LRT. In most cities, efforts have been made to furnish accessible service to the disabled through the use of technology such as lifts, ramps, high-level station platforms and low-floor vehicles. Safer and faster transport has been sought in a number of cities by increasing the level of new route segregation (without expensive tunnelling, where possible) and by giving LRT vehicles signal priority where they intersect with other travel modes. Throughout Europe and the United States, barrier free automated fare purchase with random inspection has become a common way to quicken service and make LRT more attractive. Completely automated service has also been attempted in a few cities, although such operation is difficult and less cost-effective than expected because it requires 100 per cent route segregation. Some countries have tried to reduce costs while meeting service needs by developing standard vehicle designs, but so far no dominant design has emerged and competition continues.

Managerial innovations have improved service while minimising costs. The simple fare systems now used by most LRT operators, such as zone-based and flat rates, ease passengers' price calculations and increase travel on some routes, and, as noted above, rely on honour-based purchase in order to ease passenger movement, limit personnel costs, and reduce construction costs by eliminating station access barriers. Cost-effective route design and segregation has been sought through the redesign and use of a system's existing right of way (including some tunnels), or the acquisition of previously-assembled rail routes. A few LRT operators have tried to reduce personnel expenditures, which represent a large proportion of operating costs, by increasing flexibility and decreasing required quantities of labour through open shops, flexible task assignment, part-time employment and outside contracting. Innovative personnel policies face stiff resistance from workers, but are likely to continue given the high cost of providing LRT service. All operators work to integrate LRT service with other travel modes through such mechanisms as electronic communication systems feeder and radial bus networks, links to heavy rail routes and highways and convenient mode transfer stations. In most cases, LRT is intended to serve as the primary public transportation mode in the central city.

1.4 Issues and concerns in Light Rail Transit development

Urban areas that undertook the development of LRT had specific issues and concerns they were seeking to address. The goals and objectives for the LRT systems studied were similar. LRT systems were undertaken to achieve several goals:

a) to increase mobility through the increased usage of public transportation;

b) to reduce the use of private vehicles by diverting passengers to public transportation;

c) to supplement automobile disincentive measures, and make them more acceptable;

d) to reduce transit subsidy levels as a result of higher passenger densities;

e) to reduce air pollution and energy consumption, through the reduction in private vehicle use;

f) to reduce the number of automobile accidents;

g) to generally improve urban environments so that they are more livable and environmentally benign;

h) to support central city revitalisation as part of an overall plan; and

i) to contribute to the economic stimulation of less developed regions of a country.

It was anticipated that light rail systems would attract more automobile users and provide more capacity than bus. LRT was selected rather than heavy rail because it was less expensive, could be justified with lower demand and because it was believed that heavy rail systems could be justified only in the largest metropolitan areas. LRT was considered to have a better image than buses and to be more suitable for integration into the city.

1.5 Cost-effectiveness of Light Rail Transit systems

The new LRT systems met many of the expectations of the planners and decision-makers. The systems attracted increased patronage and the costs were usually within expectations, even though they were higher than forecast in a number of instances. In one city, it was found that riders on the LRT system had higher automobile ownership rates than those using buses, indicating the ability of LRT systems to attract a greater number of choice users.

Nevertheless, the major overall objectives of significantly reducing total automobile usage and the congestion and negative environmental impacts in the cities were not achieved. All case study areas reported that in spite of the major investment in these LRT systems which may have attracted trips that were formerly made by automobile and which initially reduced congestion, automobile ownership and travel continued to grow and to cause additional congestion, pollution, accidents, noise, and energy consumption.

In order to be cost-effective, LRT systems must attract fare paying riders. In most cities studied, boardings and passenger kilometres per vehicle revenue kilometre (load factor) grew substantially during the years immediately following commencement of LRT service. A number of cities also reported that 10-15 per cent of drivers were diverted from their cars by LRT and that many bus riders switched modes. But long-term results have not been uniformly good; total rail ridership after a number of years of LRT service declined in one city and the transit proportion of total trips decreased in another. Because travel monitoring varies substantially by country in both detail and frequency, it was difficult to determine how well buses have been replaced and auto travel discouraged by LRT.

As noted above, LRT was generally selected instead of heavy rail because of its lower capital and operating costs and lower patronage required to justify investment. Capital costs per unit of service provided by the LRT systems varied substantially. Where completely new systems were constructed and important components (for example, right of way and track) were sited or assembled from scratch, such as in Grenoble, Nantes and San Diego, capital costs were relatively high. Where some portion of the proposed system (for example, right of way, stations, or catenary) already existed, capital costs were much lower. These cases suggest that LRT systems constructed based on some existing components may be less expensive. However, use of existing right of way or existing facilities might also limit the long-term cost-effectiveness of a system by forcing the use of routes that may not best serve a city's existing travel patterns and future needs and therefore may be less cost-effective than other alternatives.

10

Operating costs also varied, over a three-fold range from high to low. Per trip costs tend to be lower on systems with shorter trip lengths, but because of the dramatic differences in trip lengths among the systems studied, these figures do not provide a comparable indicator of efficiencies of service output. Costs per vehicle revenue kilometre ranged in 1989 from less than $2.5 in San Diego to more than $5.00 in Stuttgart, suggesting substantial variation in the efficiency with which LRT service is provided. Costs per passenger kilometre ranged from $0.07 in Nieuwegein and San Diego to $0.20 in Bern, which indicates differences in both appropriateness of service and levels of patronage. Without complete cost and ridership data and comparable ridership and fare expectations, however, assessments of operating costs were difficult.

Examination of combined capital and operating costs allows undistorted comparisons of LRT service efficiency and effectiveness. In the countries studied, total costs were generally lower on improved LRT routes than on entirely new systems. Long average trips also corresponded to higher costs per trip than short trips. Incomplete passenger kilometre data prevented a thorough analysis of combined LRT system costs.

Procedures for selecting LRT projects for construction varied but were for the most part not rigorous, with the notable exception of the United Kingdom which has a rigorous appraisal selection process. The United States has a formal and fairly rigorous process for selecting projects that use federal funds, but the San Diego LRT system was built with only State and local funds.

In general, analyses ranged from assessments of strict financial benefits and costs to assessments of broader benefits and costs related to amenities, air pollution, travel times and other more complex factors. These analyses, however, were often overwhelmed by other issues. Some local authorities simply regarded new transit facilities as essential to the development and status of their cities, in which cases alternatives analyses were generally no more than pro forma exercises. LRT systems were sometimes simply selected regardless of the degree of analysis, as the mode providing more capacity than buses at lower cost than heavy rail or metro systems.

For the most part, LRT systems were encouraged to operate in an efficient manner by recovering the bulk of their operating expenses through fares rather than general public subsidies. Many of the systems had cost recovery policies, some as high as 100 per cent. Some had no policy at all. The Netherlands, Switzerland and the United States provide central government assistance for operating expenses. Integrated fare systems make analysis of the separate effect of the cost recovery of LRT difficult because of the lack of data.

In all cases, national governments provide a significant share of capital investment funding for LRT projects ranging from 30 per cent in France to 80 per cent in the Netherlands. The local share of these projects is often supported by a dedicated tax or other revenue source. Recently, there has been an attempt to recover part of the cost of these projects from the private sector especially beneficiaries of the system. In no instances have the capital investment funds been recovered from transit patrons.

All of the urban areas recognised that it was not the primary objective of the LRT systems to cover operating costs from the farebox and that operating revenues would certainly not cover the capital investment cost. Although all of the systems attempted to operate in an efficient manner, they traded some financial gain to achieve social and environmental objectives. By not charging the full cost of transit service to the patrons, LRT systems sought to increase ridership and reduce the use of automobiles. To the extent that these systems achieved higher patronage, they contributed to lower traffic congestion, air pollution, accidents, noise and energy consumption.

Another important objective for LRT systems was to improve safety. Although this study does not report safety performance for each LRT system reviewed, LRT operators seek to demonstrate the safety advantages of their systems relative to other modes. A 1992 study by D.A. Walmsley of Great Britain's Transport and Road Research Laboratory suggests that well-designed LRT systems offer a number of safety advantages. On average, LRT systems have higher accident rates per vehicle kilometre but lower rates per passenger kilometre that buses. Moreover both LRT and buses are safer than automobiles.

Additionally, in response to governmental mandates, many of the LRT systems are becoming accessible to elderly and disabled persons. These mandates were reflected in the design and operation of LRT systems. Although such accommodations increased the cost of LRT systems, they were considered an acceptable and important social objective.

1.6 Conditions affecting the success of Light Rail Transit systems

LRT systems are expensive and time consuming undertakings. There is a strong interest in ensuring that they are cost-effective and successful in achieving the objectives established for them. Even though many central Governments have decentralised decision-making for urban transportation, they still provide large amounts of financing for constructing and, in some instances, operating LRT systems. Data from this study was limited because most urban areas did not perform thorough assessments of the impacts of LRT systems. Nevertheless, this study found a number of factors that contributed to and reinforced the success of these LRT systems.

As with other categories of transit, the usage and effectiveness of LRT systems increased with the population and density of the urban area. Although no threshold figures were found, LRT systems perform better in areas where there was significant traffic congestion and compact development densities.

Careful analysis and planning contributed to the success of LRT projects. This includes the establishment of clear objectives, identification of a range of alternatives to achieve these objectives such as LRT, heavy rail, buses, and traffic management measures, analysis of the overall benefits and costs of each alternative, conducting a financial analysis, and determining the supporting policies and actions to implement.

More effective results were achieved where the construction of a LRT system was part of an overall plan of central city revitalisation. Greater impact on congestion was achieved where parking controls, higher prices on automobile usage and parking and other restraints on automobiles were implemented with the LRT system. Supporting land use measures were needed to achieve desired development impacts. LRT systems were less effective where they were implemented independently of other policies and development programmes in the urban area.

LRT systems provide improved speed and service on line haul portions of trips. These systems were more effective in attracting passengers where the access portions of the trips were well served and integrated into the overall systems. In several urban areas, bicycle was an important access mode and provision was made for good access and parking for bicycles.

Higher speeds contribute to greater patronage and better service. This was achieved by the provision of separate rights of way where possible. These separate rights of way come at an additional cost for grade separations and right of way. Additionally, higher speeds and better reliability were accomplished by allowing LRT system vehicles to have signal priority, thereby reducing delays. There is also an operational trade-off between headways and load factors. Shorter headways provide shorter waiting times which attract more passengers. However, with more vehicles traversing a line, load factors can decrease.

Lower vehicle costs were sought by several urban areas. A number of strategies were employed to achieve this reduction. Several countries developed uniform vehicle design standards to reduce costs. Others combined vehicle purchases for more than one urban area to obtain lower prices per unit. A third strategy was to increase the competition in bidding for vehicle procurements.

This study found that the level of monitoring and evaluation was limited. In only one instance there was a formal and rigorous appraisal process to determine the effects of the LRT project. Considering the high cost of these systems, it is important to evaluate their effectiveness. More complete monitoring of the final costs, patronage, and impacts of LRT systems needs to be carried out to provide the information for a thorough evaluation of their cost-effectiveness and success.

II. INTRODUCTION -- OBJECTIVES FOR STUDY

In recent years there has been an upsurge in interest among the ECMT Member and Associated countries in building new light rail transit (LRT) systems and extensions to existing systems. In the last decade significant numbers of public transport operators in OECD countries have invested in new light rail systems. Large numbers of other operators are planning new light rail investments, or evaluating alternatives that include light rail.

2.1 Recent Light Rail developments

Since 1978 LRT extensions have been completed for four of the five current systems in Belgium, three of the four in the Netherlands and Switzerland, two of four systems in Sweden, and fourteen systems in the Federal Republic of Germany. In Europe, new systems have been constructed in Grenoble, Lille, Manchester, Nantes, Utrecht and Valencia. New systems are under construction or authorized in Sheffield, Genova, and Lausanne.

In North America, new systems have been constructed in the last ten years in Calgary, Edmonton, Vancouver and San Diego.

The Urban Transport Coordinating Group of the European Conference of Ministers of Transport (ECMT) has undertaken a report on the economic and other performance of LRT within six ECMT Member or Associated countries (the Federal Republic of Germany, France, the Netherlands, Switzerland, the United Kingdom, and the United States). This report provides participants with an opportunity to reflect on their national experiences with LRT over a decade in which OECD countries have made substantial investments in light rail.

The report is intended to encourage the exchange of international information on the results of recent light rail investments, and on plans for new projects. The report describes innovative technological and economic trends in light rail operations, and applies a standardized framework in case studies analysing the economic and other performance of a selected set of systems in each participating country. The report should assist Ministry officials and public transport operators to make informed decisions on investments in LRT or alternatives.

2.2 Overview of the report

The report begins by discussing the resurgence of light rail in OECD countries and providing an overview of existing and proposed LRT systems in the six participating countries. These systems are described using economic, supply, ridership, and other basic operating characteristics, with a focus on significant technological, managerial, and economic trends.

The report applies a standardized technical framework in case studies analysing the economic and other performance of new LRT systems or extensions in each participating country. These case studies are contained in Part two, Section 1. The case studies are then synthesized to produce general findings. Based on insights from the overview and case studies, the report concludes by analysing the policy and management issues raised by new LRT systems.

2.3 Definition of Light Rail Transit

Definition of light rail transit can be a matter of controversy in the international public transport industry. For the purposes of this report, a flexible rather than rigid definition will be applied. Rather than debating the correct classification of a system with characteristics of more than one mode, the report identifies and analyzes innovative applications of systems with some LRT characteristics.

As defined by the Light Rail Transit Subcommittee of the Transportation Research Board (US), light rail is "a metropolitan electric railway system characterized by its ability to operate single cars or short trains along exclusive rights-of-way at ground level, on aerial structures, in subways, or occasionally, in streets, and to board and discharge passengers at track or car floor level."

The importance of flexible definitions is apparent in considering characteristics of some systems to be discussed in this report. For example, to the extent that a system utilizes exclusive rights-of-way, with no grade crossings, and elevated structures or subways, it can be considered rapid rail. And to the extent that a system operates in mixed street traffic, it is usually considered a tramway or streetcar. Light rail systems fall in-between, and can combine characteristics of modes.

Although the Grenoble system runs at grade, as do tramways, it can be considered LRT because it is segregated from automobiles through barriers, slight rises above the road, and operation in pedestrian malls, and has other distinguishing characteristics.

At the other end of the spectrum, the Edmonton, Alberta (Canada) LRT system uses suburban rail tracks and new tunnels in a totally segregated right-of-way. Edmonton, however, is sometimes considered to be LRT because of other characteristics, including operating LRT-type vehicles singly or in pairs.

Some analysts distinguish between **tramway**, which primarily operate in mixed traffic with crossings, and **light rapid transit**, which has capacity, power, speed, and other characteristics that differ from rapid rail, but is totally segregated from traffic and **modern light rail**, which can clearly be distinguished from tramway and rapid transit, but may share some characteristics with each.

14

In another exception to the general definition, the Dutch have constructed two systems and are working on a third connecting satellite suburbs to major urban centers. Although this is contrary to the general definition that service be to urban centers, the Dutch systems have other LRT characteristics.

The definition of light rail used in this report is as follows:

A rail-borne form of transportation which can be developed in stages from a modern tramway to a rapid transit system operating on its own right-of-way, underground, at ground level or elevated. Each stage of development can be the final stage, but it should also permit development to the next higher stage.[1]

This definition allows older tram systems, even those operating primarily in mixed-traffic with no grade separation, to be included in this overview.

Light rail is distinguished from metro systems (also called rapid rail), which can be defined as follows:

Transit service using rail cars with motive capability, driven by electric power usually drawn from a third rail, configured for passenger traffic and usually operated on exclusive rights-of-way; service generally utilizes longer trains and station spacing than light rail.

Also not covered by this report are automated guideway systems which are defined as follows:

One or more automatically controlled vehicles operating over an exclusive guideway.

The lines of definition between these three modes can sometimes be cloudy. Both light rail and heavy rail can use high platform stations, but only light rail generally uses low platforms. Some metro systems use overhead wire to supply power instead of contact (third) rail, but it is very unusual for light rail to use contact (third) rail. Both metros and light rail systems can use automated technology.

III. INTERNATIONAL OVERVIEW OF EXISTING AND PROPOSED LIGHT RAIL SYSTEMS

Each of the six participating OECD countries has a number of existing LRT systems and new systems under consideration in large metropolitan areas. This section describes general trends in the development and use of LRT in each country, and identifies and describes management and technological innovations that have been implemented. Information for the following section was drawn from case studies of new LRT systems and detailed overviews of trends in four of the countries studied, which are compiled in Part 2, Section I. The discussion is supplemented by a summary of basic operating and financial data presented in Part 2, Section II.

3.1 Summary descriptions of current and proposed systems - By country

The Netherlands

Prior to the 1950's, there was a large number of local and regional tramways in the Netherlands. Some of the trams shared characteristics with modern light rail systems. In the 1950's and 1960's nearly all Dutch regional trams were abandoned, as were those in the U.S., France, and Great Britain. The only surviving regional system from this period is in The Hague, and it operates as an urban circulator and connector to Delft. In addition, urban street trams continue to operate in Amsterdam and Rotterdam.

The rebirth of light rail in the Netherlands occurred in the 1960's and 1970's, when public authorities sought ways to connect new satellite towns to major "donor" urban centers. This is noteworthy because it contradicts the conventional wisdom that light rail is most effectively applied within urban centers. During this period proposals were made to use light rail to connect Zoetermeer to The Hague, the eastern suburbs to Rotterdam, Nieuwegein to Utrecht, and Amstelveen to Amsterdam. Heavy rail was the final choice for Zoetermeer, but light rail was selected for the other suburbs. LRT is currently considered a major contender for the connection between Uithof and Utrecht.

France

Most French cities abandoned tram operations in the years following World War II. Small-scale tramway operations continued in Lille, Marseille, and St. Etienne. New light rail systems were built in Nantes (1985) and Grenoble (1987). The development of these systems originated in 1975, when the State Secretariat for Transport commissioned nine of the most populous conurbations (excluding Paris, Lille, Lyons, and Marseilles) to develop specifications for new tramway-type rail systems. The Secretariat also held a competition to promote light rail transit in France by selecting a single standard specification for light rail equipment. The standard design is intended to be marketed to other French and foreign operators. Nantes was the first operator of the French standard tram, while Grenoble operates an accessible, low floor version.

Light rail has recently been introduced in the suburbs of Paris, using equipment identical to that found in Grenoble. New equipment for Lille, however, is coming from the Italian manufacturer Breda. Strasbourg is currently constructing a new light rail system, which will use vehicles manufactured by ABB/Socimi, also of Italy.

In addition to promoting the development of light-rail, French transport and railway industries have developed the VAL automated light metro system, built by Matra. VAL systems have competed with light rail designs in several French cities. Lille constructed the first VAL system, Toulouse is constructing one, while Bordeaux and Rennes have chosen to build one. Nice has considered a VAL system.

Great Britain

As in France and the United States, almost all cities in Great Britain abandoned tram operations in favour of motor bus service in the years following World War II. Only Blackpool continued to operate trams.

Interest in light rail systems has grown rapidly in the last few years in Great Britain. The earlier perception was that the technologically-advanced heavy rail systems proposed during the late 1960's and early 1970's were unacceptably expensive in the economic climate during that period. Light rail offered the option of using existing, often dormant, British Rail rights-of-way in urban areas where rail corridors were available.

Light rail systems are operating in Manchester (1992), and a system is under construction in Sheffield. Plans for new systems are under study in Birmingham (Midlands Metro), Croydon, Leeds, Nottingham, South Hampshire and other cities.

United States

The earliest light rail systems, combining street tramway with partial grade separation, first appeared in Boston (1897), with service from the urban centre to suburbs, Philadelphia (1905), Rochester (1927, abandoned 1956), and Newark (1935). These systems supplemented numerous other street tramways that were abandoned in the 1950's and 1960's. In 1978, tram operations remained in seven U.S. cities: Boston, Newark, Philadelphia, Pittsburgh, Cleveland, New Orleans, and San Francisco.

As in many of the European countries, there has been a significant resurgence in LRT investment in the last decade. A new system has been constructed in San Diego and another new line will soon open there.

Other cities have made substantial investments to upgrade older light rail systems. In conjunction with the opening of the BART rapid rail system in San Francisco in 1972, a second level tunnel was added for the existing tramway, which runs from the city centre to provide on-street, mixed traffic service in residential areas. With Federal funding and encouragement, San Francisco and Boston sponsored a combined purchase of advanced technology light rail vehicles from a subsidiary of Boeing, an aerospace manufacturer. The attempt to establish a U.S. light rail manufacturing business ended after both systems experienced substantial vehicle reliability problems.

Germany

Unlike the United States, France, and Great Britain, Germany maintained tram service in most of its large cities and in many smaller cities.

In the former West Germany, light rail and/or tram systems are operated in more than 25 cities. Since the early 1960's, many of these systems have been updated from tram to light rail standards. Tunnels have been constructed in downtown areas, 1 000 mm gauge track has been converted to standard (1 435 mm) gauge in some areas, and efforts have been made to separate rail and auto traffic. The rail vehicle fleet has been constantly updated, and large articulated cars have replaced antiquated stock, with recent efforts focusing on developing accessible low-floor technology.

More than 25 tram systems operate in the former East Germany. Few, if any, of these systems have been developed to light rail standards, and much of their infrastructure (track, wire, and vehicles) is in need of replacement.

Throughout Germany, light rail and tram lines are the backbones of many transit systems in large and small urban areas. The best example is Frankfurt/Main, where 88 per cent of all public transit journeys are on light rail. The only large German cities where light rail is not an important part of the public transport system are those with full-scale metros (München, Nurnberg, Hamburg and Berlin). In München and Nurnberg, trams carry less than 30 per cent of all public transport riders. In Hamburg and the former western section of Berlin, trams have been abandoned entirely.

Switzerland

Like Germany, Switzerland has maintained tram service in larger urban areas and some rural areas. According to Jane's Urban Transport Systems, the Swiss cities of Basel, Bern, Bex, Geneva, Neuchatel, and Zürich have maintained tram service. Electrified regional rail operations, some having characteristics of light rail, operate throughout Switzerland. Lausanne has recently opened a new light rail line. Unlike the metre-gauge trams found in older Swiss urban operations, the Lausanne light rail line operates mostly on a segregated right of way.

3.2 Technical innovations

Accessibility

In the United States, all light rail systems built since 1978 are accessible to mobility-impaired riders under the Uniform Federal Accessibility Standards. Recent legislation (the Americans with Disabilities Act of 1990, or ADA) raised these standards and requires almost universal accessibility. Under ADA, people with hearing, visual or motor impairments cannot be discriminated against in employment or public service, including public transport. For example, all light rail systems must now provide at least one car per train and designated key stations that are accessible. Currently, all accessible light rail systems in the U.S use either car-mounted lifts, platform way-side lifts, platform ramps, or high level platforms.

The Grenoble system in France pioneered the use of low-floor technology to gain accessibility, and the equipment used in Nantes has been modified with new low-floor middle sections. New equipment for mature tram operations in Lille, Marseille, and St. Etienne is of low-floor design. New light rail lines being built in Strasbourg and Paris will also use low-floor equipment.

In Germany, many tram systems that have been converted to full light rail standards use high platforms to speed loading and unloading. If the platforms are accessible from the streets by ramps, then the systems are accessible to those in wheelchairs. Both Hannover and Stuttgart use high platforms on their upgraded lines. For German cities that operate conventional trams, several versions of low-floor cars are available in the vehicle marketplace. Attempts are currently underway to design a standard German low-floor car, but many German cities are not waiting, and are opting instead to immediately purchase low-floor cars of different designs.

In the U.K., the recently opened Manchester LRT system uses high platforms and ramps, and the system currently under construction in Sheffield will use low-floor cars.

The Nieuwegein light rail line in the Netherlands currently uses high platforms to provide access to the disabled and those with prams. Planners have also made efforts to locate LRT stops within walking distance of residential areas.

In Switzerland, low-floor technology is being tested in several cities. The suburban system in Bern has recently ordered equipment that uses low floors and ramps. Geneva uses low-floor cars (which pre-date the Grenoble cars by several years) on its remaining tram line.

The prevailing trend in the construction of most new LRT operations has until recently been to use accessible high platforms whenever practical, but low-floor cars are now the dominant technology. In cases where in-street design does not allow the installation of high-platform stations, low-floor design is the only option other than lifts, which are inconvenient and unreliable. The use of low-floor technology is also growing quickly on older, existing European tram operations.

Segregated operation and traffic priority

The feature that distinguishes most LRT systems from conventional tram operations is segregated operations, which keep rail vehicles separate from other forms of road traffic. Methods used to segregate rail include building tunnels, using former or current railroad rights of way, building reservations in roadways, and raising curbing stone on the edges of tracks to prevent automobiles from entering LRT zones.

Tunnel construction, which provides total segregation, is the most expensive method of segregating LRT traffic from road traffic. The lack of requirement for 100 per cent segregation from motor traffic is one of the primary construction cost advantages that LRT has over full metro. LRT systems can operate directly in the street, on reservations that allow automobile crossings at key intersections, or through pedestrian areas that exclude automobiles. In highly congested areas or corridors where surface alignments are not available, however, tunnels are a viable option.

In the U.S., tunnels have been used to separate tram traffic from motor traffic since 1897, when Boston opened its subway.

In western Germany, the construction of tram tunnels was initiated in several cities beginning in the mid 1960's, and has continued to grow. The following German light rail systems use tunnels: Bielefeld, Bochum, Dortmund, Duisburg, Düsseldorf, Essen, Frankfurt-am-Main, Hannover, Köln and Stuttgart.

In France and Great Britain, extensive use of tunnels for light rail operation has not been undertaken.

The conversion of unused or under-used railroad rights of way to tram operation has a long history in the U.S. The San Diego light rail system has made extensive use of railroad rights-of-way since 1979. In fact, freight railroad operations continue at night in San Diego, when the light rail line is closed.

In Great Britain, the Manchester operation makes extensive use of former British Rail rights-of-way. The Manchester LRT line directly replaced active British Rail suburban rail service.

In Germany and France, use of existing rights-of-way for LRT has been limited because these countries do not have many under-utilized rail corridors. A portion of the Nantes light rail line operates next to a railroad right-of-way, and in Karlsruhe, Germany dual-voltage light rail cars are being developed which can operate on both conventional tram and suburban railroad lines.

In Switzerland, regional railways that have been electrified for many decades have used light-rail equipment to modernize operations. Rights-of-way have generally not changed.

Traffic signal prioritization for light rail vehicles is a means for partially-segregated operations to decrease interference from auto traffic. The systems in Grenoble, Hannover, Manchester, Nantes, San Diego, Stuttgart and Utrecht use this technology. Automatic vehicle location systems increase the ability of light rail managers to maintain scheduled headways by enabling dispatchers to quickly identify late-running trains and take steps to remedy the situation. Nantes, Grenoble, Stuttgart and Hannover use automatic vehicle monitoring equipment to scan the system, assure punctual operation and timely transfers, and provide information during emergencies. Dutch systems have begun using the VETAG computer system to give priority to their LRT vehicles.

Fare collection

Proof-of-purchase, barrier free fare collection for light rail operations has become common throughout Europe and on new U.S. systems. This method encourages patrons to purchase tickets before boarding the rail vehicle, or to obtain a valid transfer or monthly pass. Fare inspectors conduct random observations of vehicles, checking valid payment. Those found without valid tickets are subject to stiff fines. This fare collection system provides the following advantages: doors on the vehicles can be used for boarding and alighting, allowing for faster station stops; vehicles on multi-car trains can operate without fare-collecting conductors, reducing labour costs; and stations can be designed with greater access because there is no need to restrict entrance only to those paying fares by using turnstiles and fences. The primary disadvantage to this method of fare-collection is potential fare-evasion if insufficient inspectors are provided.

Automation

Few existing light rail systems use automation for train operations, because one of the advantages of LRT is its ability to effectively use non-segregated rights of way. Systems that are not 100 per cent segregated from road traffic are not candidates for automation. The Los Angeles Green Line LRT, now under construction, is planned for future conversion to automated operation. The majority of systems use visual sight and traffic signals to control train movement in areas that are wholly or partially unsegregated from motor traffic. In segregated areas, automatic block or automatic train control (ATC) systems are commonly used to regulate LRT movement. While ATC signal systems can automatically control braking, the vehicle must still be manned.

Standard vehicle designs

The French have a standard vehicle design that is used in varying forms in Nantes, Grenoble, and Paris. The original design form, which is used in Nantes, is not accessible. The updated model, which is used in Grenoble and Paris, is accessible. The mature tram system in Lille and the new system in Strasbourg have purchased vehicles from Italian manufacturers, instead of using the standard car. St. Etienne is using a metre-gauge variation of the standard car which was jointly constructed with a Swiss manufacturer.

20

Attempts are being made in Germany to design a standard, low-floor light rail vehicle, but many systems are not waiting. Instead, a number of LRV operators use high-platform vehicles manufactured by the large German carmakers (ABB, AEG/MAN, Duewag/Siemans, and LHB).

In the U.S., no standard design has been used since the failure of the Boeing LRV of 1976-78, but Siemans equipment of similar design is used in San Diego. New systems and line extensions continue to shop among different vehicle manufacturers to find designs that suit their individual needs.

Great Britain and Switzerland do not have national vehicle design standards.

3.3 Managerial innovations

Fare policies

Efficient fare setting and collection can improve labour productivity, enhance service quality, and increase ridership. Different systems reviewed use automation, honour-based fares, and simplified fare structures to reduce operating costs through leaner sales and vehicle personnel requirements.

Fare policies are similar among the cities studied. Manchester, Nieuwegein, and San Diego charge zone-based fares. Bern used distance-based fares until 1991, when it switched to zones in an effort to ease price calculations and increase travel on some urban routes. Other cities have flat rates, but all systems studied rely on honour-based collection that is enforced by roving ticket inspectors. Tickets are sold by machines, at booths, or in shops rather than by drivers. Honour-based collection has a number of advantages. It eases movement on and off of vehicles, which adds to the convenience and attractiveness of the service for riders and may increase ridership . The elimination of need for enclosed stations and barriers reduces construction costs.

Automatic ticket distribution and cancellation machines in Bern allow increased service frequency without additional personnel. The major potential disadvantage, fare evasion, can be mitigated through the imposition of stiff fines on violators. San Diego describes its fare evasion rate as about 1 per cent.

Right of way use

Where right-of-way is partially or fully segregated from other modes, LRT systems can provide improved service through higher operating speeds, and increased safety. Faster speeds reduce trip times, improving service quality and the competitiveness of LRT relative to automobile travel, and reduce costs by requiring fewer trains and personnel to maintain schedules.

In San Diego, where 96 per cent of route mileage is on a private right-of-way, average speed in 1989 was 30 kph (Figure 2). By keeping the majority of its right-of-way segregated (and using an electronic vehicle tagging and signalling system that gives absolute priority to LRT), Nieuwegein achieved an average speed of 29 kph in 1989. In Hannover, where 30 per cent of LRT rails are on-street, the average 1989 speed was 24 kph. Both French systems use an electronic Operating Aid System (OAS) to manage rights-of-way. The OAS tracks the positions of all LRT cars and their intersection crossings, and regulates traffic signals, which allows better coordination with established timetables, gives LRVs priority movement, and improves safety. Grenoble and Nantes, however, integrate LRT with other modes extensively in the city centre, resulting in average speeds of 18 and 24 kilometres per hour (kph), respectively.

21

New exclusive right-of-way is difficult and expensive to construct, and may have been feasible for LRT use only in cities where existing right-of-way could be purchased. The San Diego Trolley purchased an intact, segregated right of way in 1979 from a railroad that had assembled it years earlier. Nieuwegein's right-of-way, which was new, was specially provided when the line was built. The cities with extensive mode mixes on their rights-of-way, such as those in France and Germany, might have been unwise to invest in very costly means to totally segregate lines, such as tunnel and bridge construction. These costs might have rendered their systems unaffordable.

Labour management

Personnel expenditures represent a large portion of operating costs for all transit systems. Policies that decrease required quantities and increase flexibility of labour should therefore be encouraged.

San Diego has been innovative in the area of labour management. The operation negotiated an open shop (which allows workers to decide if they wish to join the union), and is required to assign only one employee per train, regardless of the number of cars. The LRT labour contract allows flexible task assignment (whereby some workers perform different tasks and can be assigned to needed functions) and the hiring of part-time workers, thus reducing total labour requirements and the cost of staffing peak travel periods. Work may also be given to contractors, and San Diego pays a private company to provide LRT security service.

Manchester's private operator recruited its own work force.

In Nieuwegein, bus drivers will be taught to operate LRT vehicles in order to allow flexible scheduling and assignment of labour at no extra cost. Bern operates a continuing training program for which twelve tramway and locomotive drivers serve as instructors.

Train management and service integration

Effective integration of LRT with other modes provides efficient, safe and attractive service. The systems studied vary in their complexity of integration. In Bern, two interchange centers that control signals, switches, barriers, and electricity also operate a communications system that manages LRT movement and connections with feeder buses. The Nantes LRT is "the backbone" of the public transit system and is linked to thirty-one radial and circular buses in the city centre and outskirts and twenty-one feeder buses serving outlying communities. Grenoble's two LRT lines complement three trolleybus and fifteen bus routes. Nieuwegein completely redesigned its bus service to provide feeder service to the LRT lines and prevent duplication. San Diego schedules bus service to allow convenient transfer to LRT, has bus stops adjacent to LRT platforms, and uses interchangeable fares and passes between modes. Bus service has also been arranged with a private Mexican carrier to connect Tijuana to the Trolley's South terminus. The Hannover and Stuttgart LRTs are linked to both high-speed, long-distance City-Bahns (metro) and short-distance bus lines that provide feeder, terminal, and other complementary services.

IV. EVALUATION AND COMPARISON OF PERFORMANCE

Each of the LRT systems studied is expected by its operator to achieve certain goals, whether related to cost of service or promotion of desired travel behaviour. In order to compare the overall performance of the LRT systems, this section gathers and evaluates data on expected and actual benefits, costs, and service provision. A number of cost and ridership performance measures are calculated for each LRT system, and the policies of each are analyzed. Table 1 presents the raw data from which the twelve quantitative performance measures in Figures 1 through 11 in Subsection A are derived. Subsection B evaluates the relative performance of LRT systems based on these quantitative measures. Subsection C analyzes the planning and management policies that have guided the development, management and expectations of the LRT systems. The analysis in the following sections is based on case studies of new LRT systems and detailed overviews of trends in four of the countries studied, which are compiled in Part 2, Sections 1 and 2 of the overall report. Supplemental comprehensive operating and financial data are presented in Part 2, Section 3 (Annexes). These annexes outline the reporting framework that was used to attempt to establish a rigorously defined, standard set of comparable LRT performance data for participating OECD countries. Given differences in the completeness and underlying assumptions of data provided by transport authorities, performance measures should be used with caution to compare LRT systems. In order to prevent distorted assessments, the measures should be reviewed together rather than as separate components. For example, an emphasis on operating costs that excludes a consideration of capital costs will bias comparisons in favour of systems that have low operating costs, such as those that rely heavily on automation.

The intent of the performance analysis is not to establish a ranking of transit systems using individual performance measures, but to evaluate the relative performance of the different systems using a balanced set of measures. It is probable that relative performance will change over time, and is sensitive to the assumptions used in this report. Because of resource limitations, it was not possible to test the degree of sensitivity of the different assumptions, for example, use of an eight percent discount rate or different currency exchange rates.

4.1 Performance measure graphics

The following figures (pages 36 -- 46) record comparative performance measures for the systems studied. For purposes of additional comparison, a number of the figures include measures for U.S. systems that are not reviewed in the overall report. Measures are based on 1989 data provided by transport operators.

4.2 Evaluation of performance

The following analysis clarifies assumptions and data differences where possible, and draws a number of conclusions about the relative performance of the systems studied. Other analysts may apply their own assumptions to the data provided (for example, choosing asset lives and discount rates) to make system comparisons.

Because currencies and the time periods during which LRT investments were made differ among the ECMT nations studied, cost figures obtained from transportation officials were adjusted. In order to derive comparative capital costs for new systems or extensions, figures reported by the different LRT

23

operators were converted into dollars based on International Monetary Fund exchange rates at the end of November in the year during which investments occurred. These nominal dollars were converted into constant 1990 dollars based on an index of United States gross national product growth from 1950 to 1990. The resulting figures provide a reasonable estimate of total capital expenditures for the sample LRT systems. Using a standard capital recovery factor[2] that assumes asset lives of 20 years for vehicles, 40 years for construction, and infinity for rights of way, the 1990 dollar values of light rail capital investments were also expressed as annual costs. The quality of the cost estimates is dependent on the data, and more complete or desegregated figures would of course allow better and fairer comparisons of the systems.

Total capital cost figures allow a rough comparison of the magnitude of investment in the different LRT systems. Participants in this study provided data of varying levels of completeness, but the figures do illuminate some differences. Grenoble, Nantes, and San Diego provided cost data divided into expenditures for right of way, construction, and vehicles. Total reported costs for their projects (all figures are in 1990 dollars) were $246 million, $129 million, and $346 million, respectively. Bern reported expenditures between 1956 and 1990 for construction and vehicles totalling $237 million. Nieuwegein listed expenditures in 1983 for construction and vehicles totalling $100 million. Manchester provided a total uncategorized capital cost estimate for its system of $231 million. Hannover and Stuttgart reported uncategorized total annual depreciation costs for their light rail transit systems of $15 million and $16 million, respectively, which were assumed in the absence of other data to reflect their annualized capital costs but not total capital investments. The systems that reported no right of way costs (Hannover, Stuttgart, Manchester and Bern) are assumed to have been given their rights of way by other agencies and therefore to have not reported these costs, which suggests that all capital cost estimates for these systems are conservative relative to those that installed or purchased entirely new systems (Grenoble, Nantes, Nieuwegein, and San Diego).[3]

Estimated annual capital costs were used to compare the effectiveness and efficiency of capital exploitation for the various systems per passenger kilometre, vehicle kilometre, and unlinked trips in 1989. Low annualized capital unit costs indicate either intense use of capital in the form of heavy ridership, or well-planned, appropriate levels of investment. High capital unit costs, conversely, may suggest low ridership or over-investment.

Costs per unlinked passenger trip (Figure 9) suggest that the systems in Nantes ($.78/trip) and Nieuwegein ($1.24/trip) have low capital costs relative to those in San Diego ($2.70/trip) and Grenoble ($2.11/trip). Per trip costs, however, tend to be low on systems with short average trip lengths, such as Nieuwegein. More neutral capital cost figures per vehicle revenue kilometre (Figure 8) indicate that Nantes ($13.11/VKm) and Grenoble ($22.46/VKm) have relatively high capital costs. San Diego ($7.96/VKm) uses capital quite effectively according to this measure. Nieuwegein ($6.17/VKm), the German cities of Stuttgart ($0.18/Vkm) and Hannover ($0.80/Vkm), and Bern ($2.63/VKm) also invest quite well per vehicle revenue kilometre but, as noted above, their costs are comparatively lower because of the absence of reported right of way expenditures. Passenger kilometre data were incomplete, but the figures provided indicate that ridership is relatively heavy in Bern and Nieuwegein (Figure 10). When 1989 capital and operating costs are combined (Figure 11), Grenoble's costs are quite high ($27.99/Vkm) and San Diego's lower ($10.37/Vkm), while those of the cities that report no right of way costs are extremely and, it appears, unrealistically small.

Operating costs alone offer an accessible means of comparing LRT system performance, allowing at least a superficial analysis of cost effectiveness, as measured by consumption of service, and cost efficiency of output provided. The 1989 expenditures per unlinked trip (Figure 5) suggest that the French and Dutch systems operate quite inexpensively, while those in the United States, Germany and

Switzerland are costly. As noted, however, per trip costs are affected by average trip lengths. Operating cost figures per vehicle revenue and passenger kilometre (Figures 3 and 6) suggest that San Diego, where average trips are quite long, and Nieuwegein provide relatively cost efficient and effective LRT service. The German and Swiss systems still appear relatively costly. This analysis could be usefully extended by comparable information on how and at what level fares are set in different cities to achieve targeted cost recovery rates.

Operating financial performance figures indicate whether some of the systems have achieved management fare recovery targets. The San Diego Trolley recovered 92 per cent of operating costs through fares in 1990, substantially more than all other American LRT systems. Manchester estimated a recovery rate in excess of 100 per cent after an initial patronage build-up period. In France, recovery rates for all transit modes increased after LRT service began. More impressively, 1988 operating revenues in Grenoble for LRT service alone exceeded costs by 29 per cent. In contrast, Stuttgart and Hannover had recovery rates of 66 per cent and 70 per cent in 1988, and Hannover's rate had fallen from 78 per cent in 1985. It should be noted, however, that in both German cities LRT costs per passenger and vehicle kilometre are lower than those for buses, suggesting the relative success of investment in LRT. The Bern system reported a 72 per cent recovery rate for 1990. All of these figures exclude capital costs.

Combined capital and operating cost figures allow a complete and undistorted comparison of LRT systems' service effectiveness and efficiency. Because data on passenger kilometres is not collected in all the countries studied, a reliable comparison of service cost effectiveness is impossible. Combined costs per vehicle revenue kilometre and passenger trip, however, suggest a range of service efficiency (Figures 10 and 11). Grenoble's combined costs are high per vehicle kilometre and trip, while these costs are consistently low in the German cities. As expected, all costs are lower on improved or extended LRT routes (Stuttgart, Hannover) than on entirely new systems (Grenoble, San Diego). Long trips (San Diego, Bern) also result in higher combined costs than short trips (Stuttgart, Nantes, Hannover), making it difficult to rely on this indicator for comparison. More similar LRT systems and complete data would improve the comparison of systems' cost effectiveness.

Ridership provides a measure of service quality and the effectiveness of fare collection methods. The cities studied reported different LRT impacts on ridership. On the San Diego Trolley, boardings per revenue vehicle kilometres increased by 23 per cent between the first year of operation and 1988-89, and a 1985 survey indicated that 48 per cent of riders had previously made their trips by car. In Nantes, 18 per cent of LRT riders in 1987 were new to public transport and 17 per cent had formerly travelled by car. Unlinked trips there also grew by 31 per cent between 1984 and 1987, while cost per passenger mile was lower than that for buses, but by 1989 public transit accounted for a lower proportion of total trips than it had in 1980. Twelve per cent of riders were new to public transport in Grenoble in 1988, where LRT accounted for 30 per cent of all transit trips.

Total rail trips grew in Hannover and Stuttgart after LRT was improved, but ridership in Hannover actually dropped between 1985 and 1989. Nieuwegein claims that 23 per cent of its 1984 riders were new to LRT and 8 per cent were from cars. Bern decreased one-way and commuter subscription fares in 1987, resulting in an increase in ridership and costs, a decrease in receipts per passenger, and a larger operating deficit. However, transit ridership in Bern grew from 15 million to 18.3 million between 1987 and 1991, and auto traffic on the Bernstrasse has actually declined since 1985. Better data on total auto use, trip times, and emissions would indicate how well LRT has reduced congestion and air pollution in all of these cities. It is unclear how well buses have been replaced and auto travel has been discouraged.

Load factor figures (average vehicle loads) also provide some measure of how service outputs and ridership are linked. The data for this indicator (Figure 1) is imperfect, because some systems provide load figures for their entire rail systems, but it is still informative. Nieuwegein and San Diego both report more than thirty passenger kilometres per vehicle revenue kilometre (33.8 and 32.09, respectively) in 1989. This performance is particularly notable in San Diego, where vehicle travel distances are quite long. Capacity in San Diego appears to be heavily utilized. Stuttgart (27) and Hannover (26) also report respectable load factors, but they do not separate LRT service.

Relative safety

This study does not report safety performance for each LRT system reviewed, but safety is a goal of all transportation projects, and LRT operators seek to demonstrate their safety advantages relative to other transport modes. A recent study of light rail accidents, conducted by D.A. Walmsley of Great Britain's Transport and Road Research Laboratory, examines accident statistics for "new or substantially new" LRT systems in Europe and North America and compares them to figures for buses and other travel modes. The study report also breaks down safety data by passenger and vehicle kilometre, user type, severity of injury, and degree of LRT segregation from other travel modes.[4]

Walmsley's general conclusions based on the cities studied suggest that well-designed LRT systems offer a number of safety advantages. Average LRT systems have higher accident rates per vehicle kilometre but lower accident rates per passenger kilometre than buses. Both LRT and buses are safer than automobiles. New LRT systems do not appreciably affect bus accident rates, but they generally reduce total numbers of public transport accidents because they provide more passenger carrying capacity per vehicle than buses and allow displacement of bus service in busy areas. As expected, degrees of route segregation and accident rates have an inverse relationship. LRT passengers face the greatest risk of accident, and LRT passengers, occupants of other vehicles and pedestrians are at roughly equal risk from LRT and buses. Accident rates also tend to be high immediately following the introduction of LRT, and to decline with time as communities grow accustomed to new systems. The single indicated safety disadvantage of LRT is that a greater proportion of LRT accidents than bus accidents are fatal, but this indicator is biased by the extremely small total number of fatal accidents.

The British safety study provides brief data on three cities studies for this report: Grenoble, Nantes and San Diego. In Grenoble, the total number of public transport accidents fell significantly during 1987 (when LRT was introduced) primarily because of the removal of buses from busy corridors. Using a projection of the number of buses that Nantes would have had to operate in 1986 to provide a level of service equal to that of the LRT, an estimated bus accident rate, and actual 1986 LRT accident figures, Walmsley calculates that LRT reduced total accidents in Nantes by about 9 per cent. In Grenoble, Nantes, and San Diego, LRT accident rates were high at the onset of service and declined significantly in following years, although San Diego's rate has increased since 1988 (due to significantly increased vehicle miles) and Grenoble's LRT rate remains much higher than its bus rate (probably due to the low level of route segregation in Grenoble). In San Diego, Walmsley's estimated accident rates since 1981 for on-street and segregated portions of the LRT line are, respectively, 32.7 and 1.4 per million vehicle miles, suggesting the importance of separated right of way to overall safety. In San Diego in 1988, the LRT accident rate per passenger kilometre was roughly one-tenth the rate for buses.

4.3 Policy analysis

Expectations and results

Reasons for building LRT systems are similar but vary somewhat by location. Cities in the United States, such as San Diego, are experiencing explosive growth in auto trips and declining use of transit service causing congestion and air pollution. In Europe, cities such as Grenoble and Hannover face similarly growing auto travel and intensive use of public transit facilities that are either worn out or, in bus-dominated systems, increasingly in conflict with automobiles, and of limited ability to provide dependable and attractive service. All cities studied are fiscally constrained. LRT systems are intended to offer large numbers of passengers convenient transit that supplements and is more rapid than buses, but is less expensive to build and operate than metro.

New LRT systems are expected to carry passengers who might otherwise travel by auto, bus, or not at all. In the words of the Grenoble transit operator, these systems may positively alter "the quality and fabric of city life." Anticipated benefits include increased overall use of public transit, reduction in auto and bus use and the resulting congestion and air pollution, and improved mobility for the elderly and disabled. Passengers are to be drawn from peripheral bus routes and autos and channelled into concentrated rapid LRT lines, thereby easing traffic in central cities. The service is considered socially and environmentally attractive because it runs on largely segregated rights of way that reduce the conflict and delay caused by buses operating alone, entails a less disruptive construction process than metros or highways and, if well-integrated with other modes, is attractive and accommodating to riders. Reduced congestion combined with reliance on vehicles that use electricity rather than directly burning fossil fuel should also improve air quality. Not least important, LRT offers the possibility of low capital costs relative to heavy rail projects, and low operating costs relative to other transit options.

Each system seeks to maximize fare box cost recovery and ridership. These goals are difficult to achieve simultaneously and will challenge LRT managers. Low fares might both lure few new riders and fail to produce revenue sufficient to cover operating costs. High fares are likely to deter riders. More frequent service, convenient access, amenities, and wise routing are among appropriate alternatives to pricing that may induce ridership and allow reasonable fares. Given the external benefits expected from LRT use, some cost recovery may appropriately be fulfilled through public subsidies.

All of the cities studied claim that light rail has met most expectations, and each has achieved high levels of service and ridership. Though the data are sparse, cost and ridership information suggests how well LRT systems have performed. For example, after LRT was added to an exclusive bus system in Grenoble in late 1987, total kilometres of service and ridership grew while expenditures declined and cost recovery improved, suggesting that the new investment met major objectives. Bern reports that auto traffic on the local Bernstrasse actually declined after LRT service began. San Diego, Nantes, and Nieuwegein claim that many of their LRT users are former drivers. More thorough data on total auto trips, trip times, and emissions, which were not submitted, might indicate how well LRT has reduced congestion and air pollution and improved travel, particularly whether new LRT riders formerly drove alone or switched from other public transport modes.

Cost figures reported in Section IV of this report suggest that San Diego and Nieuwegein operate quite efficiently and effectively while, based on capital costs for a complete and operating system, San Diego's capital investment has been well-designed.

Project selection methodologies

Project selection methodologies, such as alternatives analysis, whether superficial or comprehensive, are fundamental to decisions about whether or not to build LRT systems. Planners seek to minimize overall public costs and therefore should evaluate alternatives before investing in and operating LRT systems. In each country studied, some alternative analysis was required and performed, but approaches differed. Incomplete responses from participants in the study, and data limitations, preclude a detailed review of the various analyses here. For example, it is impossible to determine what criteria were used to assess the relative values of project benefits and costs. We also have no indication of what project economic lives and discount rates were applied to analyses.

Available data do suggest limited conclusions about the extent of alternatives analysis in the different countries. Analyses range from assessments of strict financial benefits and costs to assessments of broader benefits and costs related to urban amenities, air pollution, travel times, and other more complex factors. Population and transit use projections appear to be done inconsistently, and it is not clear that the environmental impacts have been determined and the value of time has been calculated. Estimates of LRT's potential to divert travel from private to public transport are crucial, but appear to be gauged after installation of new systems.

Analysis of benefits and costs (even when these terms are broadly defined) is often overwhelmed by other issues. Some local authorities regard new transit facilities as essential to the development and status of their cities, in which cases alternatives analyses are generally no more than pro forma exercises. LRT systems are sometimes simply anointed, regardless of the degree of analysis, as the mode providing more capacity than buses at lower cost than heavy rail or metro systems. Without careful study of alternatives, this assumption cannot be tested.

Britain requires extensive alternatives analysis prior to government funding, which provides an incentive for the development of cost effective systems. Public projects must demonstrate that their future benefits will exceed costs. In addition, fares must be structured to recoup the cost of benefits from their beneficiaries, usually defined as the users. A demonstration of benefits accruing to non-users, however, may serve as the basis for grants from the British government to meet revenue shortfalls. This method encourages cost control and imposes discipline on processes that often overestimate benefits and underestimate costs. Consideration of many alternatives may also lead to the discovery of options for meeting a city's transport needs that were not previously considered. Such a process rationalizes expectations, reduces waste, and promotes accountability.

Before LRT was explored in Manchester, three alternative schemes for linking regional rail lines that terminate in the central city were rejected by the national government on the basis of costs exceeding benefits. Once LRT was put forth as a means of using and expanding the aging urban rail network, a five-year alternatives analysis occurred during which three options (closure of rail network and shift of emphasis to buses, retention of network as commuter/regional rail, and conversion of network to LRT) were compared. This process began with the assumption that no project was feasible that did not use the existing, and therefore less expensive, right of way. In fact, 90 per cent of route right of way ultimately used already existed. While this was a strong effort, it should be noted that even here no route corridors or land use schemes appropriate for completely different applications were considered. Other cities in Britain, however, have conducted wider strategic studies before developing specific transportation schemes for implementation.

In the United States, new LRT and other urban rail systems are almost universally built with federal financial assistance. Applicants for federal capital contributions must compare new LRT project proposals to alternatives that include Transportation System Management (TSM), which is generally a low-capital series of investments and strategies designed to improve use of existing facilities, and a "no-build" option, which is the continuation of the present investment level. Since 1980, transit agencies have been required to produce environmental impact statements for new projects. The federal government does not require that comparisons be based on benefit-cost analysis. The initial phase of the San Diego Trolley was built with state and local funds, thereby eliminating the federal alternatives analysis requirement. Metro and bus system improvements were discussed as alternatives to LRT, but analysis appears to have been minimal.

France has undertaken alternatives analyses prior to construction of LRT systems, but decision rules and the depth of evaluation are not clear. Expanded and improved bus systems seem to have been rejected because they were not able to cost-effectively meet needs using existing technology. Nantes and Grenoble sought to increase capacity, lower operating costs, reduce congestion and air pollution, and use existing rights of way. In Nantes, the assessed alternatives included shared use of existing rails, a trolleybus system, and a metro. In Grenoble, the options besides LRT were an untested POMA 2000 cable car system and a metro. Non-capacity changes or TSM changes improving the management or pricing of existing facilities were not discussed. However, the LRT system in Grenoble does cost less to operate and carry more riders than did the exclusive bus system. French grant incentives favouring dedicated right of way and infrastructure work may have encouraged the decision to build LRT.

While considering its Nieuwegein LRT, the Netherlands rejected a heavy rail system because it was too expensive. A high speed bus system was also considered, but was rejected despite a lower cost. According to a Dutch transportation official, it "was doubtful whether a fast bus system will generate the same ridership" because marketing studies indicated that passengers might not regard buses as highly as LRT. Willingness to pay premium LRT fares was not studied, indicating that this was a narrow consideration of costs and benefits. In fairness it should be noted, however, that cost and the effects of willingness to pay are not the only factors in the Dutch decision-making process. The Dutch government's policy is "to provide fast and reliable services which are sufficiently attractive to divert trips by car to public transport, particularly in congested corridors."

In Germany, the Hannover LRT was built without any analysis of alternatives. A metro was rejected because of its obvious high cost, but busways and transportation system management were not seriously considered.

In general, alternatives analysis could be more thorough. Narrow ranges of options are considered, market studies are limited, and route designations tend to be based on the existence of technology rather than travel demands. Legitimate political interests also add elements of subjectivity to the process, giving support to projects that may not prove themselves through pure benefit-cost analysis. In the same context, however, planners urged to define benefits narrowly (users only) may underestimate the value of projects. The existing costs of granting huge subsidies to auto users, through under-priced road use and car ownership, are rarely added to the comparisons. These opposing pressures may balance one another, but they distort assessments. To encourage fully informed, rational decisions, benefits and costs should be properly assessed and publicly-provided goods should be correctly priced. Alternatives analysis alone may not guarantee selection of an "optimal" investment, because transit planners operate with limited information and in a politicized environment, but careful project evaluation does discipline investment decisions.

Pricing and fare recovery policy

LRT systems seek to encourage efficiency by striving to recoup expenses through fare collection rather than general public subsidies. Ridership levels are expected to indicate reasonable fares and appropriate levels of service provision. Actual expectations vary by system. The stated purpose of the requirement is to allocate costs fairly and further encourage the local transport executive, which holds an interest in the 75 per cent private operating consortium, to set efficient service levels based on user willingness to pay. San Diego also seeks 100 per cent recovery, which is extraordinarily high for the United States. In Switzerland, most local transit systems are expected to achieve a recovery rate of 65 per cent. No fare recovery goals are indicated for France, but the involvement of private equity suggests the existence of an incentive for efficient performance. Germany and the Netherlands note no fare recovery goals; the Netherlands uses national fare collection and does not report cost recovery for each system. As noted earlier, ridership levels are affected by fare prices, and all the systems studied seek to balance cost recovery goals with ridership targets. Ambitious cost recovery and ridership growth policies require careful management.

Light Rail System ownership and operating funding policy

Ownership of LRT lines is generally under public control. Only the San Diego Trolley has facilities jointly owned by public and private entities. On the extension to the central city's Bayside neighbourhood, the transit operator and private investors built and jointly own LRT stations in two new mixed-use real estate developments, sharing costs and risks.

To encourage efficient service, three of the systems studied involve private interests in the operation of their LRT systems. In both Nantes and Grenoble, rolling stock and infrastructure are owned by the local transport organizing authorities, and operation of the systems is entrusted to mixed-economy companies in which 35 per cent of equity is held by private interests. In Manchester, the right to operate and maintain the LRT system, and set fares, was given to the same 75 per cent private consortium that designed and built the system, through a single contract. This arrangement was intended to induce efficient construction and reasonable service levels. The San Diego Trolley is publicly operated, but a private security force is used and a freight railroad company rents the right of way during hours when LRT is not in service. These innovations are designed to impose some of the discipline of a profit-seeking marketplace on enterprises that might otherwise lack incentives to operate efficiently. The Dutch and German LRT systems are entirely public and no private involvement is foreseen. In all the countries except Britain, operating deficits are covered by subsidies from federal, regional or state, and local governments. In Britain, shortfalls must be made up by the operating government or through service changes.

Capital funding policy

Capital funding requirements affect how LRT systems are designed and determine whether or not they are built. LRT investment funds come from combinations of national, state and local sources in France (30 per cent national), Germany (60 per cent national), the Netherlands (100 per cent national), and Switzerland (50 per cent national). National and local governments demonstrate need for a system together, costs are estimated, and grants and tax levies are legislated. France allows transit Organizing Authorities that are building public transport on dedicated right-of-way and have obtained national government assistance to raise local capital funds through a "Versement de Transport", a dedicated tax on wages of up to 1.75 per cent. Both Nantes and Grenoble used this device. Manchester sought public savings by funding capital with national (50 per cent) and local grants but contracting design and construction to a 75 per cent private company, thus encouraging efficiency and shifting some costs to the private sector. The British national government required such private involvement as a condition of providing the public capital grant, thus precluding an entirely public project.

San Diego's capital funding process was unusual. Most U.S. transit systems have obtained 75 per cent of their capital funds from the federal government under the Urban Mass Transit Act. In contrast, construction of the first San Diego Trolley line was financed entirely by a combination of state gas and state and county sales taxes, which allowed LRT planners to avoid complex federal grant conditions relating to material sources, cost projections, contracting, and other design features. In 1987, San Diego County adopted a 1/6 cent "transport sales tax" to fund LRT extensions. The transport sales tax is commendable because it was approved by referendum and ensures that LRT system costs are borne in part by residents of its service area. San Diego County also contributes to an annual LRT depreciation fund, depending on fare box revenues, that reflects real equipment costs and provides resources for future capital purchases. These financing mechanisms ensure that LRT planners are sensitive to the expressed interests (willingness to pay for and use LRT service) of the local population and will be able to meet long-term needs. Actual estimated annualized capital costs are discussed above in Section 4.

Trade-offs between financial and non-financial objectives

As discussed previously, fare collection and ridership goals can conflict; high fares discourage riders and low fares attract riders. Although cost recovery through fares is an objective of all case study operators, the relative importance of this objective varies by country. None of the system descriptions suggests that profitability is the major goal of LRT service, although British LRT operators are expected to recover operating costs and minimize losses.

Transit providers have a range of non-financial objectives, and governments have varying willingness to pay for them. Like ridership goals, these broad objectives can conflict with financial objectives such as fare box cost recovery. All operators seek to draw travellers out of their autos, increase overall use of transit, and conserve energy. In the United States, national ambient air quality standards (NAAQS) require metropolitan areas that are not in compliance to make efforts to reduce air pollution emissions, and transit development is one means of doing so. U.S. cities with excessive ozone and carbon monoxide levels must reduce these pollutants by specified target dates, or risk losing federal transportation grants. An explicit goal of the San Diego Trolley is to decrease emissions by encouraging drivers to switch to transit, reducing both auto trips and congestion.

Improved accessibility and mobility are also goals of all systems studied. In the United States, the Americans with Disabilities Act requires transit operators to make their systems accessible to the elderly and disabled. LRT systems in Britain, France, the Netherlands, and Germany are being made accessible through the use of equipment such as high station platforms and low-floor vehicles. The Manchester LRT uses "profiled platforms" and vehicles with doors at different levels, which together provide level access at a number of points at stations. The Bern LRT has recently purchased eleven new and accessible cars and plans to acquire more. All of these broader objectives must be carefully balanced with financial goals.

Acquisition of vehicles and equipment

LRT vehicle requirements do not generally encourage efficiency. In the United States, regulation designed to support American manufacturing mandates that all vehicles purchased with federal assistance have at least 50 per cent domestic content. Because there have been no American vehicle manufacturers until recently, LRT developers have purchased cars from foreign companies and had them assembled with domestic parts in the United States, preventing the use of off-the-shelf technology and increasing costs. Other countries studied do not mention domestic purchase requirements, and vehicle standardization (which might reduce costs) has not actually occurred anywhere. France attempted to promote the development of a standard LRT car and system type in 1975, using the Nantes project as a model, but operators have actually used the best available off-the-shelf technology. Grenoble and Nantes use different car designs manufactured in France, and systems in Lille and Strasbourg have purchased different cars made by foreign companies. Stuttgart and Hannover use German cars, but they follow no standard. British operators are free to obtain their equipment anywhere, and international competitive tender is the norm. Swiss systems have sought cost reductions by grouping together to purchase rolling stock at lower unit prices.

Right of way acquisition policy

Right of way designs are described in earlier sections, but they deserve a brief discussion as matters of policy. When deciding what type of right of way to use for an LRT system, planners make choices that affect both the cost and quality of new transit service.

Because of the organizational and compensation requirements of assembling large land parcels, the use of an existing rather than new right of way substantially reduces the capital cost of an LRT system. In Manchester, where existing public rights of way were used, the reported land costs are a small proportion of total capital expenditures. In Nantes and Grenoble, where dedicated space was also used for most of the systems, land costs were 5 per cent and 10 per cent, respectively, of capital expenditures. The San Diego Trolley had to purchase its right of way, but because it bought an entire railroad line that included routes throughout the county, land costs amounted to only 15 per cent of the capital cost of the first two stages of development, and the system began operating with substantial existing capacity for expansion.

Labour policy

LRT systems use different labour utilization policies. France and Britain report no specific policies or innovative uses of labour forces. In the United States, all transit operators seeking federal assistance are required by the Federal Transit Act of 1964, As Amended, to protect the interests of employees regarding tasks and benefits, collective bargaining, seniority, and job security. This regulation compels transit systems to negotiate any innovative labour utilization schemes with unions representing workers. Flexibility appears possible in the Netherlands. The Nieuwegein LRT system has experimented with a decentralized labour model that matches small management and operating teams in local areas to encourage common identity. The operator believes that the sense of "loyalty to the team" has reduced sick leave, which kept 10.2 per cent of labour force away from work in 1990. The Nieuwegein system has also sought to develop job diversification for its labour force in order to increase worker performance and satisfaction.

Table 1. **Performance Data for Light Rail Systems (1989)**

System	Operating Costs ($000)	Capital Costs ($000)	Revenue ($000)	Vehicle Revenue Hours (000)	Vehicle Revenue Kms (000)	Pass. Trips (000)	Pass. Revenue Kms (000)
Bern-RBS[1]	27 324	21 995	17 845		2 491[2]	16 500	15 8600
Grenoble [2]	5 131	34 769	23 088		1 910	16 500	
Hannover	72 804		60 666	752	18 336	96 501	
Manchester		19 394					
Nantes [2]	6 100	11 352	22 721		826	14 500	
Nieuwegein	4 255	10 768	N/A	45	1 746	8 685	59 053
San Diego	9 159	30 318	8 732	126	3 808	11 217	122 182
Stuttgart	98 270		73 549	727	18 363	94 383	

1. Bern RBS Revenue Kilom data is for train, not vehicle Kilom.
2. Nantes and Grenoble use 1988 data.

For Operating Costs, February 4, 1992 exchange rate to $ of 5.45 French Francs, 1.58 Deutsche Mark, 1.81 Guilder, 1.41 Swiss Franc and 0.55 Pound was used.

For Capital Costs, assumes an 8 per cent discount rate, dollar based on IMF exchange rates during November of years in which investments were made.

Notes

1. David Scott Hellewell, "Financing Light Rail -- Case Studies," International Union of Public Transport, Brussels, Belgium, 1991.

2. The capital recovery factor was derived using the formula $i/[(1+i)^n-1]+i$, where i=discount rate, which is 8 per cent, and n=years of asset life. An 8 per cent discount rate was used because it falls roughly between the 10 per cent rate used by the U.S. Office of Management and Budget and the lower rates used by European nations.

3. The value of the right of way in Nieuwegein is an estimate created by the Volpe Centre based on the per kilometre cost of land for the San Diego Trolley, which was constructed during a similar time period. The cost per kilometre in San Diego was $ 946 855 in 1990 dollars, suggesting a value of $ 17 900 238 for Nieuwegein's 19 kilometres, or $ 14 489 812 in 1983 dollars. The value of right of way land for line 2 in Grenoble is an estimate based on the proportion of total right of way costs that went to land for line 1 in that city.

4. For a longer discussion of LRT safety and the data and conclusions referred to in this section, see Walmsley, D.A., "Light Rail Accidents in Europe and North America", Crowthorne, Berkshire: Transport and Road Research Laboratory, 1992.

Figures

Figure 1. **Average Passenger Load Factor**
(Passenger KM/Vehicle Revenue KM) -- 1989

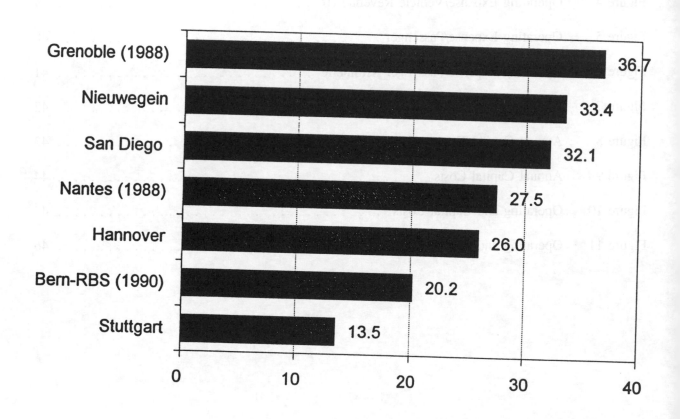

Figure 2. **Average Speed**
(Km/Hour) -- 1989

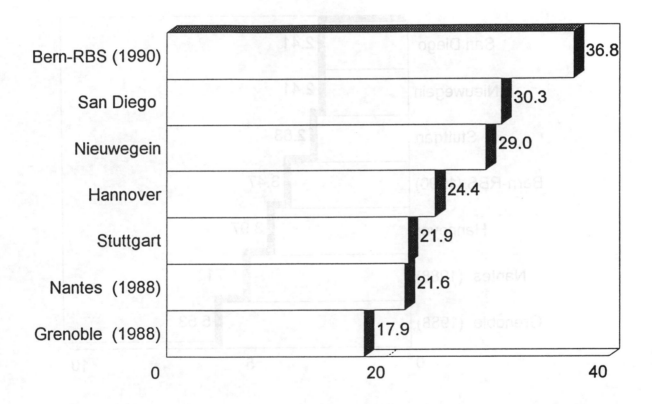

Figure 3. **Operating Expense/Vehicle Revenue Km**
($/Km) -- 1989

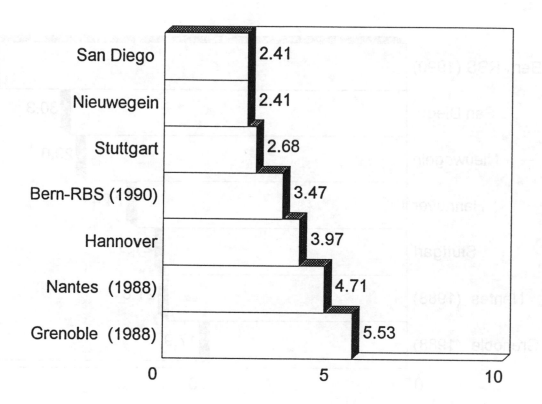

February 4, 1992 exchange rate to $ of 5.45 French Francs, 1.58 Mark, 1.81 Guilder, 1.41 Swiss Franc and 0.55 Pound.

Figure 4. Operating Expense/Vehicle Revenue Hr
($/Vehicle Revenue Hours) -- 1989

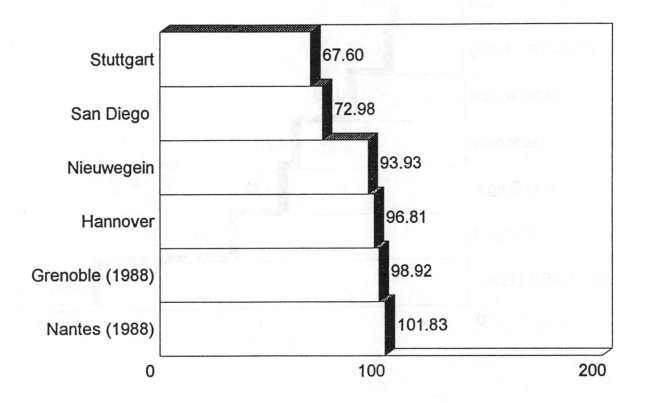

February 4, 1992 exchange rate to $ of 5.45 French Francs, 1.58 Mark, 1.81 Guilder, 1.41 Swiss Franc and 0.55 Pound.

Figure 5. Operating Expense/Passenger
($/Unlinked Trips) -- 1989

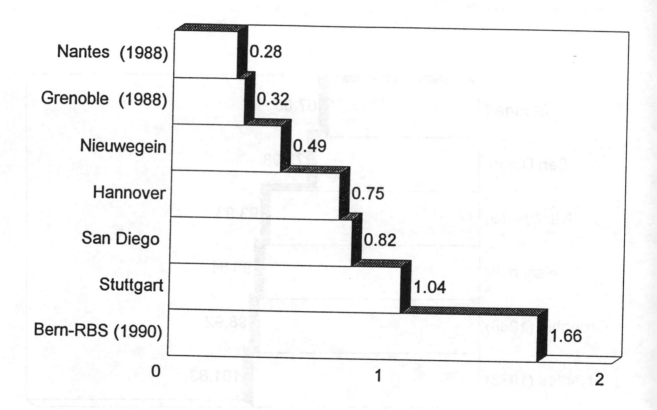

February 4, 1992 exchange rate to $ of 5.45 French Francs, 1.58 Mark, 1.81 Guilder, 1.41 Swiss Franc and 0.55 Pound.

Figure 6. **Operating Expense/Passenger kilometre**
($/Passenger Km) -- 1989

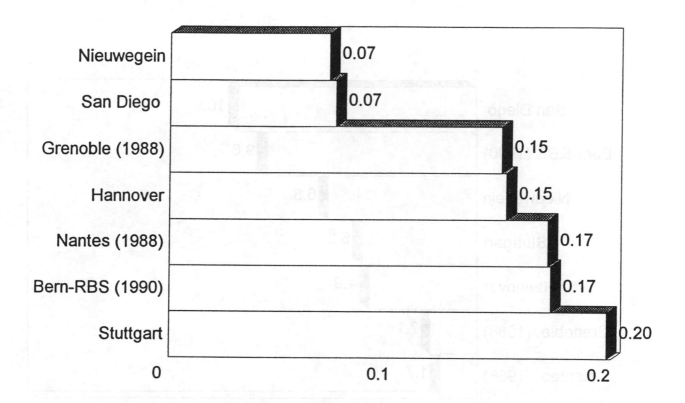

February 4, 1992 exchange rate to $ of 5.45 French Francs, 1.58 Mark, 1.81 Guilder, 1.41 Swiss Franc and 0.55 Pound.

Figure 7. **Average Trip Length**
(Passenger Km/Unlinked Trips) -- 1989

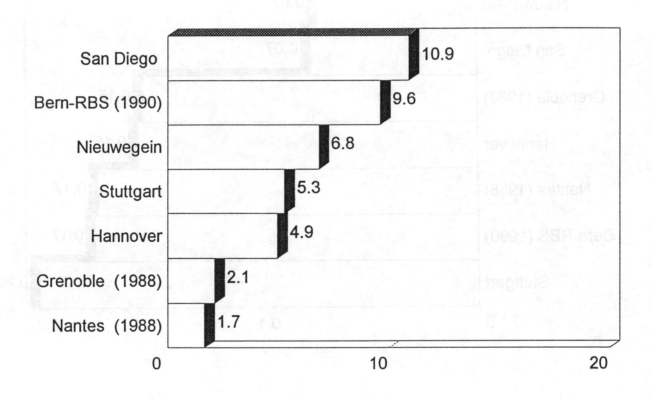

Figure 8. **Annual Capital Costs**
(\$/Vehicle Revenue Km) -- 1989

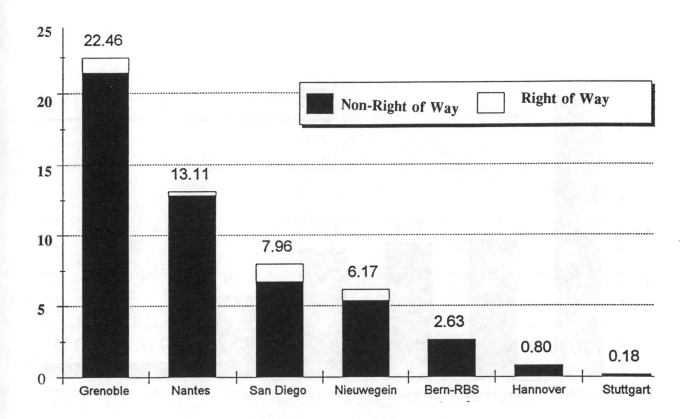

Assumes an 8 per cent discount rate. Dollars based on IMF exchange rates during November of years in which investments were made. Stuttgart, Hannover and Bern do not include right of way costs.

Figure 9. Annual Capital Costs
($/Unlinked Passenger Trip) -- 1989

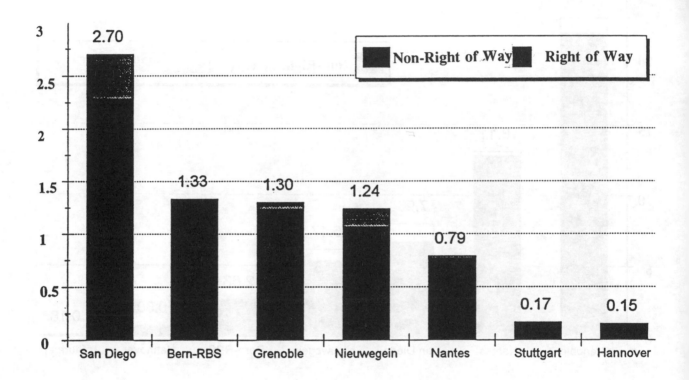

Assumes an 8 per cent discount rate. Dollars based on IMF exchange rates during November of years in which investments were made. Stuttgart, Hannover, and Bern do not include right of way costs.

Figure 10. Operating and Capital Costs
($/Vehicle Revenue Km) -- 1989

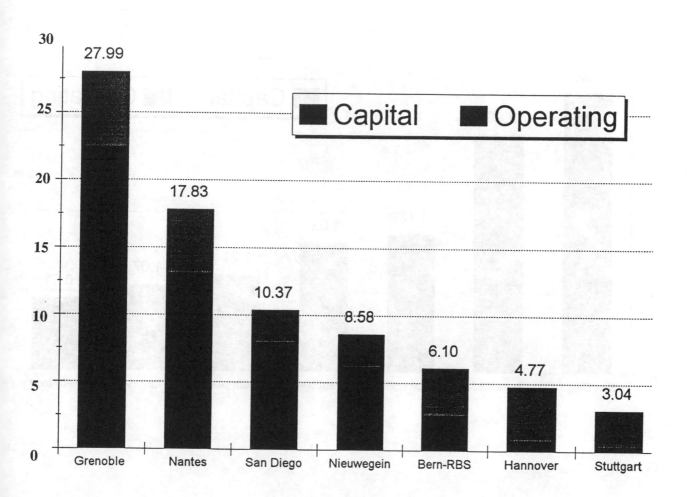

Assumes an 8 per cent discount rate. Dollars based on IMF exchange rates during November of years in which investments were made. Stuttgart, Hannover, and Bern do not include right of way costs.

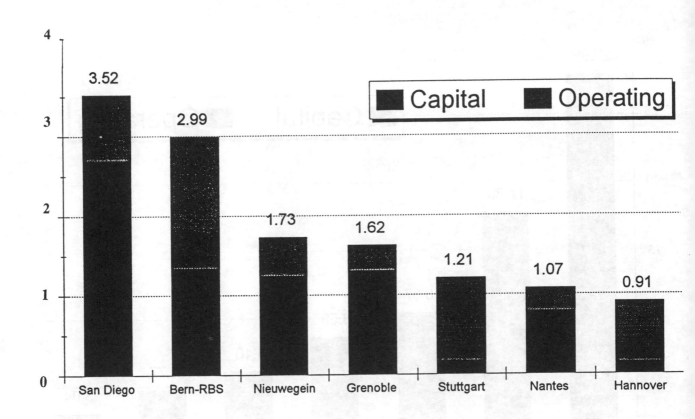

Figure 11. Operating and Capital Costs
($/Unlinked Passenger Trip) -- 1989

Assumes an 8 per cent discount rate. Dollars based on IMF exchange rates during November of years in which investments were made. Stuttgart, Hannover, and Bern do not include right of way costs.

46

Part Two

CASE STUDIES AND U.S. OVERVIEW

TABLE OF CONTENTS

I. CASE STUDIES

This section presents the case studies that provide the basis for the report's analysis and conclusions. The studies describe and evaluate the performance of eight new or improved LRT systems in the six countries that participated in this report for the European Conference of Ministers of Transport. Descriptions include goals, physical specifications, financial and operating performance, technical and managerial innovations, and future plans for the systems. Each case was written by representatives of the country in which the studied system is located.

CASE STUDY A.

The San Diego Light Rail Transit System
William M. Lyons, U.S. Department of Transportation

Table of Contents

1. OVERVIEW

1.1 Summary

The metropolitan area of San Diego, California is served by a two-line light rail transit (LRT) system, called the San Diego Trolley. The system is planning to expand to include at least three more lines.

The San Diego Trolley, which opened in 1981, was the first entirely new light rail system or extension to be built in the United States after 1963 and marked the beginning of a light rail resurgence in the United States. Since the opening of the San Diego Trolley, new light rail transit systems have been built or begun in at least seven U.S cities, and several other cities are considering the construction of light rail.

1.2 System origins

Like most large to mid-size U.S cities, San Diego had a tramway system (the early predecessor to light rail) dating from the early part of this century. In 1936, San Diego was the first transit property in the Western United States to buy P.C.C[1] cars. In 1948, however, it was the first P.C.C.-equipped American tram system to abandon electric rail service in favour of fixed route bus service. From that time until the development of the light rail system, public transport in San Diego was exclusively provided by motor buses. In 1980, prior to the opening of the first light rail line, the bus fleet for the metropolitan San Diego[2] area consisted of 514 buses, with a peak vehicle requirement of 328 coaches.

In 1971 the California legislature passed the Transportation Development Act (TDA). The act allows one fourth of the sales tax in each California county[3] to be used for transportation purposes. In 1974, the constitution of the state of California was amended to allow the use of gas taxes for public transportation. Before the amendment, state gas taxes could be used only for highway construction projects. Thus, by 1975 a process was established for local financing of public transportation projects. Prior to 1975, a regional planning agency in San Diego had proposed the construction of a "multi-billion dollar, high capacity, exclusive right of way, urban rail transit system".[4] The response to this proposal was negative, but did lead to the creation in 1975 of the San Diego Metropolitan Transit Development Board (MTDB). MTDB was created to use the newly created TDA and gas tax transit money for the construction of a fixed guideway system, and to administer all public transit agencies in the San Diego area. In reaction to the criticism of the earlier rail system proposal, the legislation creating MTDB required the following of any new fixed guideway project:

a) reliance on proven, "off the shelf" technology;

b) development on an incremental basis to allow early use of available resources and to provide for upgrading when necessary; and

c) use of existing rights of way where possible.

Initial studies of potential fixed route alignments were started in 1976. Because San Diego is confined by the Pacific Ocean on its western side, all route proposals were designed toward the Mexican border on the south, suburban communities to the east, and communities along the coast to the north.

The availability of an unused railroad right of way is one of the reasons that a South Line alignment was chosen for the initial segment. Another prime factor giving the South Line high priority was the proximity of the Mexican border, and the potential for substantial tourist and international traffic heading towards the border, in addition to the normal commuter and shopper traffic heading to and from downtown San Diego. The heaviest bus route on the San Diego Transit system at the time preliminary plans for light rail were drawn up was between the border and San Diego.

1.3 Operating environment

San Diego is located in California, in the southwestern section of the United States, and is the fastest growing major metropolitan area in the United States (see Appendix). It has a population of 1.8 million, making it the third largest metropolitan area in California, and the sixteenth largest metropolitan area in the United States. It has a population density of 7 223.5 people per square kilometre.[5] San Diego is located along the coast of the Pacific Ocean, near the Mexican border and the city of Tijuana. To the east are deserts and mountains. Because the city has a mild climate, its transit operations do not need to plan or prepare for winter conditions.

A large military base is located on the northern fringes of San Diego County. Major providers of employment include the U.S Navy, which has a large base in the immediate San Diego Trolley service area, and aerospace related industries. The Navy and aerospace industries do not dominate the San Diego economy as greatly as they did in the 1970's. In 1980 the jobs in the region were distributed as follows: 31 percent military or government, 13 percent manufacturing, 20 percent tourist related, and 26 percent service.[6]

1.4 Objectives

The initial objective of MTDB was to construct a fixed guideway transit system based on the previously mentioned principles in the legislation which created MTDB.

The initial line received no federal money for its construction, allowing the project to move forward rapidly without satisfying complex federal guidelines. At the beginning of the project, San Diego decided on a "quick build, low cost strategy". Low construction and operating costs were major objectives. To keep capital costs down, San Diego used "off the shelf" light rail equipment, existing railroad corridors, and simple and proven track, signal, and power systems.

1.5 Alternatives

Based on standards derived from the original language in the legislation that created MTDB, the Board decided that any new public transit must have the following characteristics:

-- low cost;

56

-- at-grade construction;

-- operating cost recovery through fares;

-- off-the-shelf technology;

-- ability to be part of a regional system;

-- high-speed service;

Rapid rail (metro) was rejected because it is extremely costly, would have required a long construction period, and provided more capacity than was needed. Metro would also have required completely segregated rights of way, which would have driven up construction costs and violated the at-grade requirement at street crossings. Improvements to the bus system were rejected as an alternative because they were considered inadequate for meeting trip generation, speed, and capacity goals.

In 1976, a 111 kilometre "intermediate capacity guideway system" (light rail) was chosen. San Diego officials believed that light rail could meet all of the new system criteria and provide the greatest transit improvement at a reasonable cost. No new light rail systems were under construction in the United Sates at this time. The system in Alberta, Canada, which opened in 1978 (the year before construction began in San Diego), was studied by San Diego planners as an example of a newly built light rail system operating in North America.

2. ECONOMIC PARAMETERS

2.1 Ownership

Transportation planning and funding activities for the San Diego area are conducted by MTDB, whose jurisdiction includes 1 476 square kilometre of southwestern San Diego county. The San Diego Trolley was incorporated as a separate light rail operating subsidiary in 1981 to run the light rail system. MTDB also controls the area's largest public bus operator, San Diego Transit, which was previously owned by the city of San Diego, and provides funding and planning for several other smaller public and private bus operations. All bus and light rail operations are co-ordinated and marketed by MTDB under the name Metropolitan Transit System (MTS).

2.2 Funding sources

Capital money for the San Diego Trolley initially came exclusively from local (State and County) sources. In the United States, capital and operating grants are available from the Federal Government for public transportation expansion projects. These funds are distributed and administered by the Federal Transit Administration (FTA), which is part of the U.S. Department of Transportation. In order to obtain FTA grants, local transit agencies must submit cost projections, analyses of plan alternatives, and environmental impact reviews, and must meet requirements involving labour protection, use of U.S.-manufactured materials, and the hiring of minority or disadvantaged contractors. These regulations can delay initial construction and increase costs. In San Diego, a sufficient amount of local money and a strong desire to complete the initial line quickly led to the decision not to apply for federal money.

57

When the system was expanded in 1983, federal support was requested because less local money was available. By this time, the initial line was operating and the Trolley had established its presence, decreasing the pressure to build quickly.

2.3 Private sector involvement

The private sector was involved on the construction of two downtown light rail stations, which were built as components of large, mixed-use real estate development projects. In addition, the Trolley has contracted privately for security services and the operation of freight railroad service on its right of way.

3. SYSTEM DESCRIPTION AND OPERATING ENVIRONMENT

3.1 Rail network

The current system consists of two routes totalling 61.4 kilometres, of which 58.7 kilometres are operated on private right of way. The remaining 2.7 kilometres are operated in mixed street operations, which also include a downtown transit mall.

Engineering work on construction of the first line began in 1979. The 25.6-kilometre line was finished and operating in July 1981.

The initial phase was mostly single track and used passing sidings. Simple overhead, 600 V D.C catenary was chosen for the power distribution system. These straightforward track and wire systems were relatively inexpensive. The majority of the right of way for both the first and second lines was acquired in 1979, through the purchase for eighteen million dollars of the abandoned (due to flood damage) San Diego and Arizona Eastern Railway (SD&AE). Remaining SD&AE structures (such as bridges and embankments) were incorporated whenever possible. Use of a pre-existing transportation corridor reduced land acquisition costs.

The initial single track line was expanded to double track within two years of its opening, during the second phase of construction that began in 1983. The second line or East Line has single track operation over several bridges, but otherwise is double tracked. MTDB plans to rebuild the remaining single track East Line bridges to double track.

Extensions have been built with materials of better quality than those used for the initial line. Construction proposals are now designed with greater attention to meeting capacity requirements than to minimizing costs. For example, concrete rather than wooden ties have been used on expansions. New lines are also unlikely to use single track segments and are likely to be built initially with a power system capable of serving heavily loaded and more frequently operated trains.

Stations on both the initial line and later extensions are primarily simple, unmanned, low platform structures. Trolleys are fully accessible without high level platforms because cars are lift-equipped. Parking for a total of 4 000 automobiles is provided at 16 of the 30 existing stations.[7] The recent Bayside extension of the East Line includes several stations that were constructed in conjunction with development projects. These stops are more elaborate than the standard facilities on the remainder of the system. One station has been built directly into a hotel/retail area lobby.

The initial line, opened in 1981, extends from downtown San Diego, near the city's intercity rail depot, 25.6 kilometre southward to the Mexican border at San Ysidro. The second line, which opened in two segments in 1986 and 1989, stretches 35.8 kilometres east toward the city of El Cajon. Both of these lines travel on the SD&AE rights of way until they reach downtown San Diego, where they enter street tracks. The SD&AE lines, although on private rights of way, are not grade free. Automatic crossing gates protect each grade crossing. The most recent segment to open was the 2.4 kilometre Bayside extension of the East Line. This line runs entirely on downtown Santa Fe Railway right of way, adjacent to city streets, and forms a triangle shape with the two other lines. Provision was made within the Bayside project for the next extension, north to Old Town. A signal preemption system is used to give Light Rail Vehicles (LRVs) priority over other traffic except for emergency vehicles. Automatic block signals are used on the private right of way segments.

3.2 Operational objectives

Current schedules call for 7 minute headways on the South Line and 15 minute headways on the East Line during peak hours. Both lines have 15 minute headways during mid-day, off-peak periods. Train consists are increased during peak hours to meet peak loads. Four car trains are the largest operated. Late night service has increased over the past nine years of operation, with end of service time extending from 21:00 to 01:00. Half-hour headways are maintained during late-night (20:00-01:00) and early morning (04:00-05:00) periods.

Current schedules call for trips to take 41 minutes on the South Line from San Ysidro (the southern end of the line) to Columbia Street (Downtown), and 44 minutes on the East Line from El Cajon (the eastern end of the line) to Columbia Street. The East Line proceeds into the Bayside extension. East Line trains take an additional 11 minutes to travel from Columbia Street to the Imperial & 12th Street Transit Center. The average speed on the South Line is 37.4 kilometres per hour (the 25.5 kilometre trip takes 41 minutes). The average speed on the East Line is 35.4 kilometres per hour from El Cajon to Columbia Street (this is based on the above mentioned 44 minute trip time and a route length of 27.8 kilometres), and 13 kilometres per hour on the 2.4 kilometre Bayside extension. The running time on the South Line is twice as fast as the local bus service which provided service over a parallel route until 1981.[8]

3.3 Rolling stock

The rolling stock chosen was "off the shelf, no-frills" Duewag U2 LRV's, which had been used in Frankfurt, Germany since 1968 and were chosen by Edmonton, Canada, in 1978. The use of a proven design eliminated the engineering and testing expenses of developing a completely new design.

At the time that San Diego was choosing car designs, the light rail system in Boston, Massachusetts was having difficulty with a fleet of LRV's built in 1976-78 by the Boeing company and intended to be the standard for all American light rail systems. Design and reliability problems with these American standard light rail vehicles (SLRV) made them unattractive to new systems like the San Diego Trolley. San Diego wanted to operate its new system without the problems of the SLRV, and ordered the time-proven Duewag cars.

The system currently operates 71 articulated Duewag cars, and has recently ordered 75 more to be used for extensions and increased service on existing lines. The initial 24 Duewag cars, delivered between 1980 and 1983, were built largely intact in Germany. Some final assembly work was performed at the San Diego Trolley maintenance facility. The first cars were not equipped with air conditioning. The subsequent 47 cars had more of their assembly performed in Sacramento, California (though the majority of construction still took place in Germany) and were equipped with air conditioning. The original 24 cars have since been equipped with air conditioning. Aside from the air conditioning equipment, only minor changes have been made to newer batches of cars. The cars seat 64 passengers and have a crush load capacity of 200. The center-articulated cars are 23.05 m long, 2.65 m wide, and weigh 32 600 kg. Bodies are made of lightweight welded steel with fibreglass end cabs. The recently ordered new cars are of a slightly more advanced and expensive design than the initial fleet of 71.

The cars have electric (no air) brakes, and electrical current going to the motors is regulated by mechanical, non-solid state cam controls. More efficient, solid-state "chopper" electrical control was available when San Diego purchased equipment, but it had not been well-tested in North America. San Diego's new cars will use chopper control, which has now been proven on other North American systems.

Each car is equipped with a wheelchair lift on one side. Problems were encountered with the lifts on the first batch of cars, but these were improved and all subsequent cars have had the new lift design. Lifts are used instead a high platform systems, which require segregated, raised platforms at every stop, or low-floor cars, which require neither lifts nor high-platforms. When the San Diego Trolley first purchased equipment, no low floor light rail car designs were in production.

3.4 Control and operating systems

Fares are collected using a barrier free, self-service system with roving ticket inspectors. San Diego was the first American system to use the honour system, which remains rare in the United States. Only the light rail lines that have been built since the opening of the San Diego Trolley use the honour system. Fares are based on distance travelled. Prices begin at .50c for travel between two stations, increase by .25c for each additional three to four stations travelled, and reach a maximum of $2.00 for passengers travelling a distance of twenty-three stations or more. The original 1981 fare was $1.00, regardless of the distance travelled.

Monthly unlimited ride, multi-ride, and multiple-day visitor passes are available, which are valid on all MTS bus and light rail routes. Special reduced fares and passes are available to the elderly and handicapped. Transfers are available between buses and light rail and are either free or require a small upgrade charge.

Only 1 percent of passengers are cited for not possessing a valid ticket, which is a very high compliance rate. The passenger inspection level is 20 to 25 percent.[9] If an increase in the non-compliance rate is noted, more inspectors are added in order to bring the rate down.

A conventional automatic block signal system was chosen, as opposed to more complex Automatic Train Operation (ATO) or Automatic Train Control (ATC) systems. At the time of the initial decisions concerning signal selection, several U.S. rail transit operators, most notably the Bay Area Rapid Transit (BART) metro system in San Francisco, were having well publicized problems with advanced technology automated signal systems. Keeping costs down and avoiding major signal-related start up problems were the major goals behind choosing non-automated signal systems, which also met the overall system requirements by offering off the shelf technology.

All trolley cars are radio equipped, and operators are in contact with a centralized control center. During the early phases of operation, when single track operation was extensive, radio communication played a vital role in scheduling cars and keeping 'meets' at passing sidings on schedule. The central control center also monitors fixed video cameras that are focused on fare machine equipment. Plans call for the installation of an automatic vehicle identification system in the near future.

3.5 Integration with other transport modes

Light rail is coordinated with bus service, and several bus routes connect with the current light rail system. Bus schedules are planned to allow convenient transfer between bus and light rail at most stations, with bus stops located next to light rail platforms. Regional/Commuter rail service is proposed from North of San Diego (Oceanside) to downtown San Diego. This service would use the existing intercity (Amtrak) station, which is served directly by the light rail line. Fares and passes are interchangeable between all local buses and light rail. Recently, co-ordinated bus service has been planned with a Mexican private carrier to provide international service from the end of the South Line to Downtown Tijuana.

Riders with valid permits are allowed to bring bicycles on the San Diego Trolley during off peak hours.

This table compares current bus system statistics for San Diego Transit (the largest of the area's bus operators) to those during the year of service prior to the opening of the San Diego Trolley.

	Operating Cost ($)	Farebox Revenue ($)	Total Passengers	Revenue Kilometres	Farebox Recovery %
1980-1981	33 913 545	13 991 103	33 141 011	18 613 685	41.2
1989-1990	45 496 406	19 168 856	30 487 454	17 514 494	42.2

Source: MTDB 1989-1993 Short Range Transit Plan and San Diego Transit FY 91 Budget.

3.6 Expansion plans

Proposals for system expansion include:

-- a possible 3.3 to 4.3 kilometre Airport extension;

-- a line to the north, initially extending 5.6 kilometres, reaching an additional 32.8 kilometres in a second segment;

-- a 5.7 kilometre extension of the El Cajon (East) Line to the northeast town of Santee;

-- an east to west line, to be called the Mission Valley Line, starting (on the West end) at an intersection with the proposed North Line, and ending at a junction with the current East Line; and

-- an additional new line (the I-15 Line) is also proposed in a corridor running north from the city, in an alignment running between the new North Line and the current East Line.

The East Line extension would rely on SD&AE right of way for part of its journey, and then street running to complete it. The new North Line would use Santa Fe railroad right of way, but unlike the South and East Lines, the light rail track would be next to, not the same as, the railroad track. This separation is necessary because the Santa Fe line (which extends to Los Angeles) is extremely busy now with freight and intercity rail (Amtrak), and may in the near future carry commuter rail service. The proposed Airport Line would be at grade or on an elevated structure. The proposed east to west (Mission) Line would be built next to a river channel.

Most of the currently operating light rail lines use previously existing transportation corridors (primarily the SD&AE right of way). As plans progress to expand the system into areas that have never had rail transportation services, the possibility of community opposition to right of way locations is likely to increase, according to a San Diego Trolley official. For example, residents living near proposed elevated structures may not like the change in view, or store owners on streets for which new mixed traffic lines (in traditional tram style) are planned may complain about proposed stops either being too close or not close enough to their businesses.

3.7 Freight service -- A unique aspect

Until 1992, the San Diego Trolley was the only light rail system in the United States to provide freight service at night on the same rails on which light rail cars operate during the day. The freight operation is contracted out to a private operator, and the MTDB earns a slight profit from this arrangement. The Duewag cars do not have a collision buffer strength strong enough to meet U.S. freight railroad requirements, and freight and passenger operations are not intermingled. The freight operation extends 173.7 kilometres, and travels through part of Mexico (the Mexican portion is owned by the Mexican national railroad). In 1992, Baltimore opened a new light rail line, which also accommodates freight service at night.

4. STAFFING

In September 1989, the staff of the MTS light rail operation consisted of 213 people, with 27 in Administration, 96 in Transportation, and 90 in Maintenance. Expansion of the light rail fleet in 1990 required an increase in maintenance staff of 10. Heavy maintenance of light rail car components was contracted out when the system first opened, but because the Trolley's maintenance facilities have been enlarged since, almost all work is now done in house.

Fare inspectors are employees of MTDB itself, not the San Diego Trolley operating company, and their costs are charged to the Trolley by MTDB. On site security needs are contracted out to a private firm.

The San Diego Trolley has unusual union contracts for a U.S. transit system. The system has one agreement with one union, while the majority of other U.S. transit systems have multiple contracts with multiple trade unions. The contract includes no reference to specific job categories, giving the Trolley great flexibility in the assignment of employees. The operation is an "open shop", which allows employees to choose whether or not to join the union. The contract also allows for the use of part-time employees and the contracting out of work.

5. CAPITAL EXPENSES

The initial phase one single track line cost $ 86 000 000 to construct in 1980 (this price includes 14 vehicles), or $ 3 360 000 per kilometre. The phase two work, which included double tracking, boosting power, and purchasing 10 vehicles cost $ 31 000 000, which comes to $ 1 240 000 per kilometre. The total cost for both phases of line one construction came to $ 116 600 000, or $ 4 664 000 per kilometre.

The San Diego Trolley has an unusual approach to replacing capital equipment. As indicated in the operating expense table in Section VI below, the Trolley funds a capital depreciation account which it contributes to MTDB. This amount was $ 910 000 in 1990. Actual estimated annualized capital costs, based on total project life for all lines (which cost about $ 305 million in 1990 dollars to build), was $ 30.3 million in 1990. (See next two pages for a breakdown of capital costs).

Capital Expenses by Project

Project	Year(s) built	Cost (in $ millions)
SD&AE acquisition	1979 (purchased)	18.1
South Line	1980-1983	95.7
East Line -- initial (Euclid)	1984-1986	33.6
East Line -- ext (El Cajon)	1987-1989	108
Bayside	1989-1990	48
Proposed Projects		
East Line extension (Santee)		85
North Line -- initial		89
North Line -- phase II		365
Airport Extension		75
Mission Valley Line		460
Park Blvd		80
Mission Beach		80
I-15 Line		385

Source: Metropolitan Transit Development Board fact sheets. Costs are unadjusted historical costs.

Estimates of Annual Capital Costs for Most Recent Fiscal Year*

Asset category	Depreciation estimates ($ 000)	Asset life (years)
Right-of-way	4 651	Infinite
Tracks, signals, catenary, buildings, other equipment	17 068	40
Revenue vehicles and revenue vehicle equipment	8 599	20
Total	30 318	

*   Assumes an 8 per cent discount rate.

Source: ECMT/VNTSC Study capital cost estimates.

6. OPERATING EXPENSES

Operating expenses for the San Diego Trolley for Fiscal Year 1990 are separated into major cost categories in the following table. The table indicates that the greatest portion of the San Diego Trolley's operating budget went to labour costs, which are reported in the Personnel category.

Contractual Services	$ 2 125 000	12.9%
Materials and Supplies	$ 1 200 000	7.3%
Personnel/Labour	$ 7 020 000	42.8%
Utilities	$ 2 250 000	13.7%
Casualty & Liability	$ 1 000 000	6.0%
Administrative	$ 435 000	2.6%
Non-Operating Expenses	$ 581 385	3.5%
Start-Up Expenses	$ 355 000	2.0%
Insurance Reserve	$ 500 000	3.0%
Miscellaneous Reserve	$ 15 320	0.05%
Capital Depreciation Payment	$ 910 000	5.5%
Total	$ 16 391 705	100.0%

Source: San Diego Trolley Fiscal Year 1991 Operating Budget

Section 15 data indicate that the San Diego Trolley pays 15.3 percent of expenses for operators salaries and wages, 27.8 percent for other salaries and wages, and 8.0 percent for fringe benefits (for example, sick and vacation time). The total for salaries and fringe benefits of 51 percent compares favourably to the U.S. public transport average of 72.1 percent (all modes combined). When the 14.4 percent of the budget spent on contract services is added, which brings the total to 65.5 percent, the comparison is less favourable.

As indicated in the table, the San Diego Trolley is not responsible for capital project construction, funding or planning, which are provided by MTDB. The Trolley does make an annual capital depreciation payment to MTDB to be used to fund replacement of capital equipment.

7. REVENUES AND FINANCE

Gas and sales taxes provided most of the money for the construction of the system. A statewide sales tax of 1/4 percent is collected for transportation purposes, with money allocated to individual counties using a population-based formula. Additional money for transit purposes is provided by a county 1/6 percent sales tax, which was approved by San Diego voters in 1987 through a measure called Proposition A, which stipulated that most of the money raised would be used for San Diego Trolley extensions. In 1990, California voters approved a tax to be used to fund statewide transportation improvements. It is not yet clear how much of the statewide money will be available to San Diego.

A small amount of additional local money for capital projects has been raised through sale/leaseback contracts for light rail equipment negotiated with foreign (German) corporations. Under these agreements, new equipment is sold to private companies, which in turn lease the vehicles back to MTDB. The private companies benefit by owning additional equipment which they can depreciate for tax purposes, while the transit agency benefits from a one-time infusion of additional cash.

Federal money was not requested for the first phases of construction because of the availability of local money, and the desire to construct the line quickly and cheaply. Some federal funding (Sections 3, 8 and 9 monies) was used to construct the second phase of the East Line.

MTDB is the recipient of public funds. It administers all tax money received and implements all capital project construction. The San Diego Trolley operating company receives its operating subsidy from MTDB, not directly from collected tax money.

The Bayside extension was built entirely with local funding from the following sources:

-- San Diego Unified Port District: $ 10 million;

-- City of San Diego's Transient Occupancy Tax: $ 32.68 million;

-- Central City Development corporation: $ 4 million;

-- County of San Diego: $ 0.4 million.

One reason that local Government agencies not directly involved with transit operations and planning contributed funds for the Bayside project was to encourage development in an under-developed area of the city.

The Bayside extension includes two public/private sector joint development projects at station sites. At the Imperial & 12th Street Transfer Station (where all lines intersect) a ten-story office building and parking garage were built. The primary tenants of the office building are MTDB, the San Diego Trolley and county agencies. At the Kettner and C Street station, the light rail stop will be incorporated into a large hotel and tower complex, which includes a 34-story office tower and a 15-story hotel, is constructed on two city blocks, and costs more than $ 200 million. The trolley station is located in the center of the complex in an area adjacent to retail shops and a cafe.

The Bayside extension also includes the development of a linear park parallel to the light rail line.

The following table describes the San Diego Trolley's record on the recovery of operating costs from farebox revenue, which includes cash and pre-paid or pass revenues.

Farebox recovery figures by Fiscal Year

Fiscal Year	Operating Cost ($)	Farebox Revenue ($)	Farebox Recovery Ratio (%)	Operating Cost + Depreciation Payment ($)	Farebox Recovery Ratio with Depreciation Payment (%)
81-82	3 453 804	2 787 175	80.7		
82-83	4 101 325	3 037 204	74.0		
83-84	4 950 481	3 976 264	80.3		
84-85	5 516 600	4 753 300	86.2		
85-86	6 116 199	5 560 148	90.9		
86-87	7 379 527	6 336 741	85.9		
87-88	8 280 085	7 362 028	88.9		
88-89	8 313 691	7 160 000	86.0	10 616 454	67.0
89-90	8 865 000	7 630 000	86.0	10 684 900	71.0
90-91	14 030 000	12 600 000	89.0	16 391 605	76.8
91-92 proposed budget	16 600 000	14 906 800	89.8	18 630 000	80.0

Source: Metropolitan Transit Development Board fact sheets

The next table describes the operating cost recovery performance from the farebox of the two original lines. In 1988, the South Line recovered almost 100 percent of its costs from fares, according to MTDB. In contrast, the East Line recovered only 50 percent. The data for the East Line is from 1988, a year before the opening of a lengthy extension into a heavily populated area.

Operating costs and revenues by line

Line	Operating Cost ($)	Fare Revenue ($)	Subsidy ($)
South-1988	6 494 000	6 456 000	38 000
East-1988	1 806 000	912 000	912 000

Source: Metropolitan Transit Development Board fact sheets.

Operating Costs per passenger

Fiscal Year	Operating Cost ($)	Passengers	Operating Cost Per Passenger ($)	Operating Cost + Depreciation Payment ($)	Operating Costs + Depreciation per Passenger ($)
81-82	3 453 804	3 885 703	0.89		
82-83	4 101 325	4 137 928	0.99		
83-84	4 950 481	5 437 091	0.91		
84-85	5 516 600	5 942 858	0.93		
85-86	6 116 199	7 003 283	0.87		
86-87	7 379 527	7 974 058	0.93		
87-88	8 280 085	9 280 612	0.89		
88-89	8 313 691	11 216 631	0.74	10 616 454	0.95
89-90	8 865 000	16 005 726	0.55	10 684 900	0.67
90-91	14 030 000			16 391 605	
91-92 proposed budget	16 600 000			18 630 000	

Source: Metropolitan Transit Development Board fact sheets

8. OPERATIONS -- SERVICE OUTPUTS

The following table describes the total service output of the San Diego Trolley for the years 1987, 1988 and 1989. These figures are used to derive the cost and service efficiency and effectiveness measures. They also provide a sense of the total magnitude of service provided by the Trolley over the time period.

Performance of San Diego Trolley					
Year	Vehicle Kilometres (000)	Vehicle Revenue Kilometres (000)	Vehicle Hours (000)	Vehicle Revenue Hours (000)	Capacity Kilometres (million)
1987	3349	3283	114	108	733
1988	3443	3271	117	108	753
1989	n/a	3806	132	125	817

Source: UMTA Section 15 Data 1987-1989

9. PATRONAGE -- RIDERSHIP

The following table summarizes nine years of ridership on the San Diego Trolley. Revenue passengers are unlinked trips or boardings, and do not necessarily indicate complete origin-to-destinations trips, which may require transfers to other modes. Ridership has steadily increased since the opening of the system, growing more than 312 percent from 1981-82 to 1989-90. Although much of the increase can be attributed to service expansions, the increase in ridership has been greater than that in revenue kilometres. From 1981-82 to 1988-89, ridership increased by 189 percent, compared to a 136 percent increase in revenue kilometres. Boardings per revenue vehicle kilometre, which measures passenger demand per unit of service supplied, has increased by 23 percent since the opening year, with substantial increases after 1987-88.

Revenue Passengers and Kilometres by Fiscal Year

Fiscal Year	Revenue Passengers	Revenue kilometre	Revenue Passengers/ Revenue kilometre
81-82	3 885 703	1 616 821	2.40
82-83	4 137 928	2 037 507	2.03
83-84	5 437 091	2 594 829	2.10
84-85	5 942 858	2 574 766	2.31
85-86	7 003 283	2 889 337	2.42
86-87	7 974 058	3 290 133	2.42
87-88	9 280 612	3 426 399	2.71
88-89	11 216 631	3 807 698.5	2.95
89-90	16 005 726	6 460 927	2.48

Source: Metropolitan San Diego -- Short Range Transit Plan FY 1989-93, San Diego Trolley Inc. -- ridership Statistics, and UMTA Section 15 Data.

Original ridership projections anticipated 9 800 trips per day during the first year on the first line, growing to 28 000 to 30 000 per day on the entire network by 1995.[10] Actual first year ridership averaged 11 000 riders per day, and in September 1990, an average of 49 260 passengers per day were carried on the two light rail lines.[11]

The following information is drawn from a 1985 San Diego Association of Governments (SANDAG) passenger survey of ridership on the South Line only. Of riders:

54%	are men and 46% women
68%	use the system between 4 and 7 days a week
26%	prefer light rail to their own car
30%	made the trip driving alone before light rail
18%	made the trip as a passenger in a car before light rail
28%	are between 19 and 24 years old
40%	are between 25 and 44 years old
12%	are between 45 and 59 years old
9%	are 60 years old or over
85%	are local residents
15%	are visitors/tourists
14%	had incomes below $ 5 000
21%	had incomes between $ 5 000-$ 10 000
17%	had incomes between $ 10 000-$ 15 000
15%	had incomes between $ 15 000-$ 20 000

14%	had incomes between $ 20 000-$ 30 000
9%	had incomes between $ 30 000-$ 40 000
10%	had incomes over $ 40 000
34%	of the trips included a U.S./Mexican border crossing

Although the survey data are now 7 years old, they allow some interesting observations about the characteristics of San Diego Trolley riders. The system is predominantly used by commuters, as indicated by the 68 percent who used the system 4 to 7 days a week. Cross-border travel is a very important component of service, although it is likely that many of the 34 percent crossing the border do so for work trips and are included in the 68 percent who ride daily. Almost half of the riders would have travelled by automobile if LRT had not been available. Of these, 30 percent previously drove alone. It is assumed that many of the other half of the riders formerly used bus or other modes of public transport. The average incomes of riders were relatively modest -- 53 percent had incomes below $ 20 000.

10. PERFORMANCE EVALUATION

10.1   Productivity measures

Compared to other U.S. LRT systems, the San Diego Trolley is characterized by high degrees of efficiency, cost-effectiveness, and service utilization.

As indicated in the following figure, San Diego has the lowest operating expenses per kilometre in the U.S.. Explanations for this may include:

--   newer infrastructure that does not require as much maintenance as older systems;

--   reliable vehicles that do not require as much maintenance as old ones;

--   efficient employee utilization; the San Diego system requires only one person to operate a light rail train, regardless of the number of cars. Some other systems require one person on each car to collect fares or because of union-management agreements.

70

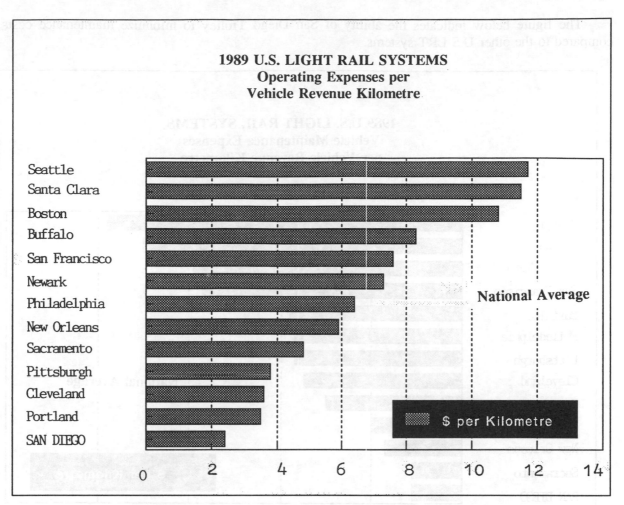

1989 U.S. LIGHT RAIL SYSTEMS
Operating Expenses per
Vehicle Revenue Kilometre

National Average

$ per Kilometre

Seattle
Santa Clara
Boston
Buffalo
San Francisco
Newark
Philadelphia
New Orleans
Sacramento
Pittsburgh
Cleveland
Portland
SAN DIEGO

0   2   4   6   8   10   12   14

1989 UMTA Section 15 Data

The figure below indicates the ability of San Diego Trolley to minimize maintenance costs, compared to the other U.S LRT systems.

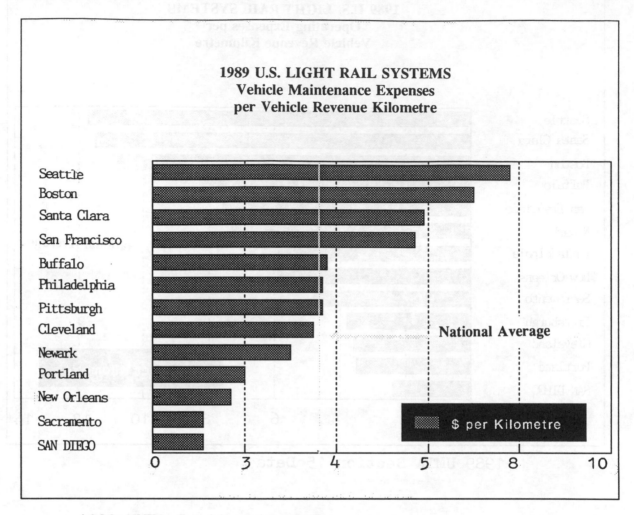

1989 UMTA Section 15 Data

The next figure and table should be considered together to indicate the cost effectiveness of the San Diego Trolley.

The figure below presents operating expenses per unlinked trips, which is of limited value as a basis of comparison of the cost-effectiveness of systems with different characteristics and operating in different environments. Variation in the cost of trips provided by different operators is caused by extreme differences in average trip lengths. For example, Boston has a high number of transfers and short average trip lengths (2.2 kilometres), while San Diego and Pittsburgh have average trip lengths over 10 kilometres, which distorts comparisons of these cities. Operating costs per passenger kilometre, which adjusts for different trip lengths, is a better measure of cost-effectiveness. Based on cost per passenger kilometre, which is presented in the following table, the San Diego Trolley exhibits a high level of cost-effectiveness relative to other U.S. systems.

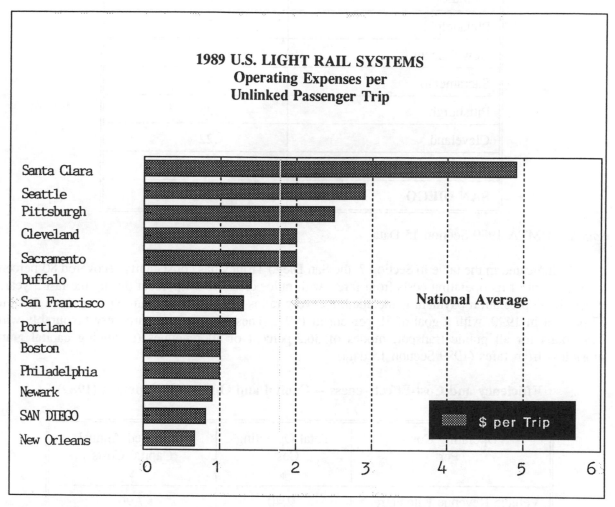

1989 UMTA Section 15 Data

1989 U.S Light Rail Systems sorted by
Operating Expenses / Passenger Kilometres

Seattle	1.7
Santa Clara	.93
Boston	.44
Buffalo	.35
San Francisco	.31
Newark	.28
Philadelphia	.27
New Orleans	.24
Sacramento	.23
Pittsburgh	.23
Cleveland	.22
Portland	.14
SAN DIEGO	**.07**

Source: UMTA 1989 Section 15 Data

As indicated in the table in Section 7, the San Diego Trolley has consistently recovered 80 percent to 90 percent of its operating costs from fares, with ratios closer to 90 percent during the last 5 years. When the depreciation payment is included, recovery ratios have climbed from 67 percent in 1988 to 77 percent in 1990, with a goal of 80 percent in 1991. These figures compare very favourably with U.S. totals for all public transport modes of 36.2 percent of all revenues (excluding capital grant subsidies) from fares (1989 Section 15 data).

Efficiency and Cost-Effectiveness -- Capital and Operating Expenses (1989)

Operating Costs Per	Total Operating Costs $	Estimated Annual Capital Costs $
Vehicle Revenue Kilometre	2.40	7.96
Vehicle Revenue Hour	73.00	
Unlinked Trip	0.55	2.70
Passenger Kilometre	0.07	0.25

Source: 1989 UMTA Section 15 Data for operating costs. ECMT/VNTSC study estimates for capital costs, based on an 8 percent annual discount rate and 1989 performance figures.

The following table presents load factors for U.S. light rail systems. Load factor, or passenger kilometres per revenue vehicle kilometres, is an important measure of the utilization of service. It indicates the extent to which outputs supplied are actually consumed by riders. San Diego had the highest load factor of any U.S light rail system in 1989. When additional LRVs were added, the headways on the South Line should have been reduced. This provides a superior level of service, it will also reduce the reported load factor.

1989 U.S Light Rail 000 Systems sorted by Load Factor, defined as Passenger Kilometres / Vehicle Kilometre

Seattle	6.6
Santa Clara	12.3
Newark	13
New Orleans	15.9
Sacramento	20.4
Buffalo	21.4
Philadelphia	21.6
Boston	24.2
Portland	24.9
San Francisco	26.3
Cleveland	28.1
Pittsburgh	31.9
SAN DIEGO	**32.0**

Source: UMTA 1989 Section 15 Data

The next table compares average trip lengths, which presents another perspective on differences in the types of trips taken on each system. The statistics indicate that San Diego riders travel on average the second greatest distance.

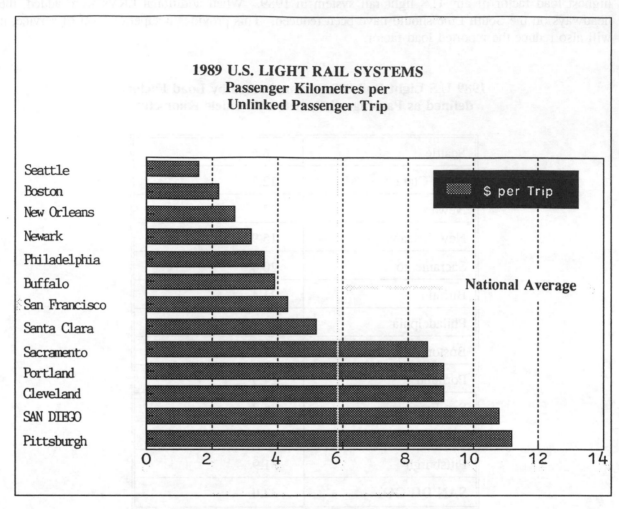

1989 U.S. LIGHT RAIL SYSTEMS
Passenger Kilometres per
Unlinked Passenger Trip

1989 UMTA Section 15 Data

76

The next table presents average LRT speeds in the U.S. Although this measure indicates one aspect of the ability of a system to use its equipment and labour effectively, numerous local characteristics that influence speed, cannot be controlled by operators or managers. These include the extent of grade separation, congestion, and station spacing.

Speed -- Kilometres per Hour -- 1989

Seattle	8.0
Philadelphia	14.3
New Orleans	14.4
San Francisco	16.8
Buffalo	18.0
Santa Clara	20.7
Average	22.5
Newark	23.8
Boston	23.9
Pittsburgh	24.1
SAN DIEGO	**30.4**
Portland	30.8
Sacramento	31.8
Cleveland	37.4

Source: UMTA Section 15 table 3.182

When compared to bus operations in San Diego, the light rail system has lower per trip and per kilometre operating costs, three times the load factor, and twice the average trip length, according to the next table. This is not a fair direct comparison, however, because the light rail system consists entirely of heavy trunk line routes, while the bus system includes trunk lines, feeder lines, and socially necessary services to low traffic-generating areas.

Comparison of San Diego Trolley to San Diego Transit (bus) for 1989

	San Diego Trolley	San Diego Transit (bus)
Operating Expenses/Actual Vehicle Revenue Kilometre	2.40	2.50
Operating Expenses/Unlinked Passenger Trip	.81	1.39
Operating Expenses/Passenger Kilometre	.074	.181
Load Factor -- Passenger Kilometres/Vehicle kilometre	32.08	13.8
Speed -- Vehicle Kilometres per Hour	30.4	12.4
Vehicle Operations Expenses per Vehicle Revenue Kilometre	2.57	3.7
Vehicle Maintenance Expenses per Vehicle Revenue Kilometre	1.12	1.44
Average Trip length -- Passenger Kilometres/Unlinked Trip	10.8	5.2

Source: 1989 UMTA Section 15 Data

10.2   Projected compared to actual performance

The system has maintained ridership greater than original expectations, and has maintained a high farebox recovery ratio, which was originally projected when construction began.

10.3   Managerial, policy, and technological innovations

When compared to other American light rail systems, San Diego seems to have achieved its original goal of developing a fixed route, high capacity system at a low cost.

The use of an honour-based roving inspector fare collection system allows for improved employee productivity, because it allows operators to operate a train, regardless of the number of cars in the consist. The only increased costs of running longer trains are for power consumption, added car maintenance (because more cars are being used), and more fare inspectors as ridership increases.

The use of existing railroad rights of way combined with proven, simple vehicles, power systems, and signals contributed to a low initial capital cost per kilometre of construction.

The securing of local funding and an expedited construction period allowed the system to be built on schedule and within budget. Simple system designs reduced the likelihood of cost overruns, construction delays, and cost increases due to inflation.

The San Diego Trolley's annual depreciation fund payment is an innovative method of partially funding long term capital costs. The calculation of the annual payment entails dividing capital cost objects into specific categories and determining a standard estimated life for each group. For example, San Diego uses a 30 year estimate for light rail vehicles, 16 to 30 years for tracks, and 20 to 30 years for traction power equipment. The annual payment is determined using the following formula:

$$AP = [(BP\text{-}D) \; X \; CPI1] + [(AV\text{+}DP) \; X \; CPI2]$$

Where   AP   = Annual Payment
            BP   = Base Payment ($500,000 in year 1)
            D   = Deletions
            AV   = Added Value Fixed Asset Valuation
            DP   = Depreciation Period
            CPI1 = Consumer Price Index
                      (cumulative change since initial year of account)
            CPI2 = Consumer Price Index
                      (annual change, for this year)

The amount of the annual depreciation payment is also affected by achieved farebox recovery ratios. If the farebox recovery ratio drops below that which is budgeted, the depreciation payment will be lowered accordingly. For every one percent that the farebox recovery ratio falls below budget, the payment is lowered by five percent.

10.4   Social policy -- analysis of ability to meet local objectives

The system appears to be meeting the original objectives set forth when the MTDB was created. It was inexpensive to build, recovers a high percentage of its operating costs through fares, uses off the shelf technology, is well integrated into the regional transit system, and operates at a relatively high speed (when compared to other U.S light rail systems and the San Diego Transit bus system).

The statistics presented indicate that the San Diego Trolley has successfully redirected work trips from automobiles, particularly single occupant drivers, to LRT. The impact on congestion will be modest, given the small share of total trips made on public transport (well below 10 percent in San Diego, as in most U.S. cities). The system also appears to be serving middle and low income riders, and capturing tourist trips. It is reasonable to assume that, although tourists may be one time only riders, each tourist on the Trolley might otherwise have been driving and competing for road space.

11. CONCLUSION

San Diego has constructed a light rail system that is relatively inexpensive to operate and consistently maintains high ridership. The system has also been able to rely on high levels of dedicated local financial support. If San Diego is to be used as an example for other cities, a couple of factors should be remembered:

-- San Diego is one of the fastest growing metropolitan areas in the United States. Increasing ridership may owe as much to population increases as it does to improved service. Cities with declining or slower growing populations should not necessarily expect the same levels of ridership increases;

-- unused railroad corridors through major population areas were available at a low price in San Diego, partially due to flood damage. Other cities may face a lack of unused rail corridors, unused rail corridors that do not serve the major population areas of a city, or rail corridors that serve prime areas but are available only at a high price.

The San Diego experience proves that an LRT system can be efficiently operated with little or no application of advanced technology. Effective planning can enable the integration of systemwide elements into a workable end product. If experienced personnel are used throughout various levels of management and implementation, a public light rail system can be operated safely and efficiently.

In addition, cities can use a business management approach as opposed to the public agency/bureaucratic standard normally associated with transit agencies. While this may be difficult in cities that implement LRT systems as part of an existing transit agency, the experience of the San diego trolley can guide innovation elsewhere.

Much was done during the early phases of the San Diego Trolley project without the benefit of actual operating experience. For similar projects elsewhere, it would be wise to develop extensive design criteria based on industrywide standards. This would encourage a more uniform approach to the design and construction of facilities. Systems should anticipate future expansion and build-out of the system, even though such expansion might occur many years in the future.

APPENDIX

The figures below apply only to specific city populations and do not include total urban area populations.

	City	1980 Population	1990 Population	% Change	Transit Modes
1	New York	7 071 639	7 322 564	3.5%	Metro, Bus, Commuter rail
2	Los Angeles	2 968 528	3 485 398	17.4%	Bus, new Light rail, Metro (under construction), Commuter rail planned
3	Chicago	3 005 072	2 783 726	- 7.4%	Metro,Bus, Commuter rail
4	Houston	1 617 966	1 630 553	.8%	Bus
5	Philadelphia	1 688 210	1 585 577	- 6.1%	Metro, Light rail, Commuter rail, Trolley bus, Bus
6	**San Diego**	**875 538**	**1 110 549**	**26.8%**	**Light rail, Bus, Commuter rail planned**
7	Detroit	1 203 369	1 027 974	-14.6%	Bus, Automated Guideway
8	Dallas	905 751	1 006 877	11.2%	Bus, Light rail planned
9	Phoenix	790 183	983 403	24.5%	Bus
10	San Antonio	813 118	935 933	15.1%	Bus
11	San Jose	640 225	782 248	22.2%	Bus, Light rail
12	Indianapolis	700 974	741 952	5.8%	Bus
13	Baltimore	786 741	736 014	- 6.4%	Metro, Bus, Light rail under construction
14	San Francisco	678 974	723 959	6.6%	Light rail, Metro, Trolley bus, Commuter rail, Bus, Cable Car
15	Jacksonville	540 920	672 971	24.4%	Bus, Automated Guideway
16	Columbus	565 021	632 910	12.0%	Bus

	City	1980 Population	1990 Population	% Change	Transit Modes
17	Milwaukee	636 298	628 088	- 1.3%	Bus
18	Memphis	646 170	610 337	- 5.5%	Bus
19	Washington	638 432	606 900	- 4.9%	Metro, Bus, Commuter rail
20	Boston	562 994	574 283	2.0%	Metro, Light rail, Commuter Rail, Bus, Trolley Bus
21	Seattle	493 846	516 259	4.5%	Bus, Trolley Bus (includes bus tunnel)
22	El Paso	425 259	515 342	21.2%	Bus
23	Nashville	477 811	510 748	6.9%	Bus
24	Cleveland	573 822	505 616	-11.9%	Metro, Light rail, bus
25	New Orleans	557 927	496 938	-10.9%	Bus, Light rail
26	Denver	492 694	467 610	- 5.1%	Bus
27	Austin	372 536	465 622	25.0%	Bus
28	Fort Worth	385 164	447 619	16.2%	Bus
29	Oklahoma City	404 551	444 719	9.9%	Bus
30	Portland	429 400	437 319	1.8%	Light rail, Bus

Vehicle Operations Expenses per Vehicle Revenue Kilometre, 1989

Santa Clara	9.8
San Francisco	9.4
Boston	9.3
Seattle	7.8
Philadelphia	6.7
Pittsburgh	5.3
Average	5.2
New Orleans	4.0
Newark	3.8
Cleveland	3.8
Buffalo	3.8
Portland	3.2
Sacramento	2.5
SAN DIEGO	**2.5**

Source: UMTA Section 15 table 3.182

Vehicle Maintenance Expenses per Vehicle Revenue Kilometre, 1989

Seattle	7.8
Boston	7.0
Santa Clara	5.9
San Francisco	5.7
Buffalo	3.8
Philadelphia	3.7
Pittsburgh	3.7
Average	3.6
Cleveland	3.5
Newark	3.0
Portland	2.0
New Orleans	1.7
Sacramento	1.1
SAN DIEGO	**1.1**

Source: UMTA Section 15 table 3.182

U.S Light Rail Systems sorted by
Operating Expenses / Unlinked Passenger trips, 1989

Santa Clara	4.9
Seattle	2.9
Pittsburgh	2.5
Cleveland	2.0
Sacramento	2.0
Buffalo	1.4
San Francisco	1.3
Portland	1.2
Boston	1.0
Philadelphia	.99
Newark	.90
SAN DIEGO	**.81**
New Orleans	.67

Source: UMTA 1989 Section 15 Data

U.S Light Rail Systems sorted by
Average trip length -- Passenger kilometre / Unlinked Trips, 1989

Seattle	1.6
Boston	2.2
New Orleans	2.7
Newark	3.2
Philadelphia	3.6
Buffalo	3.9
San Francisco	4.3
Santa Clara	5.2
Sacramento	8.6
Portland	9.0
Cleveland	9.1
SAN DIEGO	**10.8**
Pittsburgh	11.2

Source: UMTA 1989 Section 15 Data

U.S Light Rail systems sorted by
Operating Expenses / Actual Vehicle Revenue Kilometre, 1989

Seattle	11.7
Santa Clara	11.5
Boston	10.8
San Francisco	8.3
Buffalo	7.6
Pittsburgh	7.3
Cleveland	6.4
Philadelphia	5.9
Sacramento	4.8
New Orleans	3.8
Newark	3.6
Portland	3.5
SAN DIEGO	**2.4**

Source: UMTA 1989 Section 15 Data

Notes

1. P.C.C. (President's Conference Committee) cars were the standard American streamlined streetcars. Introduced in 1936, they were produced until 1952. During this time they were considered the state of the art in tram design.

2. Total is a combination of the fleet requirement for San Diego Transit and North San Diego County Transit District.

3. A multi-city regional government.

4. Transit Australia, March 1988 Vol 43, N°3 "The San Diego Light Rail Transit Program" by Senator James R. Mills and Thomas F. Larwin.

5. Source: 1989 UMTA National Urban Mass Transportation Statistics Section 15 Annual Report.

6. Source: San Diego Trolley: The First Three Years San Diego Association of Governments for UMTA Nov, 1984.

7. Source: Metropolitan Transit Development Board Fact Sheet.

8. Source: Trends Before the San Diego Trolley. Prepared by the San Diego Association of Governments for the Urban Mass Transit Administration, 1982.

9. Metropolitan Transit Development Board fact sheet.

10. Source: Trends before the San Diego Trolley.

11. Source: San Diego Trolley ridership statistics.

CASE STUDY B.

The Bern-Solothurn Regional Transport System
P. Frezza (Switzerland)

Table of Contents

90

The RBS (Regionalverkehr Bern-Solothurn) regional light railway has been chosen for this study because it came closest to matching the definition of a light rail system given in the ECMT reference document. The only other system in Switzerland which might have come closer, the Lausanne TSOL (Tramway Sud-Ouest Lausannois), has not been in operation long enough to permit meaningful analysis.

1. GENERAL FOREWORD

Most of the data given in this paper have been taken from annual reports published by the RBS (from 1985 to 1990) or from internal files supplied by the RBS management. These documents have allowed us to gain an insight into the operator's business concept, which sets out the ground rules for policy formulation, its supply philosophy and its long-term investment projects. Other confidential documents have helped us to clarify our approach to the study itself. We have also made use of official statistics on public transport published by the Federal Statistical Office in 1989 (data for 1990 were not available), as well as the legislative texts governing relations between the Confederation and cantons, communes and railway operators.

1.1 Introduction

The RBS system is both a regional and a suburban rail network in that it not only provides rail links between the centre of Berne and the suburbs, but also between Berne and Soleure via Zollikofen. The network appears to have grown naturally, not only in terms of new lines but also through the gradual concentration/merger of different companies into a single enterprise. This pattern of growth has produced a rather disparate network that includes both metre-gauge railway lines and bus services.

The first rail link (Soleure-Zollikofen-Berne) entered into service on 10 April 1916. The success of this line may be attributed to the central location of stations, the frequency of trains and the relatively high speed of transport. It would now seem inevitable that train capacity will have to be increased to cope with rising demand as a result of the stricter parking regulations planned by the city of Berne, the constraints arising from implementation of the Ordinance on air pollution and the segregation of residential areas, leisure centres and the workplace.

This trend is fairly typical of a number of other major cities in Switzerland and reflects the growing desire of city-dwellers to solve the two-fold problem of pollution and congestion in their city centres.

1.2   Historical background

The canton of Soleure's original plan, as far back as 1899, had been to build a standard-gauge railway link to Schönbühl, from where passengers could travel to Berne on lines operated by Swiss Federal Railways (SBB). The canton of Berne, however, had been opposed to the idea, preferring simply to extend the existing suburban tramway line. A compromise was finally reached in 1912 when the two cantons decided to install a metre-gauge line built to Rhaetian Railway (RhB) standards. The Soleure-Zollikofen link was subsequently extended to Berne in 1924.

The advantage of this system lies in the fact that rolling stock built to RhB standards has virtually the same carrying capacity as standard-gauge wagons. Furthermore, the fact that the SBB used a different gauge, despite posing problems for freight transport, meant that innovations, such as the introduction of automatic couplings to rationalise marshalling operations, could be implemented more speedily.

The following chronological table illustrates how the network has grown since its inception:

-- Opening of the Berne-Muri-Worb (BWB) steam railway line	21/10/1898
-- Electrification of the line	21/07/1910
-- Opening of the Berne-Zollikofen (BZB) railway line	13/07/1912
-- Opening of the Worblental (WT) railway line	25/08/1913
-- Electrification of the Solothurn-Berne (ESB) electric railway railway line	10/04/1916
-- Merger of BZB and ESB to create the Solothurn-Zollikofen-Berne railway (SZB)	01/01/1924
-- Introduction of an uninterrupted service between Solothurn and Berne	01/10/1924
-- Merger of BWB and WT to create the joint Berne-Worb railway (VBW)	01/01/1927
-- Opening of the SZB underground station in Berne	20/11/1965
-- Extension of the WT line to the SZB station in Berne	25/05/1974
-- Merger of SZB and VBW to create the Regionalverkehr Bern-Solothurn (RBS)	30/11/1984

1.3 Geographical, economic and political context

The city of Berne is located in the Swiss Mittelland facing the entrance to the Bernese Oberland. The conurbation of Berne covers an area of 325 square kilometres and has a population of some 258 600 inhabitants, giving it a population density of 796 inhabitants per square kilometer (1991 figures; the decline in population noted over the last few years is expected to end shortly). In 1991, Berne had a working population of approximately 147 200. The economy of the region consists mainly of tertiary sector activities with a large proportion of small and medium-size enterprises. Berne is the fourth largest city in Switzerland after Zurich, Geneva and Basle. The city is located at the centre of a major tourist area extending from Lakes Neuchâtel, Murten and Biel to the west and south of Berne to Lakes Thun and Brienz in the foothills of the Bernese Alps to the north. While the climate is relatively mild, heavy snowfalls are common in winter and require the use of appropriate equipment.

Transport systems within the Berne region are organised highly efficiently under an integrated planning policy. The Berne conurbation has an extremely dense public transport network with strict policing of parking spaces within the city boundaries; park-and-ride facilities for commuters have been provided on the city outskirts. The city authorities have also introduced schemes designed to funnel traffic into a network of designated roads and to limit traffic in residential areas. Priority is given to public transport (co-ordinated traffic lights, dedicated roads in parts of the network, etc.), and the city centre has been transformed into a pedestrian area (with access restricted solely to delivery services). The RBS has embraced this move towards more environmentally-aware methods of land use and transport planning and is now an important player in terms of regional logistical planning. The RBS supplements the basic SBB network by providing passenger connections to destinations outside the city centre, and also helps to cut down on road traffic-related disamenities by providing attractive services for several categories of travellers (commuters, tourists, schoolchildren, leisure activities and others) (see Figure 1.3.).

The population of the communes served by the RBS network totals 272 249 inhabitants (1985), for (potentially) 77 696 of whom access to the SBB public network is provided solely by the RBS (estimate based on figures given in the RBS brochure "Bahn und Bus verbinden Stadt und Land -- Der Regionalverkehr Bern-Solothurn stellt sich vor, 1987").

2. ECONOMIC PARAMETERS

2.1 System of ownership

The Regionalverkehr Bern-Solothurn enterprise is a private company with head offices in Soleure. The public authorities hold a 94 per cent stake in the company's total equity capital of SF 22.4 million. Two thirds of the shares are held by the Confederation and the canton of Berne; the remaining shares are divided between the canton of Soleure, certain communes in the Berne and Soleure conurbations and private shareholders, as shown in the following table.

Capital Shareholdings in Bern Light Rail Systems

Shareholder	%
Confederation	31.4
Canton of Berne	34.7
Communes in Berne	17.9
Canton of Soleure	7.9
Communes in Soleure	2.0
Private shareholders	6.1
TOTAL	100.0

2.2   Sources of funding

Passenger fares and revenue from other sources cover approximately 70 per cent of the network's operating costs.

The **operating deficit** is governed by Article 58 of the Federal Law on Railways which states that the Confederation may give financial assistance to loss-making railway operators provided that the services they supply are needed to maintain traffic movements at either national or regional level. The operator must demonstrate that its revenues are not enough to cover its operating expenditures and the depreciation on railway facilities and rolling stock allowed under law. Support from the Confederation may be subject to special requirements such as the introduction of technical, structural and legal measures to improve the financial position of the operator, including merger with other enterprises (as was the case with SZB and VBW in 1984 when they merged to form the current RBS).

As a general rule, aid is provided in the form of subsidies or, if circumstances permit, short-term interest-free loans to be repaid from future operating surpluses (once the requisite depreciations have been calculated).

The provision of financial assistance by the Confederation is also contingent on support being provided by the cantons concerned. The amount that the cantons are required to pay is calculated according to both their ability to pay and the size of existing financial commitments they may have as a result of subsidies they have to pay to railway operators under federal law.   In cases where several cantons are required to provide financial aid, their share of such aid is calculated on the basis of the number of stations located within their canton, the importance of such stations in terms of overall traffic on the line, and the length of track exploited within their boundaries (Article 60 of the Federal Law on Railways).

The cantons are entitled to ask communal authorities and other public corporations in the canton to share the cost of such support.

The Confederation covers approximately 50 per cent of the operating deficit of the RBS;   the remainder is divided between the canton of Berne (88 per cent) and the canton of Soleure (12 per cent).

With regard to **investment**, funding is provided under a number of agreements with the Confederation which set out the overall amount of credit to be allocated, depreciation rates, the share of funding to be provided by the cantons and the share of funding which the enterprise must provide from its own capital resources.

Under the above agreements (Article 56 of the Federal Law on Railways), concession-holders are allowed to build new facilities, to upgrade existing installations and to purchase new rolling stock, provided that by doing so they can significantly increase either the efficiency or the safety of their operations. In the case of RBS, the Confederation's share of investment funding amounts, in principle, to some 50 per cent of the amount specified in the agreement, the remainder being split between the cantons of Berne and Soleure in the proportion of 80-88 per cent and 12-20 per cent respectively (depending upon the relative impact of the investment on the two cantons, the benefits that will accrue to the network as a whole, etc.) in the form of subsidies and grants.

As part of plans to modernise the railway system (assistance to private railways, Article 56 of the Federal Law on Railways), the Confederation and the RBS signed two new funding agreements in 1990. Under one of these agreements, the Convention of 18 May 1990, the Confederation will provide funds to build a double-track line, including a bridge, between Urtenen and Schöbühl. The line will be 0.842 km long and construction costs are expected to amount to around SF 6 570 000 per km (Table 2.2.a provides a breakdown of the share of the funding to be provided by the Confederation, the canton of Berne and the canton of Soleure respectively).

3. DESCRIPTION OF NETWORK AND SYSTEM OPERATION

3.1 Rail network

The 56 km (1990) of track operated by the RBS consist of a regional line to Soleure, two suburban lines to Worb and Jegenstorf and a line that is virtually a closed loop serving part of the Berne conurbation. The bus routes are designed primarily to act as feeders for the rail lines, both in Soleure and in Berne. The RBS serves a total of 43 stations (see Figures 3.1.a and 3.1.b).

SBB type I, 46 kg/m rails have been used for the track.

The network has three tunnels (the Schanzentunnel in Berne, 1 318 metres; Station Tiefenau, 510 metres; Altikofen, 125 metres), five bridges more than 10 metres long and 15 private branch lines for goods traffic whose aggregate length is 5 km. The entire network comprises 69 level crossings with public highways and roads (1989).

The track is metric gauge with a maximum gradient of 3 per thousand (4.5 per thousand at a few locations).

At present, platform height is generally 18 cm. This year the RBS is introducing new rolling stock offering easier access for physically handicapped passengers (see paragraph 3.3.). In the longer term, the RBS intends to raise the height of all its platforms (to 32 cm). Initially, this requirement will apply solely to new platforms, but will subsequently be extended to all other existing platforms (see Figure 3.1.c).

The RBS network is already integrated into the SBB network (including timetables) by virtue of the fact that RBS trains are routed directly into the SBB station in Berne, which has its own taxi rank and is linked directly to the public transport system (buses, trams, PTT) operated by the city of Berne. The same is true of Soleure. In addition, RBS stations are served by feeder buses (urban transport bus lines, RBS suburban bus lines, PTT buses in rural areas), which provide extensive coverage of the entire conurbation.

Furthermore, the RBS has provided park-and-ride facilities (offering an aggregate total of 250 parking places) in a dozen or so stations, thus allowing it to cater more effectively for demand -- particularly from commuters travelling in from communes that are not connected by bus to the RBS network.

There is little space available for such facilities in densely populated areas within the conurbation, however, and land prices are more or less prohibitive. Owing to problems arising from the limited number of places in the car parks, and the use made of such car parks (i.e. car drivers not using the RBS network), the RBS has had to introduce modest fees for car parking at some stations (40 centimes for 1 hour; 1 franc for 2 hours; 5 francs for the day; 15 francs for a monthly pass. Car parking for passengers, is still free however).

3.2 Operating objectives

The primary vocation of the RBS is to provide a public (mass-transit) rail service that meets the needs of the region while respecting an environmentally-friendly transport policy. In particular, the RBS aims to:

-- attract car drivers, especially commuters and other potential passengers such as shoppers;

-- provide an efficient mass-transit system over medium and long distances;

-- provide transport services throughout the region;

-- restrict its activities to the region;

-- co-operate closely and actively with other transport operators within the region.

Furthermore, the most important function of the RBS is to provide a rapid, punctual and if possible comfortable means of transport for commuters travelling between their place of residence and their workplace or school. Existing capacity will have to be increased to cope with projected future demand. Even if seating cannot be provided for all passengers during peak operating hours, passengers must not have to remain standing for more than 15 minutes. Lastly, no more than one train in ten trains operating during peak hours is allowed to arrive more than 2 minutes late. RBS has made a special effort to increase the frequency of trains running during peak hours. The interval between suburban trains is 15 minutes, and intercity trains between Soleure and Berne run at 30-minute intervals. Additional trains have therefore been brought into service outside the school holidays to meet the growing demand during peak hours. The RBS now operates trains from 05.12 to 00.35 hours between Berne and Soleure, representing a daily service of 19 hours and 23 minutes. Night buses have been introduced between 00.45 and 02.00 hours on Saturday and Sunday mornings to provide transport within the suburbs.

Transit times on the Berne-Soleure line have fallen as follows:

1916	75 minutes
1973	57 minutes
1985	43 minutes
1987	42 minutes
1993	36 minutes

The reduction in travel time to 36 minutes is primarily due to the introduction of new cars (higher speeds, wider doors, etc.) as well as to other network improvements (double tracks, elimination of level crossings, etc.).

In addition, the RBS has set itself the following objectives:

-- to increase the number of passengers carried outside peak hours;

-- to upgrade facilities, provided that costs are covered by passenger receipts and subsidies;

-- to improve management efficiency (streamlining);

-- to make safety a priority;

-- to motivate its personnel, by providing adequate staff training and by gearing manning to requirements;

-- to lay special emphasis on relations with the public.

Most of these objectives have been written into medium-term (i.e. over a period of around five years) corporate programmes at every level (finance, operations, personnel, etc.). In principle, RBS should be able to achieve all of these objectives by around 1997, except in cases where basic principles governing corporate policy are involved.

3.3 Rolling stock

The rolling stock in use on the RBS network reflects the way in which equipment has been steadily improved over time. Although some of it might seem relatively old to be still in use on a light rail system (some stock has been in service for over thirty years, with an average usage factor of 100 000 km a year), passenger cars have been regularly upgraded and renovated, thus increasing their useful life while at the same time ensuring that they are still attractive to passengers. Nonetheless, all this rolling stock is due to be replaced under the Confederation's eighth funding plan, which should reduce axle-km costs by 42 per cent (by lowering maintenance costs from SF 0.40 to SF 0.28 per axle-km). There are other reasons, too, why this older rolling stock should be rapidly phased out: safety requirements, braking systems, transmission of information, couplings incompatible with newer passenger cars, etc.

The rolling stock inventory in 1989 was as follows (see also Figure 3.3.):

Number	Type of equipment	Number of axles	Seating capacity
45	Electric railcars	264	3 946
4	Electric locomotives		
32	Passenger cars	108	1 730
3	Brake vans and mail vans	12	

Source: Statistical data No. 11: "Les Transports publics 1989", Federal Statistical Office, Berne 1991.

The most commonly used, and also the newest, rolling stock consists in 21 Be 4/8 41-61 (1974/1977/1978) electric railcars, each of which has a seating capacity of 128 and a top speed of 75 km/h. These train-sets account for almost half of the seating capacity of the RBS network and operate at a line voltage of 1 200 V dc.

RBS has ordered 11 new type (A)Be 4/8 low-deck cars (length: 40 metres; tare weight: 55 tonnes; top speed: 90 km/h) from Schindler Waggon in order to improve access for physically handicapped passengers; these cars are to be delivered in 1992. Each two-car unit will cost SF 5 million (by placing a bulk order with other light rail system operators RBS was able to reduce the purchase price by around 15 per cent); three units will be used for suburban services and the remainder for intercity services. The interior design of these new units has also been improved through the use of glass partitions. The greater visibility they afford should improve passenger safety, particularly at night.

3.4 Operating system

The RBS has been operating suburban services without ticket collectors since 1974. Single tickets are sold to passengers through automatic vending machines which can give change and which can also process multi-journey tickets. Tickets are periodically inspected at random by special teams of inspectors. The use of this system has enabled timetables to be streamlined and the number of trains increased without a concomitant increase in staff. Passenger information is provided by electronic display screens on the platforms in Berne station. Train delays are announced over a public-address system.

A heavily utilised network consisting mainly of single-track lines needs a control centre to manage and co-ordinate train movements. Since 1974, Worblaufen has gradually emerged as the nerve centre for lines leading to Berne, Soleure and Worb. Concurrently, a second remote-dispatching centre has been set up at Worb for the tramway-type line G. These two centres monitor and control all signals, crossing barriers and points, and will ultimately control the power supplies for the entire network. A two-way radio communications system provides links to trains and buses, thereby enhancing safety, improving interconnections and allowing information to be clearly and rapidly circulated within the network. This streamlining of control operations has lessened the workload of station personnel, who are now free to concentrate on marketing and customer services.

4. STAFF

In 1991 the RBS had a total staff of 357 employees (annual average and solely railway workers), compared with 353 in 1990. The staff were employed as follows: 45 in the administration department; 55 in the stations; 28 as travelling train crew; 3 in the ticket-machine maintenance service; 87 as train drivers; 13 in the traffic department; 13 as carriage cleaners; 30 in the facilities maintenance shop; 21 in the electrical shop; 60 in the repair and servicing shop; 2 as assistants. In 1990 (figures are not available for 1991), the staff turnover rate fell slightly to 7 per cent.

The six staff committees provide a forum in which to discuss all kinds of technical and operational problems and allow close contact to be maintained between management and "front-line" operatives.

In 1990, 35 people took part in in-house management training schemes (lasting 2.5 days). In addition, the company ran a series of other job training programmes (transactional analysis, bus-driving lessons, ticket inspector training, etc.). Ten train drivers and two tram drivers were given training by an instructor.

5. OPERATING COSTS

The operating costs for 1990 (figures for the bus service are not included) are set out in the table below.

	SF.	%
Wage costs	26 238 046	55.7
Equipment	9 767 830	20.7
Construction and renovation costs which cannot be entered as assets	5 176 996	11.0
Depreciation	5 940 881	12.6
TOTAL	47 123 753	100

Wage costs account for 55.7 per cent of network operating costs, 10.7 per cent up on the previous year's total. The sharp increase in labour costs is primarily due to inflation, improved overtime payments as well as the increase in real salaries in 1991.

In contrast, the increase in expenditure on equipment has remained below the rate of inflation, and construction and renovation costs that cannot be included on the assets side of the balance sheet are slightly down from the previous year's level.

Equipment costs include advertising, insurance, rents, power supplies, contract maintenance services, operating supplies and office overheads.

6. FINANCING AND REVENUES

6.1 Funding of investment

Depreciation allowances (SF 4.3 million) can be reinvested; for the remainder, see paragraph 2.2.

The following table lists sources of funding (as percentages):

Source of funding (as a percentage)	1956-1986	1987	1988	1989	1990
Confederation	32	46	54	44	50
Canton of Berne	40	35	46	34	39
Canton of Soleure	2	15		11	11
City of Berne	8				
Communes	3				
RBS	15	2	(0.6)	3	
Other (private)				8	
Total	100	100	100	100	100
TOTAL (SF million)	252	2.6	27.3	8.3	17.1

The above funding was used as follows (nominal values):

Year(s)	Equipment	SF millions	%
1956-1986	Rolling stock	87.00	34.0
	Worblaufen station	29.00	11.5
	Double track between Worblaufen and Berne	29.00	11.5
	Underground station at Berne	28.00	11.0
	Double track and new lines	38.00	15.0
	Stations and workshops	32.00	13.0
	Electrical installations	9.00	4.0
	Total	252.00	100.0
1987	25 pairs of carrying boogies	2.58	100.0
1988	9 x Be 4/8 articulated train-sets (trams)	26.00	97.0
	Spare parts for vehicles	0.80	3.0
	Total	27.00	100.0
1989	Loading facilities	1.20	15.0
	Double track	5.20	63.0
	Replacement of old catenaries	1.80	22.0
	Total	8.20	100.0
1990-1993	Extension of Soleure depot	4.50	26.0
	Worblaufen depot No.3 (equipment)	2.10	13.0
	Works unit	1.60	9.0
	Radio communications system (phase 1)	2.20	13.0
	Diesel locomotive	1.30	8.0
	Double track	5.50	32.0
	Total	17.10	100.0

Other solutions have been considered such as the construction of a new station in partnership with a private company (Migros Shoppyland) or working with the private sector within the framework of Canton development policy (Technoparks).

6.2 Operating accounts

The following table provides a breakdown of the operating results for the period 1985-1990 in SF million.

Year	Expenditure (E)	Revenue (R)	Operating results	% coverage of expenditure
1985	36.4	27.4	-9.0	75.2
1986	37.2	29.2	-8.0	78.4
1987	39.5	30.1	-9.4	76.2
1988	41.4	30.6	-10.9	73.8
1989	44.4	32.9	-11.5	74.1
1990	47.1	33.9	-13.2	71.9

Network income has covered more than 70 per cent of expenditure since 1984 (date on which SZB merged with VBW), despite falling slightly in 1990 as a result of reduced revenues (introduction of the Bäre Abi flat-rate fare scheme in the Berne region) and increased costs (inflation, increased number of employees).

The following table provides an overview of the operating costs per passenger carried over the period 1984-1990:

Year	Number of passengers (P) (Millions)	Operating costs (C) including depreciation	C/P (SF)
1984	13.1	35.4	2.7
1985	13.8	36.4	2.6
1986	14.1	37.2	2.6
1987	15.6	39.5	2.5
1988	16.0	41.4	2.6
1989	16.5	44.4	2.7
1990	17.5	47.1	2.7

It should be noted that the relative costs shown in this table, i.e. costs per passenger carried, have remained constant despite inflation (4-6 per cent over the last few years).

6.3 Revenues

The following table provides an overview of income, income per passenger and income per passenger/km (see Figure 3):

Year	Income (I)	Income per passenger (SF)	Income per passenger/km (SF centimes)
1984	16.9	1.29	13.2
1985	19.2	1.39	14.3
1986	20.0	1.43	14.8
1987	21.0	1.34	13.8
1988	20.8	1.30	13.4
1989	22.4	1.36	14.1
1990	22.3	1.27	13.2

The fall in real income per passenger carried from SF 1.43 to SF 1.34 in 1987 was a direct outcome of the introduction of price controls by the Confederation, which reduced the price of a half-price season ticket from SF 360 to SF 100 as well as the price of season tickets for commuters. As a result of these measures, the RBS was obliged to increase the frequency of trains. The Confederation compensated for this increase by topping up income in absolute terms, but not in terms of the average income per passenger carried, hence the fall in the latter.

The decline in real income per passenger from SF 1.36 to SF 1.27 in 1990 amounts to some 16 per cent since 1984 if account is taken of inflation. Much of this fall in income was off-set by streamlining, which led to a real increase of 6 per cent in operating losses (since 1984). The reason for this decline lies in the introduction of "Bäre Abi" season tickets in the Berne region which reduced income from sales of individual tickets (ticket-vending machines, multi-journey cards) by 20 per cent, the equivalent of SF 2 million a year. Given the ceilings placed on local government subsidies, the loss of income from sales of season tickets is only partially made up by the canton and the communes. Revenues from season tickets sales are currently calculated on the basis of the figures established for the year preceding the introduction of a flat-fare area. In time, prices should eventually be based on figures obtained from market surveys.

7. SERVICES PROVIDED

7.1 Vehicles

The figures given in the table below are for train movements on RBS's own network. Swiss statistics are not given in vehicle-km but train km, which limits the scope for comparison with other case-studies in this area.

Year	Train-km	Passenger train-km	gross tonnes-km
1984	2 592 081	2 491 011	167 002 482
1985	2 585 009	2 490 094	170 584 857
1986	2 594 397	2 492 526	172 319 363
1987	2 591 085	2 497 069	175 024 236
1988	2 646 399	2 548 794	189 132 569
1989	2 728 112	2 637 696	193 166 545
1990	2 732 361	2 638 966	199 148 946

7.2 Passengers

The following table indicates the use made of trains:

Year	Passengers carried (millions)	Passenger-km (millions)	Average trip per passenger (km)
1984	13.1	128.1	9.8
1985	13.8	134.8	9.8
1986	14.1	136.9	9.7
1987	15.6	151.5	9.7
1988	16.0	155.2	9.7
1989	16.5	158.6	9.6
1990	17.5	168.1	9.6
1991	18.3	175.3	9.6

With regard to transport within the conurbation, the use of passenger services has increased for a number of reasons such as favourable weather conditions, increased commuting between the conurbation and the city (due as well to a shortage of flats in the city) or between the city of Soleure as dormitory and the city of Berne as a place of work, as well as the number of sales of "Bäre Abi" regional season tickets. However, since the introduction of season tickets in June 1990, it is no longer possible to calculate passenger numbers on the basis of ticket sales. The increase of 6 per cent in passenger use of the network is based on a comparison of numbers of passengers at Berne in December 1989 and in 1990.

Passenger use of the network outside peak hours has also risen steadily since the mid-1980s due to the introduction of improved interval timetabling. The capacity of trains running before 9.00 a.m. and at certain times in the afternoon has thus had to be increased to avoid passengers having to travel standing up.

Using the same procedure applied in 1985, a census was made of the number of passengers getting into and out of trains in all stations on a given day in December 1990. The results of this census were as follows:

Lines	1990	1985	% difference
Z	8 531	7 266	+ 17
W	24 474	17 781	+ 38
S/SE	22 881	20 086	+ 14
G	19 806	11 773	+ 68
Berne	40 885	33 984	+ 20

These figures show where the greatest number of passengers change trains, as well as the lines on which traffic has risen the most steeply since 1985. These considerations will therefore be used as criteria in deciding what measures will have to be taken in the future in terms of the management of passenger flows and investment in platform widening programmes.

The RBS currently makes use of almost all its carrying capacity. Capacity will therefore have to be increased in the future, particularly in view of forecasts for the period 1995-2000 which show that the overall seating capacity of the light rail network will have to be increased by 850. These forecasts do not however take account of any emergency or policy measures that may be introduced by the authorities (pollution abatement, etc.) or any further reductions in fares on public transport networks, despite the fact that implementation of the Ordinance on air pollution could potentially boost passenger traffic by 15-20 per cent at peak hours within the next ten years. As already mentioned in paragraph 3.3., the RBS will be bringing eleven train-sets into service in 1992/3 and intends to purchase a further seven train-sets in 1996/7 for use on the busier lines. Another problem that will have to be resolved is that of platform crowding at the terminus in Berne. Because the platforms there are too narrow, passengers waiting for trains get in the way of passengers trying to get off trains, resulting in log-jams on the platforms. The RBS will begin by reviewing the problem of "passenger management" with experts from the Paris metro system (RATP), following which platform widening would seem to be inevitable.

7.3 Fares and timetables

With the introduction of regional season tickets, the fare zones were restructured and the price of tickets and season tickets increased on 1 May 1991. The zone system replaced a precise fares scale based on the distance travelled, meaning that passengers now pay a flat-rate fare within each zone regardless of the number of stations covered or the distance travelled.

The new fare system offers the following advantages:

-- fare calculations have been simplified by reducing the number of zones;

-- the price of tickets to complement the regional season ticket is also easier to calculate;

-- certain journeys have now become cheaper;

-- the zoning system matches that of the "Bäre Abi".

But also the following disadvantage:

-- some journeys are now more expensive not only as a result of inflation but also because fares have had to be readjusted under the new system.

Fares are based on the number of zones involved as well as the distance travelled (1991):

Zones	Adult fares (SP)	Reduced fare (children half-price) (SF)
Less than 1.5 km	1.20 frs	1.20
1	1.70	1.70
2	2.60	1.70
3	4.00	2.00
4	5.20	2.60

There are relatively few, if any, problems in co-ordinating traffic within the conurbation with the SBB network and its Rail 2000 programme (under which regular thirty-minute or one-hour services, depending on the importance of the destination, are gradually being introduced. The frequency of RBS trains ranges from 30 to 15 minutes, depending on the line.

For intercity traffic, however, the RBS network will have to integrated into the Rail 2000 network in order to optimise interconnections. Passengers on the inter-city line must wait 12 minutes at Berne station, the hub for the railway network, to make a connection with the Rail 2000 system operated by SBB, with the result two single-track lines (one at Bätterkinden and the other at Zollikofen-Moosseedorf) will have to be converted to double-track lines so that trains to and from Berne can cross each other.

7.4 Safety and industrial accidents

The accident statistics for 1990 are given below:

	Injuries	Deaths	Damage to property (SF million)
Passengers and employees	36	--	1.9
Others	3	2	0.2

These statistics are high because two trains collided just outside Berne station in November 1990 and 36 people were injured in this accident, 12 of whom had to be treated in hospital. It is therefore worth noting that in 1989 there were only four accidents in which people were injured (three people: a motorcyclist and two pedestrians), all of which occurred at level crossings.

7.5 Projected safety measures

Investment designed to improve safety will not be reduced. Such investment is aimed not only at basic safety equipment (signalling systems, automatic controls to stop trains, elimination of level crossings) but also systems designed to improve working conditions by reducing the stress generated by heavy work loads.

A continuous speed monitoring system is to be installed throughout the network and should be a significant additional safety factor.

Traffic has now reached the level where the RBS is obliged to convert its radio communications system into a data transmission network with remote controls for the rectifying system, TV platform monitoring system, etc. In addition to which, as mentioned earlier, rolling stock built to higher safety specifications is to be brought into service this year.

8. CONCLUSIONS

A rail system such as the RBS offers a number of major advantages that can help to improve the co-ordination of transport in cities, reduce car traffic and thus protect the environment, improve passenger safety and safeguard the economic appeal of a region. These benefits, most of which have already been touched upon in this paper, may be summarised as follows:

-- regional devolution and integration of the region into the national network (feeder services and interconnections);

-- punctuality (which is relatively unaffected by weather conditions), speed and comfort of trains, due to dedicated track and high train frequency;

-- stations located in town centres, near to shopping and administrative areas, as well as at other major logistical centres;

-- highly reliable mass-transit systems;

-- reasonable fares and frequent trains, even outside peak hours;

-- supply tailored to user groups (in terms of fares, carrying capacity, routes, etc.);

-- a healthy, balanced financial base (commercial management), considerable freedom to take decisions;

-- provision of over 300 jobs and training at all levels.

Even though there are some negative aspects too, such as operating losses, rising investment costs, land and energy use, such drawbacks are primarily of a financial nature. In contrast, the impact that this system can have on the quality of life in the region cannot really be quantified and can only be outlined roughly by tables or charts.

Figure 1.3 **The number of passengers carried by RBS through Zollikofen as compared with the number of cars using the Bernstrasse between 1981 and 1987**

Daily Traffic At Zollikofen

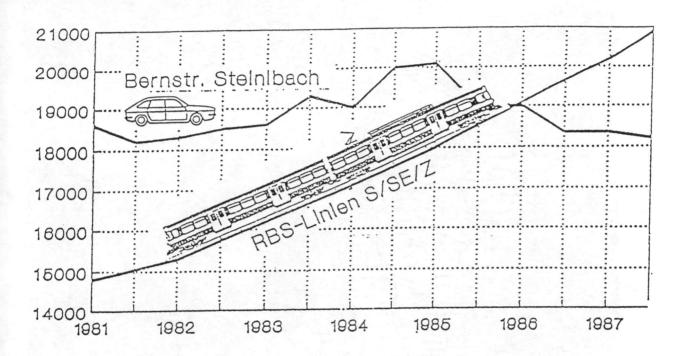

Surveys of car traffic in Zollikofen have clearly shown that the increase in the number of people using RBS trains reflects not only the greater mobility of the population, but also the ability of the rail system to reduce car traffic.

At present, there are more people using the RBS network to travel through Zollikofen than there are car drivers on the Bernstrasse.

Table 2.2.a. **Convention of 18 May 1990: allocation of subsidies**

Confederation   49.2%
Canton of Berne   36.8%
Canton of Soleure   14.0%

Figure 3.1.a. **RBS Regional network**

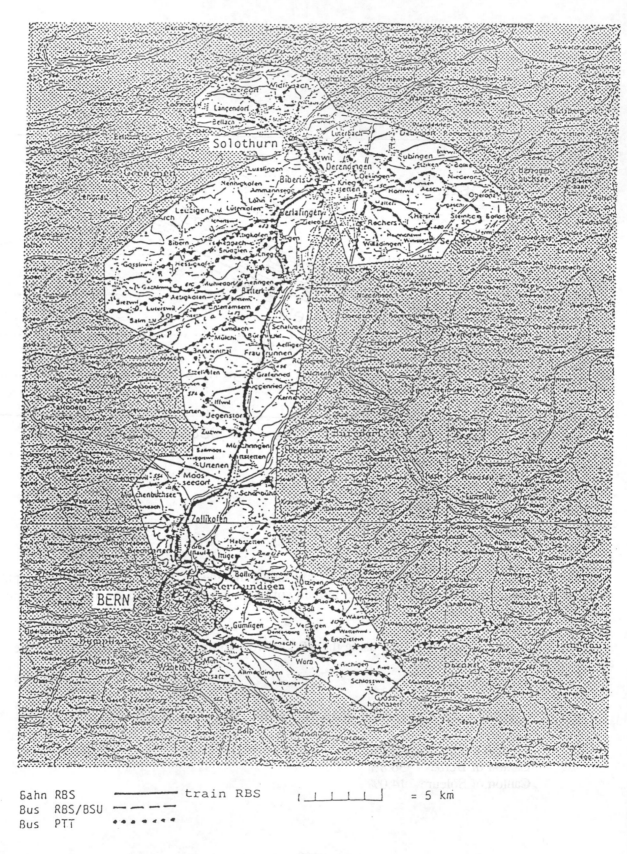

Bahn RBS	————————	train RBS
Bus RBS/BSU	– – – –
Bus PTT	•••••◄◄◄

⊢—⊢—⊢—⊢—⊢—⊣ = 5 km

Figure 3.1.b. Plan of the RBS network

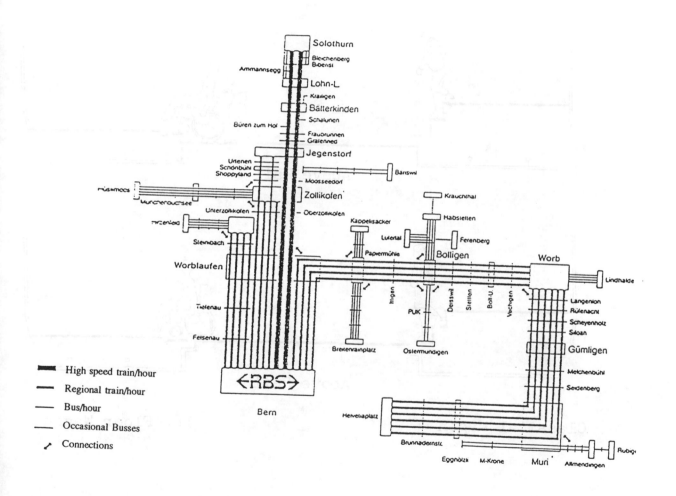

111

Figure 3.1.c. **Impact of different platform heights on access to rolling stock in service**

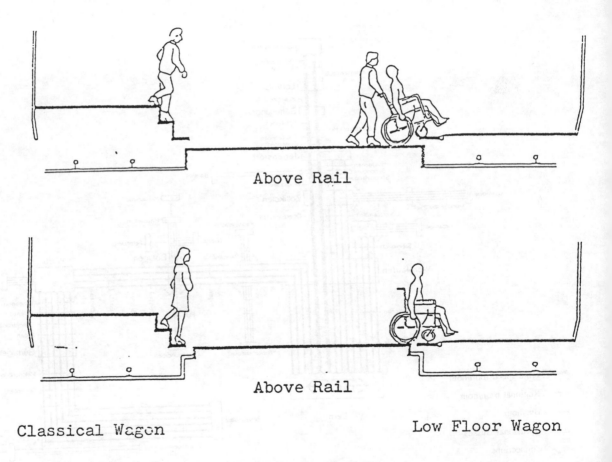

Above Rail

Above Rail

Classical Wagon

Low Floor Wagon

Figure 3.2. **Rolling Stock in Service**

Bre 4/4 "Pencer Pintli" 1916, renovated in
1959, 1987; 1200 V. 75 km/h
44 seats, Line SE, extra trips

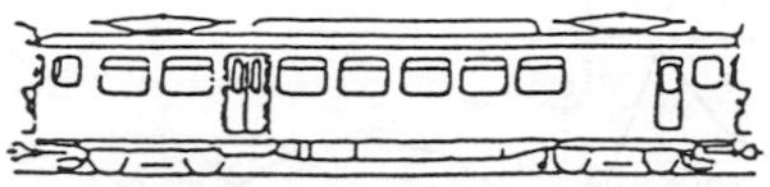

Bre 4/4 1929, renovated in
1955-1988; 1200 V. 75 km/h
64 seats, SE Line

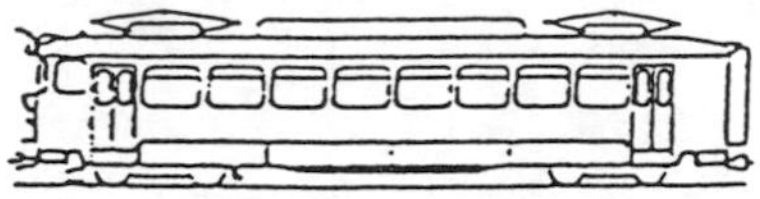

BDre 4/4 4 "Billet-Bar" (Prototype) 1950,
renovated in 1976-1981; 1200 V. 512 kW
75 km/h. 46 seats, SE Line

BDre 4/4 4 21-23 "Billet-Bar" 1955,
renovated in 1971-1979 and 1983/1984/1986;
1200 V. 512 kW. 75 km/h; 40 seats. SE Line

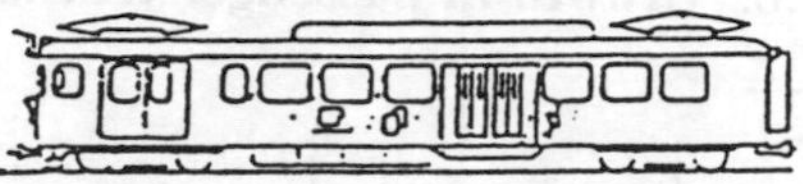

ABt 201-207, 1974/1980.
18 places 1st Class
31 places 2nd Class. SE Line

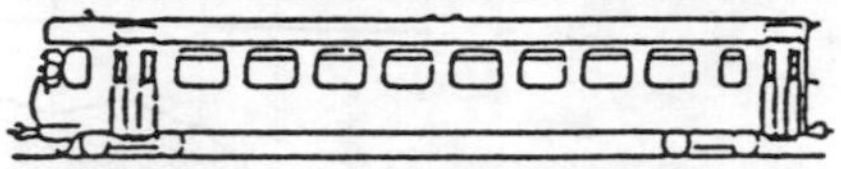

Bt 211-216. 1950/1953/1957,
renovated in 1981-1985; 72 seats.
SE Line

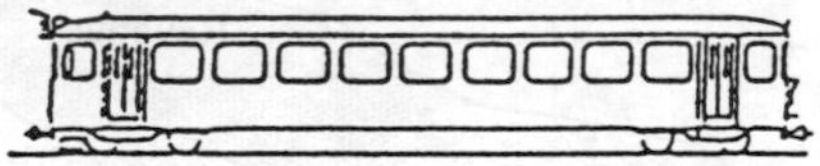

Bt 221-223, 1954;
renovated in 1977/1979.
56 seats, SE Line

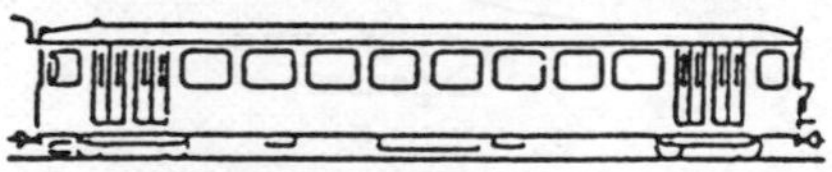

Zt 261-262 1957;
renovated in 1984/1985.
SE Line

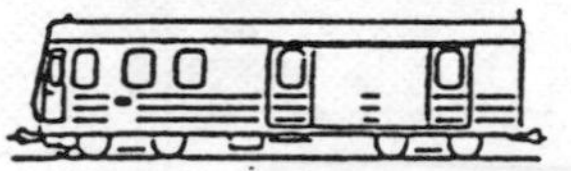

De 4/4 103. 1973 (# 101 and 102 are similar
1200 V - 547 kW, 50 km/h

Ua 401-450 1986
60 km/h when empty,
50 km/h when loaded.

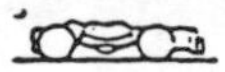

Be 4/8 **41-61** 1974/1977/1978
1200 V - 314 kW; 75 km/h
128 seats. S, W, Z Lines

Be 4/8 **81-89** 1987
600 V - 300 kW
65 km/h. 74 seats, G Line

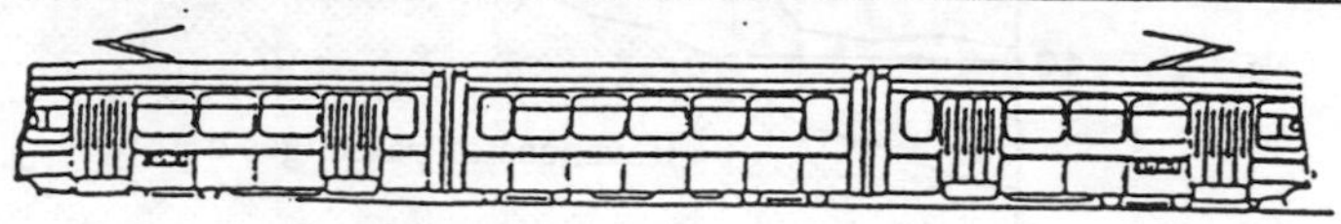

Key:
A = 1st Class
B = 2nd Class
D = Baggage compartment
Z = Mail
Va = Carrying bogies
e = Electric motors
r = Restaurant car
t = Driving trailer
4/8 = 4 = number of trailer axles
      8 = total number of axles

Figure 3.3.a. Degree of cost coverage (%)

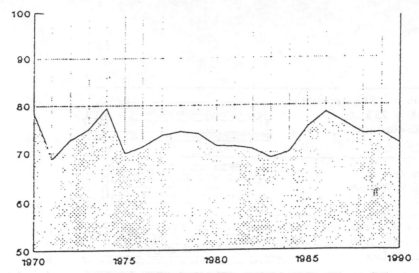

Figure 3.3.b. Growth in passenger traffic (in millions SF)

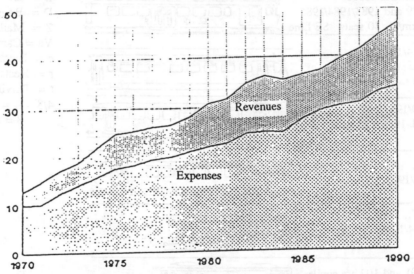

Figure 3.3.c. Growth in passenger traffic (in millions SF)

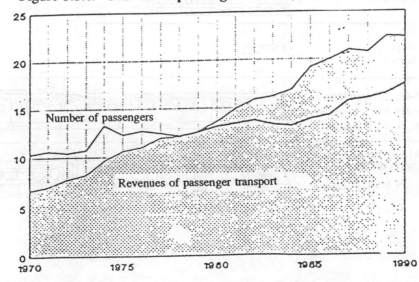

CASE STUDY C.

The Grenoble Tramway System
J. Lesne
Centre d'Etudes des Transport Urbains (CETUR)

Table of Contents

116

1. GENERAL DESCRIPTION

1.1 Resume

The Grenoble urban area is the second largest conurbation in the Rhône-Alpes Region, after the Lyons Urban Community.

It is served by a two-line tramway network.

-- Line 1, commissioned in 1987, connects the South of the city with the Commune of Fontaine on the West side of the urban area, via the inner city, the railway station and a bridge over the Drac. It is 9 km long and has 22 stops;

-- line 2 is about 5.8 km long (including 4.7 km of new infrastructure) and has 14 stops (9 of them new). It connects the railway station with the University complex in the Commune of Saint-Martin d'Hères, via 1.5 km of Line 1, the eastern part of the city, a bridge over the Isère and the Regional Teaching Hospital of La Tronche.

The idea of a tramway system grew from a transport policy designed to meet the needs of the urban area, whose population had in less than a century grown from 100 000 to 400 000. This rapid growth had resulted in a traffic build-up that had gradually brought a number of the city's thoroughfares to saturation point.

1.2 History of public transport in Grenoble

At the beginning of the century, the Grenoble city area was served by a tramway system built between 1897 and 1902.

The decision was taken between 1947 and 1952 to phase it out and replace it with buses and trolley-buses. As in most of France, infrastructure and rolling stock had deteriorated or been badly damaged during the Second World War. No specialised tramway industry existed to build new equipment. Priority was being given to developing the automobile industry and new urban thinking was giving preference to individual private transport.

From 1950 to 1973, the population of the Grenoble urban area grew considerably (from 165 000 to 385 000). The subsequent heavy increase in private car traffic made it urgent to develop a comprehensive urban transport policy.

In 1973, the Syndicat Mixte des Transports en Commun (SMTC) of the Grenoble conurbation was created, bringing together the conurbation's 23 Communes and the Isère Department. The SMTC's task was to organise and fund public transport in the conurbation. It set itself the following objectives:

117

-- to restrict motor vehicle traffic in the city centre by introducing a traffic plan giving priority to public transport and making it easier to travel by foot or bicycle;

-- reorganising and developing the public transport system;

In 1975, the city's former private operator of the public transport system was replaced by the Société d'Économie Mixte des Transports Publics de l'Agglomération Grenobloise (SEMITAG), two-thirds of whose equity was held by local authorities and one-third by private interests. One of the private shareholders of SEMITAG is TRANSCET, the second most important French urban transport operator.

The impact of the SMTC's policy was marked. Whereas from 1968 to 1973 the number of trips by public transport users had declined by 2 per cent, it rose from 17.3 million trips in 1973 to 38.1 million in 1983.

From 1978 on, this policy ran into serious obstacles:

-- the difficulty, despite the introduction of articulated units and stepped-up trip frequency, in increasing the capacity of the busiest bus routes;

-- heavier operating losses on public transport.

For these reasons, the SMTC decided to revive the feasibility studies that had been undertaken, first in 1972, on a dedicated right-of-way public transport system (a cable scheme called "POMA 2000") and, then in 1977, on a tramway line, with the twin objectives of improving public transport capacity and holding down operating costs.

After comparing the various possible modes of transport in terms of capacity and cost, the studies proposed a reorganised system featuring:

-- dedicated right-of-way tramway lines on the busiest routes;

-- trolleybus lines in heavily built-up areas with high traffic density;

-- bus services.

The summary draft project for building the two tramway lines was worked out between 1981 and 1983, the year in which a new political majority took charge of the municipality. In line with its campaign promise, the new mayoral team held a referendum on the project, which was approved on 22nd June 1983 by a 53 per cent majority.

The administrative (impact assessment, public enquiry) and financial (raising the Transport Contribution rate, obtaining a government subsidy) formalities for building the first line were then embarked upon. Preparatory work began in September 1984. Construction proceeded according to plan and the line was commissioned on 5th September 1987.

The building of the second line followed almost immediately. Work on it began in October 1988 and was completed in November 1990.

1.3 Geographical and economic background

a) The main socio-economic features of the conurbation

In 1985, the population of the Grenoble urban area numbered 380 000, corresponding to 145 090 households.

The labour force totalled 152 481, i.e. a participation rate of 40 per cent, and an average of 1.05 employed persons per household.

Households possessed 155 673 private vehicles, so that the car ownership rate was 107 per cent and the equipment rate (household units equipped with private vehicles) was 79 per cent (26 per cent of households having two vehicles or more).

b) Catchment areas for the tramway system

In 1987, inhabitants and jobs located within a 400-metre radius of stops made up respectively 20 per cent of the urban area population and 31 per cent of its jobs (42 per cent of its services jobs).

	Population served	% share of total population	Jobs served	% share of total jobs	Population & jobs served
Line 1	59 000	(15)	33 700	(22)	92 700
Both lines	78 000	(20)	47 300	(31)	125 300

c) Travel patterns

The modal breakdown of motorised travel practised by the urban area's inhabitants has been ascertained by 4 household surveys. The trends are as follows:

Year	Private car	Public transport	Two-wheeled vehicles
1966	55%	13%	32%
1973	63%	13%	24%
1978	65%	17%	18%
1985	75%	18%	7%

A forthcoming household survey will be used to assess the impact of the introduction of the tramway system on urban area travel patterns.

1.4 Objectives

a) National and local context

Beginning in the early 1970s, a national policy to develop public transport was launched, the idea being to relieve inner city congestion due to increased motor traffic by encouraging the use of public transport.

In order to implement this policy, local authorities were entrusted with organising and financing urban transport. The government promised to grant them financial aid for carrying out the necessary work (building up transport capacity, creating reserved bus routes and dedicated infrastructure).

In Grenoble the local authorities assumed responsibility for organising public transport from 1973 on by setting up the SMTC.

From the outset, the SMTC pursued a vigorous policy of public transport promotion and development with the twin aims of improving the mobility of people without motorised transport and providing an alternative to the private car.

The policy called for reorganising the public transport network and doubling its capacity; public transport vehicles would benefit from important right-of-way measures.

The policy eventually resulted in the commissioning of the two tramway lines.

b) Why a tramway service?

The SMTC opted for a modern tramway service for the following reasons:

-- increased vehicle unit capacity;

-- use of dedicated routes, avoiding general traffic unpredictability and guaranteeing better punctuality, with priority at light-controlled intersections ensuring competitive commercial speeds;

-- improved inner city service, bus services from the outskirts being linked up with the tramway system;

-- curbing operating costs and improving productivity;

-- reducing air pollution by reliance on electric power;

-- availability of government investment subsidies and entitlement to raise the Transport Contribution rate (from 1 to 1.5 per cent at the time).

The SMTC decided that tramway facilities should offer easy access, even for handicapped persons. New rolling stock design was required, differing from that of the future Nantes system where car floors would be practically level with tramstop platforms.

Passengers in wheelchairs could board cars by means of a system of retractable bridges between the car floor and the platform.

The Grenoble tramway system acted as more than a simple public transport mode -- it was also instrumental in changing the quality and fabric of city life.

It meant that some inner city thoroughfares in Grenoble and Fontaine were converted to pedestrian use and re-vitalised. Various neighbourhoods along the route were redeveloped or renovated, and improvements were made at many points along the line (squares relandscaped, car parks built, planted areas created).

1.5 Alternative possibilities

A number of other solutions were adopted or considered during this time.

Back in 1974, as part of the reorganisation of the public transport network, the emphasis had been laid on improving the bus and trolleybus traffic flow. A jointly used route across the inner city was provided for the main bus services.

The number of public transport vehicles using this route doubled in 6 years and gave rise to a spate of problems: unpunctuality, slower speeds, higher operating costs, disamenities, annoyance to people living along the route.

Other solutions were then sought.

A local firm's proposal to build "POMA 2000" (cable-drawn cars either suspended or supported on viaducts) was rejected because its technology was untried and the infrastructure would have been difficult to integrate.

In February 1975, the Secretary of State for Transport instructed 9 of France's most populous conurbations (excluding Paris, Lyons, Lille and Marseilles) to join in drawing up specifications for a new tramway-style rail system. In August 1975, he announced an international competition aimed at choosing firms who could later be called on to build the system after submitting tenders. Preliminary plans for a tramway line in Grenoble were then drawn up but were considered difficult to implement (building the inner city section without disrupting motor traffic) and expensive.

However, the spiralling operating costs of the bus and trolleybus services (falling commercial speed and unpunctuality), combined with a decline in fare revenues, meant that a new high-capacity transport system with dedicated routes had to be introduced. Fresh studies for a tramway service were therefore commissioned by the SMTC and were subsequently used for the system now in operation.

Underground options such as a metro system were rejected. Not only were they too costly but the closeness to the surface of the water table would have made construction difficult and raised expenditures even further.

1.6 Construction

a) Line 1

The contracting authority for the tramway project was the SMTC, which had the necessary administrative and technical services.

It delegated the SEMITAG as assistant for the technical supervision of the operational aspects (choice of rolling stock, track, electric power supply, overhead lines, operating facilities).

It subcontracted construction of bridges over the Drac and of a new bus depot to the Société d'Aménagement de l'Isère (SADI).

The role of prime contractor was shared among:

-- the firm GMS, which also ensured general co-ordination of the operation;

-- the municipal Technical Services of Grenoble and Fontaine;

-- Central Government Services (*Direction Départementale de l'Équipement*).

Small co-ordinating groups were set up in both of the Communes concerned to work out the best solutions for putting in the line, organising traffic, maintaining relations with the public, those living along the route and elected officials, and keeping the public informed.

Preparatory work began in September 1984. The works programme went entirely according to plan, so that the line opened on schedule on 5th September 1987.

The timetable was as follows:

-- Detailed preliminary plans	June 1983
-- Public interest clearance	April 1984
-- Bridges over the Drac	November 1984/July 1986
-- Depot-workshop	October 1985/December 1986
-- Route detours and railbase	March 1985/September 1987
-- Tracklaying	July 1985/September 1987
-- Overhead line	June 1986/October 1987
-- Delivery of rolling stock	November 1986/September 1987

b) Line 2

A different procedure was followed in building Line 2. In order to have better control over time and costs, the SMTC decided to contract out the infrastructure work (but not the procurement of rolling stock) to the SATURG, a consortium of the firms which had helped to build Line 1.

Work on Line 2 began in October 1988 and was completed in November 1990.

2. ECONOMICS OF THE OPERATION

2.1 System of ownership

In France, the organisation and financing of urban public transport are the responsibility of local government or, more specifically, of Urban Transport Organising Authorities (OAs) which may be either Communes or groups of Communes.

The decision to build tramway-type infrastructure and its financing are, in other words, devolved to the OAs.

The public transport network is operated by an OA-controlled service, by a public undertaking (mixed economy company) or by a private company.

In Grenoble, the SMTC is the OA; it represents 23 Communes with a total area of 212 sq.km. and a population of 380 000, and the Isère Department.

The SMTC owns the infrastructure and rolling stock built according to its instructions as contracting authority; it has "property rights" over infrastructure built by the consortium contracted to lay down Line 2. This infrastructure is legally considered as a reversionary interest.

Urban transport operation is entrusted to the SEMITAG.

2.2 Source of funds

OAs are able to draw on several sources to finance their investment programmes:

-- the funds of the Communes and the Isère Department forming the SMTC;

-- the "Transport Contribution", which is a tax instituted by the Act of 11 July 1973 for financing (investment and operations) urban public transport. Its base consists of the wages paid -- within the ceiling fixed for ordinary social security contributions -- by all employers of more than nine employees located on the territory of an OA with a population of more than 30 000. The OA decides whether to impose the tax and is free to set its rate within the ceiling fixed under the Act, viz. O.5 per cent for OAs with a population of 30 000 to 100 000, 1 per cent for OAs with a population of more than 100 000, or 1.5 per cent (raised to 1.75 per cent since early 1989) for OAs that have undertaken projects for dedicated right-of-way public transport and have obtained a government grant for that purpose.

-- the Government grant reserved solely for infrastructure work. The government awards grants based on the estimated cost of each infrastructure operation (excluding rolling stock) up to a maximum of 30 per cent;

-- loans.

3. FEATURES OF THE NETWORK AND ITS OPERATING SYSTEM

3.1 Description of the transport network and two tramway lines

The routes of the two tramway lines were determined after study of the principal traffic corridors and of:

-- patronage on the various public transport routes;

-- the present and future shape of the conurbation, numbers of people and jobs needing transport provision, the location of major public amenities;

-- comparative travel times with and without tramway.

As each tramway line was opened, bus and trolleybus routes were restructured with a view to:

-- ensuring complementarity between modes of transport;

-- keeping down the number of bus services running through or ending in the inner city by linking them up with tramway services further out;

-- enabling staff and vehicles made available by the replacement of buses by trams to be redeployed in outlying districts and Communes;

-- avoiding radical changes to the network structure so as not to disrupt user habits.

In 1990, the Grenoble urban area transport system consisted of:

-- 15 bus routes, served by 200 standard and 50 articulated buses;

-- 3 trolleybus routes (43 trolleybuses);

-- 2 tramway routes (35 car-sets);

The laying of the tramway tracks along dedicated lanes called for a change in the way the carriageway is used. Private transport was not placed at a disadvantage, but traffic flows were reorganised so as to maintain volume and fluidity, local provision, access to buildings and shops bordering on routes, deliveries and parking space (no reduction in capacity).

3.2 Service specifications

In 1989, the tramway service ran during the same hours as the other main network services, from 04.51 to 00.21, that is, a little under 20 hours per day.

In 1988, the commercial speed on line 1 was 18 km/h, varying between 16.7 and 19.8 km/h depending on the time of day (initial estimates had predicted an average commercial speed of 18.3 km/h).

The observed commercial speed of line 2 is 18.9 km/h. At peak hours, waiting time between cars on both lines is 4 minutes (i.e. 2 minutes on the jointly used section).

3.3 Rolling stock

a) Technical specifications

The Grenoble rolling stock is a version of that used in the Nantes system.

It also was designed to meet travel needs on busy routes in conurbations of over 200 000 inhabitants. In addition, it is remarkably easy to board. Its low floor, only 345 mm above rail level, extends over two-thirds of the length of the car-set and permits easy boarding from an ordinary pavement.

The low floor entailed incorporating some specific features, such as specially designed articulation and carrying boogies.

The following technical choices governed the design of the Grenoble rolling stock:

-- each car-set is made up of two steel cars connected by a central articulating compartment containing 860 mm of corridor space and a low floor with housings for the carrying boogie wheels;

-- a low floor in the middle of the unit, and raised-floor (875 mm above rail level) compartments at either end, three steps up from the low floor;

-- most of the electrical machinery is housed on the roof;

-- 4 double 1.50 m wide doors on each side provide access to the low floor (the two central doors have a retractable bridge system for use as and when required across the gap between platform and car floor);

-- extra low central carrying boogie with independent wheels and crank axles;

-- microcomputerised non-skid system to ensure rail/wheel adhesion during acceleration and braking;

--   electronic signalling devices for obtaining right-of-way at intersections where lights are controlled by the Operating Aid System;

--   car-sets are reversible with two driving cabs.

b) Performance details

Each car-set is 29.4 m long and 2.3 m wide. Tare weight is 44.6 tonnes and the maximum permissible load is 62.2 tonnes.

Unit capacity is 174 passengers (54 seated and 120 standing) with a standard occupancy of 4 passengers per sq.m. Under exceptional load conditions (8 passengers per sq.m.), the capacity indicated by the constructor is 293 passengers.

Maximum speed is 70 km/h and cruising speed is 60 km/h. On Line 1 of the Grenoble service, the commercial speed from terminus to terminus is 17.9 km/h.

The average rate of acceleration from O to 40 km/h is 0.92 m/s^2; deceleration with normal braking is 1.2 m/s^2 (2.9 m/s^2 with emergency braking).

Fully loaded, trams can climb inclines of up to 8 per cent (1 in 12). With only one motor boogie operating, the maximum incline is 6 per cent (1 in 16).

The first tramway line went into operation with a fleet of 20 car-sets. A further 15 car-sets + 3 end 1991 were acquired for operating the second line.

3.4 Operating system

Tramcars are visually operated, more like road than rail vehicles since, despite their dedicated right-of-way in running sections, they are required to mix with other traffic at certain places such as intersections.

Although the fleet is provided with radio communications, the visual driving mode can adversely affect punctuality. In an attempt to remedy this defect, two systems have been installed on Line 1 and will be extended to Line 2:

--   the Operating Aid System (OAS) enables traffic control in the Central Command Post (CCP) to track the positions of cars at all times and so to spot those running ahead of or behind schedule. The CCP can intervene to correct timetable fluctuations. The fact that a tram driver knows when he is ahead of or behind time means that he can adjust his speed to correct the error;

--   intersections have been equipped to take account of tramcars crossing. On Line 1, every light-controlled intersection is linked to a central computer. A connection between it and the OAS computer factors in the exact position of an approaching tram and regulates lights so as to anticipate a change or hold them on green until the tram has passed.

3.5 Integration with other modes of transport

The tramway lines are fully integrated into the Grenoble conurbation public transport network and are, in fact, the network's lead element.

Under the pricing system adopted, a single ticket enables each passenger to use all connecting services within one hour of boarding.

3.6 Planned extensions

After studying a number of projects, the SMTC has prepared a master plan for extending the tramway system in the Grenoble urban area.

Extending the two existing lines is the first priority.

The preliminary plans for these extensions have already been drawn up.

4. MANNING

In 1989, the SEMITAG's average annual payroll comprised 824 employees (including employees of subcontractors) engaged in operating the entire Grenoble area public transport network (buses, trolleybuses and tramway Line 1); of these 517 were vehicle crew. The comparative figures for 1985 were 863 and 539.

The tramway service employed 58.6 persons as follows:

-- 37.6 vehicle crew;

-- 1 other operating staff;

-- 20 maintenance workers.

The clerical staff dealing with tramway operations are included with the workforce of the SEMITAG, which handles the whole of Grenoble's public transport system.

5. INVESTMENT COSTS

Total investment for building tramway Line 1 amounted to FF 1 300 million before taxes (in January 1987 francs). It was made up as follows:

ITEM	ACTUAL COST (in FF million)
Purchase of land and buildings, rights of way	65
Civil engineering Infrastructure	466 215
Rolling stock (20 car-sets)	250
Allied operations	186
Consultancy and sundry expenditure	100
TOTAL (in January 1987 francs)	1 282

Investment for Line 2 amounted to FF 780 million before tax (in 1990 francs), broken down as follows:

ITEM	ACTUAL COST (in FF million)
Infrastructure (under contract)	514
Rolling stock (15 car-sets)	190
Consultancy, allied operations, purchase of land and buildings, sundry	76
TOTAL (in 1990 francs)	780

6. OPERATING COSTS

In 1988, tramway-related costs amounted to FF 28.8 million, broken down as follows (in millions of francs):

Personnel	56.25 %
Operating costs	9.72 %
Vehicle maintenance and cleaning	5.56 %
Installation maintenance	5.90 %
Structural charges	22.57 %
TOTAL	100.00 %

7. FINANCING AND REVENUES

7.1 The Investment package

The investment package consisted of funds from several sources -- the "Transport Contribution", the government grant and loans.

The Transport Contribution had been introduced at 1 per cent in the Grenoble area on 1 January 1974; the rate was raised to 1.5 per cent in 1984 when the decision was taken to build Line 1 of the tramway and once the first instalments of the government grant had been negotiated (it may be noted that receipts from the Transport Contribution in 1989 amounted to FF 171 million).

The Government gave the SMTC a grant equal to 50 per cent of the amount eligible for subsidy (excluding rolling stock). Investment costs for Line 1 had been estimated at FF 790 million before tax (in January 1983 francs). The eligible amount for Line 1 of the tramway service was fixed at FF 584 million and the corresponding subsidy at FF 292 million.

The SMTC was also able to borrow at preferential rates (soft loans) from the Caisse des Dépôts et Consignations (this possibility no longer exists) as part of the programme of the Fonds de Développement Economique et Social (loans at 12.5 per cent repayable over 25 years).

For the construction of Line 2, the SMTC received a government subsidy of approximately FF 150 million (in the meantime the subsidy rate had been cut to 30 per cent).

7.2 Operating revenues

a) Revenues from the whole network

The introduction of the tramway service, along with the streamlining of the bus network, had a beneficial effect on the city transport operating account. Operating costs were brought under control and passenger revenues increased sharply. Not only that, but the annual subsidies paid out by the SMTC were also reduced as shown in the following table (amounts in millions of current francs):

	1982	1983	1984	1985	1986	1987	1988	1989	1990	1991
Expenditure[1]	147	167	199	206	212	216	215	226	239	246
Revenues[2]	58	60	64	62	68	90	105	115	126	133
Revenues/ Expenditures	0.39	0.36	0.32	0.30	0.32	0.42	0.49	0.51	0.53	0.54
Subsidies paid by SIMAN	103	118	130	129	109	108	98	95	95	

1. Does not include investment-related costs, financial costs or miscellaneous charges.
2. From ticket/travel card sales.

b) Revenues from the tramway service

In 1988, revenues from the tramway service alone amounted to FF 37.1 million.

8. TRANSPORT CAPACITY

Since the opening of Line 1 of the tramway service, the trends in transport capacity have been as follows:

Year	1982	1983	1984	1985	1986	1987	1988	1989	1990	1991
Number of buses	285	291	289	276	286	281	257	254	259	204
Tramway sets	-	-	-	-	-	11	20	21	34	35
Total supply (km x 1000)	11229	11225	10871	10315	10549	10427	11646	12157	12540	12992
Of which tramway (in car/km x 1000)	-	-	-	-	-	578	1 910	1 951	2 237	3 381

9. PATRONAGE

a) Trends in patronage

The trends in number of trips on the tramway service have been as follows:

-- end 1987   35 000 trips per day

-- end 1988   50 000 trips per day

-- during 1990 88 000 trips per day (includes 33 000 on Line 2)

-- during 1991 95 000 trips per day

Traffic trends (in units x 1000) on the whole Grenoble area network have been as follows:

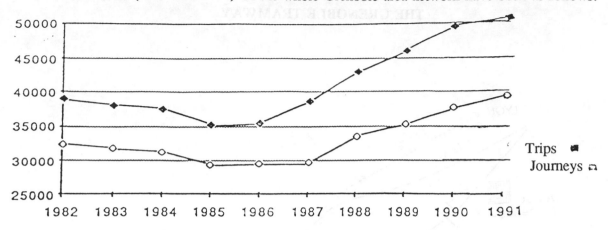

The number of tramway passengers per year increased as follows:

Year	1987	1988	1989	1990	1991
Passengers (in millions)	4 420	13 274	14 314	16 286	22 281

b) Description of clientele

12 per cent of the tramway Line 1 passengers surveyed said that during the previous year they had travelled by means other than public transport; they are the "new clientele" mentioned in the table below.

While 75 per cent of them explained that the choice of the tramway corresponded with a change of place of residence or work, 25 per cent said that they had been attracted by the advantages of the tramway service. The latter comprise an equal proportion of women and men in the 20-50 age group, from the better-off social and economic categories, owners of private cars and only occasional users of public transport.

	New Clientele	Clientele surveyed
Wage-earners	37%	30%
School pupils/students	38%	37%
Supervisory staff	7%	3%
Non-workers	19%	29%
Women	60%	65%
Men	40%	35%

The survey findings give a good idea of the make-up of the new clientele of the tramway.

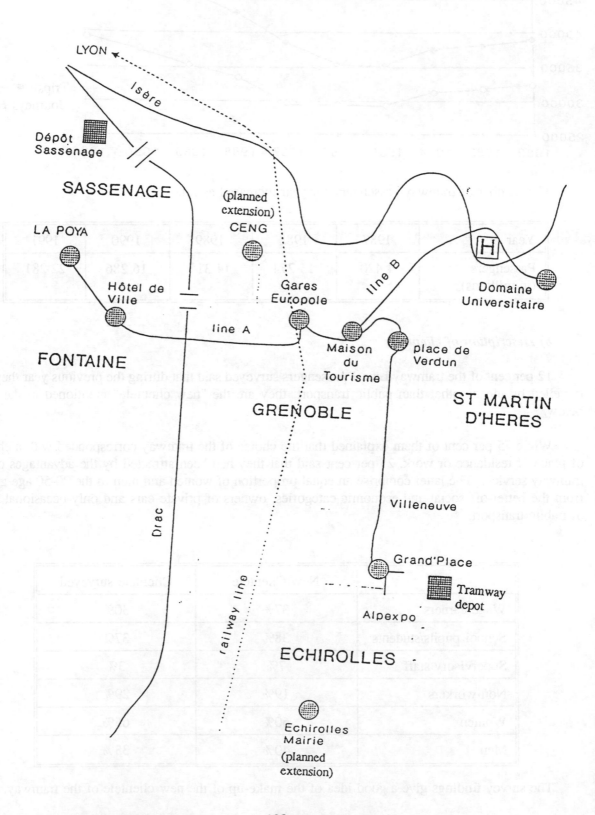

CASE STUDY C.

The Nantes Tramway System
J. Lesne, CETUR

Table of Contents

I. GENERAL DESCRIPTION

1. Resume

The Nantes urban area, the largest in West France, is served by a tramway system. The network will be extended by a second line, currently under construction, and later by a third line. Tramway Line 1, commissioned in 1985, connected Bellevue in the West with Haluchère in the East, via the edge of the inner city. The Haluchère-Beaujoire extension, opened in April 1989, increased the length of the line from 10.6 to 12.6 km and the number of stops from 22 to 24.

The route layout of the first line was decided on the basis of the following factors: ease of track insertion in the city; suburban bus feeder service possibilities; population, job and public amenity service requirements; future urban development.

2. History of public transport in Nantes

2.1. The history of the city is interwoven with that of public transport

The entry into service on 7th January 1985 of the first modern tramway service in Nantes signalled the renaissance of this mode of transport in France after more than fifty years during which lines were being closed.

It was the first time in France since the 1920s that a new line equipped with rolling stock of modern design had been built (only three conurbations -- Lille, Marseilles and Saint-Etienne had kept their trams in service). Since then, other large cities have followed suit -- or are about to do so: Grenoble, Rouen, Reims, Strasbourg, Brest, for example.

It is not surprising that Nantes should have been the site of this innovation since the city's public transport network had acted as pioneer several times before. In 1825, it had adopted the first "omnibuses" and, in 1879, it had conducted the first experiments with compressed air-driven tramcars.

2.2. 1825, the first "omnibuses"

Nantes was the town where the first commercial service of horse-drawn city buses was created in 1825. The term "omnibus" was, incidentally invented for this service. Two inhabitants of Nantes were the originators. One, Louis Bureau, was the grandson of a ship-owner whose premises were located on the site of the Place du Commerce (formerly the Place du Port-aux-vins) and whose clerks spent a great deal of their time travelling from there to the Salorges customs depot. Louis had the idea of designing a vehicle that could make the journey more quickly, cheaply and comfortably.

The idea was picked up by Stanislas Baudry, owner of a steam-powered flour mill at Richebourg. Baudry had decided to use his condensed steam to supply a public bathing establishment but, since the clientele for his baths, which were a long way out from the city centre, had trouble travelling to them, he introduced a horse-drawn vehicle to carry customers there. He then discovered that quite a number of people used the vehicle not to go to his baths but to travel to other destinations on the way. This set him thinking and, not long after, with the approval of the Nantes city fathers, he introduced a regular public transport service which was soon followed by another.

The vehicles set out from in front of the shop of a hatter named Omnés, who had adorned his shopfront with the Latin motto "Omnes omnibus" (All things to all men). The term "omnibus" stuck, and finished by being universally adopted.

Stanislas Baudry next went to Paris to set up a similar omnibus network, the first service of which was opened in 1828. His Paris company -- l'Entreprise Générale des Omnibus -- was the forerunner of today's RATP.

The success of the omnibus spurred competition. Several transport companies sprang up in Nantes, where city growth would soon require a tramway network to be built.

2.3. 1879, the first air-driven tramcars

In 1878, the Nantes City Council granted a 40-year concession on a tramway route between the tollhouses of the Boulevard de Sébastopol and La Grenouillère to the Compagnie de l'Air Comprimé directed by a M. Mekarski. Mekarski was the inventor of a traction system using compressed air. He intended to use his system to drive his tramcars.

The concession agreement was signed on 7th November 1876 and the Compagnie des Tramways Nantais was formed immediately afterwards.

Operations began on 13th February 1879 on a first section of line between Doulon and the Gare Maritime. By 1880, the line extended to Chantenay. In the next few years, the compressed-air tramway network expanded rapidly -- by 1910, there were 39 km of lines, 94 motor units, 3 locomotives and 10 trailer cars. The last of the omnibuses went out of service in 1898. The decision was taken in 1911 to modernise the network by switching over to electric power, but compressed-air trams remained in service until 1917.

2.4. The gradual replacement of trams by motor-buses

Not long after the introduction of the first electrified tramways in 1913, and while new extensions were being carried out (14 routes by 1932), the first motor-buses appeared. They were used to provide service to an exhibition in 1924. By 1926, they were in regular operation on three routes with low levels of patronage.

The Second World War air-raids seriously damaged the tramway network. Given the heavy cost of restoration, it was decided to phase out the tramway system and replace it with buses. The first bus service dates from 1949, and the last tram service was discontinued on 25th January 1958.

In 1973, the Compagnie Nantaise des Transports en Commun (the new name of the Compagnie des Tramways de Nantes) owned nearly 200 buses.

2.5. *Construction of the first new tramway line*

In February 1975, the Secretary of State for Transport commissioned nine of the most populous conurbations (excluding Paris, Lille, Lyons and Marseilles) to join in drawing up specifications for a new tramway-type rail system. In August of the same year, he launched an international competition aimed at choosing firms who could later be called upon to build the system after submitting tenders.

In February 1978, the Government and the SITPAN (Syndicat Intercommunal des Transports Publics de l'Agglomération Nantaise) signed a development contract under which work on a first tramway line would be begun by 1980-81. The studies were entrusted to the SOFRETU which handed its summary draft project to the SITPAN in December 1978.

The SITPAN approved the summary draft project in February 1979 and decided to go ahead with the detailed draft project. It requested a matching grant from the Government, which was approved in March 1979.

The detailed draft project was drawn up between June 1979 and January 1980. In March 1980, the SITPAN called for tenders on the rolling stock from the winners of the 1975 international competition. A special rolling stock committee was set up in July 1980. Early in 1981, the Government announced that it would subsidise the project, and the Prefect of Loire-Atlantique declared the operation to be in the public interest.

In November 1981, the Minister of State for Transport, signed an agreement with a construction consortium, headed by Alsthom Atlantique, for developing "Tramway Français Standard" equipment, which would be first introduced on the Nantes Urban Area line.

The way was now clear for construction to proceed. It remained to define and establish the general pattern of organisation for the contracting authority and prime contractor.

As Urban Transport Organising Authority, the SITPAN was the contracting authority and, more specifically, arranged the funding (State grants and part of the Transport Contribution ("Versement de Transport")[1] to its ceiling level of 1.5 per cent on 1st July 1981, without reliance on local taxes).

In February 1979, the SITPAN assigned to the SEMITAN responsibility as contracting authority and prime contractor. A works service was created within the SEMITAN in April 1979 to manage the tramway project.

3. Geographical and economic background

3.1 *Main features*

The Commune of Nantes lies in the Loire Atlantique Department in West France. The population of the Communes covered by the SIMAN (see D-a below) numbered 502 000 in 1989 (an annual increase of O.7 per cent since 1982) and accounted for almost half the population of the Department (1 O69 000 in 1989). Population density was 1 103 per square kilometre. In population terms, the

Nantes conurbation ranks seventh after Greater Paris, Lyons, Lille, Marseille, Bordeaux and Toulouse. It is an important hub for national and regional road, rail, air and maritime traffic.

It has a temperate maritime climate.

The conurbation's 156 665 jobs (public sector excluded) are distributed among 27 111 enterprises (5 373 of them small businesses) which break down as follows:

-- 2 177 in industry (34 435 employees);

-- 2 103 in contracting and public works (13 197 employees);

-- 5 629 in wholesale and retail trades (12 720 employees);

-- 17 202 in the services sector (73 616 employees).

The 473 concerns employing over 50 persons account for 52 per cent of the wage-earners in the Nantes Urban Area.

3.2 Travel patterns

In 1980, Nantes Urban Area residents made 1 333 000 trips daily.

In 1990, they made 1 700 000 trips daily, an increase of 31 per cent.

Nearly two out of three trips (59 per cent) are made in private cars.

The private car fleet rose from 150 000 in 1980 to 225 000 in 1990. There were 87 cars per 100 households in 1980, 109 per 100 households in 1990.

In 1990, 54 per cent of trips were made during peak hours (8-9 a.m., 12-2 p.m., 4-6 p.m.). This percentage is lower than it was in 1980.

4. Objectives

4.1 National and local context

Beginning in the early 1970s, a national policy to develop urban public transport was launched, the idea being to relieve inner city congestion caused by increased motor traffic by encouraging the use of public transport. In order to implement this policy, local authorities were entrusted with organising and financing urban transport. The government promised to grant them financial aid for carrying out the necessary work (building up transport capacity, creating reserved bus routes and dedicated infrastructure).

In 1973, the Nantes municipal authorities began to take over the organising of public transport, first by buying new buses for the operating company and then by establishing reserved lanes.

Another step forward was the creation in 1975 of the SITPAN (Syndicat Intercommunal des Transports Publics de l'Agglomération Nantaise). The introduction of the Transport Contribution in 1975 provided the SITPAN with the money needed to carry out its projects.

In 1979, the former operating company was replaced with a mixed economy corporation, the SEMITAN, whose majority shareholder was the SITPAN and which was chaired by a local elected representative.

In 1983, the SITPAN became the SIMAN (Syndicat Intercommunal à Vocation Multiple de l'Agglomération Nantaise) with responsibilities that extended beyond public transport. The SIMAN conducted a general review of transport policy for the Nantes Urban Area on which a supplementary works programme was based:

-- construction of a ring road around Nantes crossing the Loire upstream (Bellevue bridge) and downstream (Cheviré bridge) of the city, with the purpose of diverting through traffic (completion planned for September 1991);

-- introduction of a fast, punctual, comfortable, high capacity public transport network designed to serve the city centre.

The new scheme will provide means of promoting urban public transport by, first, creating reserved lanes, second, procuring articulated buses, third, going ahead with Line 1 of the new tramway service.

4.2 Why a tramway service?

There were a variety of reasons for adopting the tramway option:

-- continued promotion of public transport services be providing room for them on the road system and setting aside dedicated ways on the surface;

-- operation of large-capacity cars providing more comfort, punctuality and a higher commercial speed than motor buses;

-- introduction of modern rolling-stock with low energy consumption and ground space requirements per person carried;

-- reorganisation of bus routes around the new tramway line, considered as the backbone of the urban area's public transport system

and two major objectives:

-- to encourage people to use public transport more and private cars less and;

-- to keep network operating costs in check.

Studies established the feasibility of building a two-line tramway network within a reasonably short period of time: one extending North-South, the other East-West. Priority was given to the second, as it would be easier to put through: it would not cross the central city area and, to the East, would use

140

existing rail corridors. It would also be easier to incorporate into with the existing street system, while catering (directly or by feeder services) for 20 per cent of the population and almost one-third of urban area jobs.

5. Alternative possibilities

A number of other solutions were considered.

A study of the rail option (using existing track) showed that combining several kinds of rail traffic (goods, city transit and trunkline passenger) would have entailed heavy transformation costs and introduced constraints irreconcilable with a workable urban transport system.

The trolleybus option, requiring dedicated ways, was rejected because of insufficient passenger capacity.

The Metro option was too expensive (needing five times the investment and costing three times more to operate) and could not have been geared to the expected growth in patronage.

6. Construction

6.1 General organisation

The overall organisational structure was as follows:

Decision-making authorities

-- Steering Committee: made up of the Mayor of Nantes (and the Deputy Mayors concerned), the Mayors of Rezé, Saint-Herblain and Carquefou, and the Managing Director of the SEMITAN. The Committee took all the decisions dealing with works organisation and financing;

-- Tenders Board: made up of elected representatives and local government officials. It awarded the contracts.

Planning and consultancy bodies

-- Technical Committee: composed of representatives of the major partners in the project. As studies and work progressed, it acted in an advisory and supervisory capacity;

-- Consultants: owing to the highly innovative character of the undertaking, French and foreign tramway experts were consulted;

-- Architects: teams of architects worked on the design of the stops and, more generally, on the problem of incorporating the line into the urban fabric.

Other partners

In carrying out its task, the SEMITAN needed the collaboration of other partners to conduct studies (SOFRETU and SEMALY, for example) and certain kinds of work (municipal technical services, SIMECSOL, SOFRETU, architectural firms, etc.).

6.2 *Construction proper*

Once the organisation was in place, work could start. The works programme (November 1981 -- December 1984) was broken down into a number of specific tasks:

-- preliminary operations (transport rerouting, demolition work);

-- roadway alterations, track bed (earthworks, embankments, street lighting, signals, etc.) and civil engineering (Moutonnerie bridge, Rue Curie overpass, Railway Station underpass, Ste-Luce Road and Rue P. Bouger crossings);

-- tracklaying;

-- overhead power supply installation;

-- power substations;

-- stop construction and fitting;

-- construction of the Dalby operations centre (depot-workshop).

The first job was the demolition of the old Etablissements Brissonneau so as to build the Dalby operations centre.   Work on the actual tramway line began with the West section (Bellevue-Médiathèque), continued with the East section (Hôpital Bellier-Haluchère) and ended with the central segment (Médiathèque-Hôpital Bellier), in accordance with the timetable given.

Total time elapsing between the start of the preliminary work and the opening of the line was 33 months. Allowing for a 5-week halt in May 1983 due to a change in the Nantes City Council and a one-month period of uncertainty leading up to it, the original timetable was kept to.

II. ECONOMICS OF THE OPERATION

1. System of ownership

In France, the organisation and financing of urban public transport are the responsibility of local government or, more specifically, of Urban Transport Organising Authorities (OAs) which may either Communes or groups of Communes.

The decision to build tramway-type infrastructure and its financing are, in other words, devolved to the OAs.

The public transport network is operated by an OA-controlled undertaking, by a public undertaking (mixed economy company) or by a private company.

In Nantes, the OA is the SIMAN (Syndicat Intercommunal à Vocation Multiple de l'Agglomération Nantaise) which has other responsibilities in addition to the organisation and financing of public transport, such as the urban road system, project studies, environment, refuse disposal. 20 Communes with a combined population of 500 000 and an area of 455 sq.km. are grouped in the SIMAN.

Operation of the urban transport network is entrusted to a mixed-economy company, the SEMITAN, in which the SIMAN holds 65 per cent of the capital. The SEMITAN is also responsible for building the tramway system.

The SIMAN owns the rolling stock and infrastructure.

2. Source of funds

The OA was able to draw on several sources to finance its investment programme:

--   the funds of the Communes in the SIMAN;

--   the "Transport Contribution" (see note 1);

--   the government grant reserved solely for infrastructure work. The government awards grants based on the estimated cost of each infrastructure operation (excluding rolling stock), up to a maximum of 30 per cent;

--   loans.

III. FEATURES OF THE NETWORK AND ITS OPERATING SYSTEM

1. Nature of the transport network and tramway service

The Lines of the tramway service are intended to be the backbone of the Nantes Urban Area public transport system, enabling a maximum of passengers to benefit from their punctuality, speed and capacity.

The network is made up of various services each having a specific function:

--   the tramway service lines are diametrical; they extend to the edges of the built-up area; they carry the heaviest traffic;

--   radial bus routes (10) or diametrical routes (12) provide a secondary service between the tramway routes;

--   ring road bus routes (9) link the city outskirts without passing through the central area;

143

-- feeder bus routes (21) serve outlying Communes and industrial zones; they will connect with the tramway and the other bus services through special connecting terminals.

Tramway Line 1 connects BELLEVUE in the West with HALUCHERE in the East, via the edge of the inner city. The HALUCHERE-BEAUJOIRE extension, opened in April 1989, increased the length of the twin-track line from 10.6 to 12.6 km and the number of stops from 22 to 24.

Careful analyses and studies were carried out regarding the way in which the tramway would fit into the city and enhance the quality of urban life, a comprehensive approach that covered every aspect of the service: track, overhead lines, stops, etc.

1.1 Track

The type of track was selected in the light of proven techniques for providing maximum operating reliability.

It is of standard gauge and uses 50kg/m UIC or normal Broca rail. Bed width (not counting dividers) is 6.10 m; the distance between twin track centrepoints is 3.20 m.
In order to blend with the Nantes cityscape and match locally available or formerly available materials, three construction techniques were adopted in laying the tracks:

-- in densely populated areas (from the Gare Maritime to the Gare SNCF) and at intersections, track is embedded in the road surface ("Dortmund" laying technique). The track bed is overlaid with granite (a Brittany-quarried stone much used in Nantes) paving blocks;

-- in less densely populated areas (from Bellevue to the Gare Maritime and from the Gare SNCF to Hôpital Bellier), the track is ballasted (railway technique) and gravelled up to the rail head base;

-- the bed running parallel with the railway line (from Hôpital Bellier to Haluchère) is ballasted and the track is laid in standard railway style.

On running sections, the bed is separated from the roadway by dividers of 0.75 m minimum thickness. Where separation is wider, grassed or planted dividing strips have been created.

1.2 Overhead contact line

The overhead line studies focused on power supply, site installation and the shape and colour of line supports.

The electric cabling for the overhead line was laid underground, making it possible to have just one overhead contact wire (without catenary) in each direction.

Use of high-tension wire with a 1.5 tonne breaking-point (using the "tension-regulated" technique) made it possible to cut down the number of supports -- they are spaced at an average distance of 60 m except on curves. The placing of the supports makes for easy identification of the tramway route and avoids confusion with the street lamp posts. In front of the Château des Ducs de Bretagne, the street lighting standards have been moved for aesthetic reasons to the other side of the tramway track where

144

they have been interspersed with the plane trees, thus avoiding a visual clash with the overhead power posts of the tramway.

The choice of central support posts with double sidearms is space-saving. To make the supports even more inconspicuous, the usual glass or porcelain insulators have been eliminated. The inside of the sidearms conducts electricity whereas the outside works as an insulator. The posts have an H-shaped cross-section for good stress resistance. The H-design also houses the power cables inconspicuously and hides the weights used for tautening the wires.

1.3 Stops

Tramway service stops comprise two low boarding platforms, 60 m long by 2.50 m wide, able to accommodate double-length trams. Stops are equipped with shelters, seating, signs and other fittings, and ticket machines.

2. Service specifications

In 1989, the tramway service ran during the same hours as the other main network services, from 4.30 a.m. to 12.48 a.m., i.e. a little over 20 hours per day.

Also in 1989, travelling time between Bellevue and Haluchère, a distance of 12.6 km, was 35 minutes, the average speed being 21.6 km per hour.

During weekday off-peak hours, waiting time between cars is 7.5 minutes; during peak hours, it is 5.5 minutes for single cars and 7 minutes for 2-car sets.

The introduction of 3-car sets should enable waiting time to be reduced to 5 minutes on Lines 1 and 2.

3. Rolling stock

3.1 Technical specifications of the new rolling stock

The new tramway equipment was designed to cater for requirements on routes carrying heavy traffic in urban areas with a population of over 200 000. It therefore combines the advantages of a modern rail system (high capacity, reliability, economic running, comfort, attractiveness) with the reasonable investment cost of a mainly surface mode of transport.

The completely novel design of the Nantes tramway system is attributable to the following technical choices:

-- body in lightweight aluminium alloy with detachable side guards;

-- monomotor end boogies, directly based on the RATP model (MF 77), with rubber-steel secondary suspension;

-- articulated carrying boogies; double-articulated cars with tight-sealing doors;

-- 660 mm rubber wheels with removable tyres;

-- 2 275-kW chopper-controlled motors (1 for each end boogie) with freon-cooled thyristors (motors modelled on the MF 77);

-- wholly electric systems operating on 750 V direct current (compressed air used only for sand expulsion and wheel flange lubrication);

-- electric regenerative braking (disk brakes on all boogies and magnetic shoes for emergency braking);

-- electronic controls which trigger traffic lights to ensure right of way at intersections; an electronic voice synthesizer announces the name of each stop;

-- units are reversible with two driving cabs and are equipped with automatic coupling for forming double-length trams.

3.2 Performance details of the new equipment

Units are 28.5 metres long and 2.3 metres wide. Tare weight is 40.8 tonnes and the fixed maximum load is 56.7 tonnes.

Unit capacity is 168 passengers (60 seated and 108 standing) with a standard occupancy of 4 passengers per sq.m. Under exceptional load conditions (8 passengers per sq.m.), the capacity indicated by the constructor is 276 passengers. Considerations of comfort, based on the 4 passenger per sq.m. norm, governed the size of the Nantes tramway fleet. The norm may be exceeded only exceptionally (rising to 6.6 passengers per sq.m. at peak hours, for example). Maximum speed is 70 km/h and cruising speed is 60 km/h. In Nantes, the commercial speed from terminus to terminus is between 21.5 and 23 km/h depending on the extent to which right-of-way is allowed at traffic lights on the route. Average journey time between Bellevue and Beaujoire is approximately 35 minutes; when right-of-way is allowed at all traffic lights, the time should be cut to 32 minutes.

Average rate of acceleration from 0 to 40 km/h is 1.1 m/s2; deceleration with normal braking is 1.25 m/s2 (2.75 m/s2 with emergency braking).

Fully loaded, trams can climb inclines of up to 8 per cent (1 in 12). With only one motor boogie operating, the maximum incline is 6 per cent (1 in 16).

Theoretical maximum throughput per hour in each direction, with single units running at 3-minute intervals, works out at about 3 500 passengers (7 000 with double-length trams). This estimate is based on the assumption that traffic flows regularly over the period in question, so no account is taken of momentary variations during peak hours. Traffic surges or "super peaks" are factored in by using a peak indicator, defined as the ratio between the heaviest passenger volume in a 15-minute period and a quarter of peak-hour traffic. The indicator is used to calculate how many trams are needed to cater for requirements. In Nantes, the ratio is very high and has an influence on the make-up of the fleet.

The first tramway line went into operation with a fleet of 20 units. In view of the success of the operation, eight new units were purchased in 1988.

3.3 Rolling stock developments under consideration

The Nantes public transport authorities are currently working on several problems:

-- how to cater for the increased traffic on Line 1;

-- building up the fleet sufficiently to implement phase one of Line 2;

-- improving access to tramcars, particularly for handicapped persons.

To deal with the last point, it is planned to put a third car between the two cars of the existing sets. These would be separated at the link point and a third car with a carrying boogie and lowered floor would be added, giving optimal access from existing platforms. The third car would be 10.65 metres long and its lowered floor would have a usable length of 6.40 metres. Its two double doors would have retractable ramps for easier boarding by wheelchairs. The total length of the new trains would be 39.15 m. A full-scale mock-up will enable the various technical and ergonomic problems to be ironed out with the help of disabled persons' associations and an industrial architect.

The current fleet consists of 28 single units. Since September 1988, double-length trams have been used at morning and evening peak hours, producing a 22 per cent increase in throughput per day. At the heaviest peak hours this has led to a significant increase in the peak indicator. Surveys conducted in 1988 and 1989 revealed increases in the 15-minute "super peak" volume, so that it is now necessary to revise capacity upwards.

Based on the above factors, the tramway system will have 34 3-car sets, 18 of which will work Line 1, 10 will work phase one of Line 2 and 6 will be undergoing maintenance or on standby. The new equipment procurement programme will therefore concern 6 2-car sets and 34 central cars.
Later on, tramway network extensions will be equipped with a new kind of "built-in dropped floor". The major European constructors have begun design studies and should have several versions off the drawing-boards in the next few years. Of course, such equipment must, for the sake of consistency, be compatible with the main characteristics of the Nantes tramway system.

4. Operating system

Tramcars are visually operated, more like road than rail vehicles since, despite their dedicated right-of-way in running sections, they are required to mix with other traffic at certain points such as street crossings.

Although the fleet is provided with two-way radios, the visual driving mode can affect punctuality. In an attempt to remedy this defect, two systems have been installed on Line 1, and will be extended to Line 2:

-- the Operating Aid System (OAS) enables traffic control in the Central Command Post (CCP) to track the position of units at all times and so to spot units running ahead of or behind schedule. The CCP can intervene to correct timetable fluctuations. The fact that a tramdriver knows when he is ahead of or behind time means that he can adjust his speed to correct the error;

-- intersections have been equipped to take account of tramcars crossing. On Line 1, every light-controlled intersection is linked to a central computer. A connection between it and the OAS computer factors in the exact position of an approaching tram and regulates lights so as to anticipate a change or hold them on green until the tram has passed.

5. Integration with other modes of transport

The tramway service is fully integrated into the Nantes Urban Area public transport network and, in fact, is the system's lead element.

Connections between the tramway and the bus services -- including those which run only at extended intervals -- have been programmed to suit user requirements. A feeder bus at a terminus may leave only when ordered; a warning is sounded to signal the tram's approach, and the bus must await its arrival.

Under the pricing system adopted, a single ticket entitles each passenger to use all connecting services within one hour of boarding.

6. Planned extensions

A second tramway line, running more or less North-South and passing through the city centre, is under construction:

-- the Centre-South section will be commissioned in September 1992. It is 5.1 km long and will have 13 stops. For 3 km of its length, it runs alongside a dedicated way for buses phased into service between 1985 and 1987. It has its own bridges for crossing two branches of the Loire river and the Sèvre Nantaise;

-- the Centre-North section, 8.6 km long with 18 stops, will be commissioned in two stages, in September 1993 and September 1994.

Line 3 will link the North-West Communes of the conurbation with the South-East ones, via the city centre. As with Line 2, the first step in its construction will be a dedicated way for buses. Line 3 should be ready by the year 2000.

148

IV. MANNING

In 1989, the SEMITAN's average annual payroll comprised 966 employees engaged in operating the Nantes Urban Area public transport network (buses and tramway combined); of these 640 were vehicle crew. The comparative figures for 1984 were 955 and 619.

The tramway service employed 81.2 persons, distributed as follows:

-- 42.3 vehicle crew

-- 4 other operating staff

-- 26.1 maintenance workers

-- 8.8 office staff.

V. INVESTMENT COSTS

After it had examined the detailed draft project, the SEMITAN took as its basis an investment of FF 403 million, before taxes (in January 1980 francs) and this figure was used for reference when negotiating the government grant with the Ministry of Transport.

The actual costs after completion show that the target was met -- the amount was, in fact, slightly less than the estimates: FF 380 million in 1980 francs. It was made up as follows:

Item	Estimated cost (in FF million)	Actual cost (in FF million)
Purchase of land and buildings	17	9
Infrastructural work	111	107
Stops	14	13
Track	49	35
Power	24	24
Operational facilities	18	9
Rolling stock	94	111
Dalby operations centre	40	37
Overheads and consultancy	36	35
Total (in January 1980 francs)	403	380

Actual costs for most items of expenditure, rolling stock excepted, were lower than the estimates.

The cost per kilometre of the first Nantes tramway line was lower than that of other completed or planned operations in France. This may be explained by the fact that it was easier to carry out the project as existing rights-of-way could be used and those concerned were determined to create an efficient system that would be economically viable. The Nantes tramway system thus showed that new public transport infrastructure could be laid down without pushing local authorities too deeply into debt.

VI. OPERATING COSTS

In 1988, tramway-related costs amounted to FF 33.290 million, broken down as follows:

Personnel	13 030 MF	(39.1 %)
Power	2 195 MF	(6.6 %)
Spare parts	1 833 MF	(5.5 %)
Maintenance and cleaning	1 952 MF	(5.9 %)
Insurance	0.332 MF	1.0 %)
Commercial costs	0.805 MF	(2.4 %)
Other external charges	0.935 MF	(2.8 %)
Taxes	1 222 MF	(3.7 %)
Reserves and sundry expenses	0.157 MF	(0.5 %)
Depreciation	10 829 MF	(32.5 %)
Total	33 290 MF	(100.0 %)

VII. FINANCING AND REVENUES

1. The investment package

The investment package drew on several sources of funding -- the "Transport Contribution", the government grant and loans.

The Transport Contribution had been introduced at 1 per cent in the Nantes area in 1976; the rate was raised to 1.5 per cent in 1981 when the decision was taken to build Line 1 of the tramway and once the first instalments of the government grant had been negotiated (it may be noted that, in 1984, receipts from the Contribution amounted to FF 165 million). It was possible to lower the rate of the Contribution after the tramway service came into operation.

The Government gave the SIMAN a grant equal to 50 per cent of the amount eligible for subsidy (excluding rolling stock). The eligible amount for Line 1 of the Nantes tramway service was fixed at FF 264 million and the corresponding subsidy at FF 132 million.

The SIMAN was also able to borrow at preferential rates (soft loans) from the Caisse des Dépôts et Consignations as part of the programme of the Fonds de Développement Economique et Social (loans at the rate of 12.5 percent over a period of 25 years). (This possibility no longer exists).

Expressed in millions of current francs, the financing of Line 1 of the tramway service may be outlined as follows:

	1979	1980	1981	1982	1983	1984	1985	1986	1987	Total
SIMAN										
Loans			13.4	44	106.2	98.1	12.6	-	-	**274.3**
Self-financing (including Transport Contribution)	1.6	4.8	5.5	16	18.8	32.8	33.5	8.5	7.3	**128.8**
GOVERNMENT										
Grants	-	0.9	-	11.4	40.6	52.5	47	26	2.7	**181.1**
Total	1.6	5.7	18.9	71.4	165.6	183.4	93.1	34.5	10	**584.2**
Inflation[1] (%)		13.5	13.3	12	9.4	7.7	5.8	2.5	3.1	

1. Corresponds to the increase in consumer prices from one year to the next (ratio of sum of 12 months of year n + 1 to sum of 12 months of year n).

The above figures should be increased by FF 7.8 million for 1986, FF 28.6 million for 1987 and FF 42.5 million for 1988, used to buy 8 additional tram units.

2. Operating revenues

2.1 Revenues from the whole network

The introduction of the tramway service in January 1985, along with the streamlining of the bus network and the creation of a new travel card ("young people's monthly travel card"), had a beneficial effect on the SEMITAN'S urban transport operating account, as can be seen from the following summary table (amounts in current FF millions):

	1981	1982	1983	1984	1985	1986	1987	1988
Expenditure[1]	140	169	192	204	228	233	239	237
Revenues[2]	62	77	85	93	107	114	125	124
Revenues/ Expenditures	0.44	0.45	0.44	0.45	0.47	0.49	0.52	0.52
Subsidies paid by SIMAN		89	104	104	109	112	111	133

1. Does not include investment -- related costs, financial costs or miscellaneous charges.
2. From ticket/travel card sales and sale of advertising space.

151

The new tramway service not only increased transport quality and capacity -- for virtually the same vehicle-kms as in the past -- but operating costs were also brought under control and have been stable since 1985.

The improvement in transport facilities generated a marked growth in patronage which was reflected in appreciably higher sales of travel cards from 1984 to 1987 (the social unrest in 1988 affected the financial results for that year).

Both of these trends naturally boosted the revenues/expenditure ratio which rose by 18 per cent over the period in question.

2.2 Tramway service revenues

In 1987, revenues from the tramway service proper amounted to FF 24.967 million.

VIII. TRANSPORT CAPACITY

Since the opening of Line 1 of the tramway service, the trends in transport capacity have been as follows:

Year	1982	1983	1984	1985	1986	1987	1988	1989
Number of buses	378	391	389	361	365	367	373	399
Tramway sets	-	-	-	20	20	20	27	28
Total supply (km x 1000)	14 928	15 428	15 491	15 448	16 175	16 286	15 731	16 995
Of which tramway (in 1000 km/cars)	-	-	-		1818	1798	1746	2362

IX. PATRONAGE

1. Trends in patronage

The tramway service was brought into operation in several stages:

-- 7th January to 6th February 1985: Eastern sector with trams every 15 minutes;

-- 18th February to 15th April 1985: complete line opened with same service frequency;

152

--   from 16th April 1985: network streamlined, service frequency improved;

--   September 1988: double-length trains run at peak hours (8 new units acquired);

--   end April 1989: opening of Eastern extension (to the Beaujoire Exhibition Centre) with 2 new stops.

Weekday average passenger volume grew as follows:

--   February 1985   8 200 trips per day

--   June 1985   35 500   "   "

--   March 1986   43 800   "   "

--   March 1987   45 080   "   "

--   January 1989   47 700   "   "

--   November 1989   58 900   "   ".

Over the whole Nantes conurbation network, traffic (in thousands of trips and journeys) developed as follows:

Entry into service of tramway

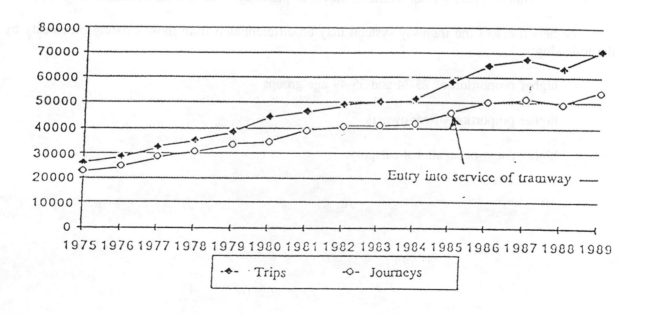

The number of tramway passengers per year increased as follows:

Year	1986	1987	1988	1989
Passengers (in millions)	11 860	13 076	12 455	14 480

2. Description of clientele

The introduction of the tramway system brought about an appreciable change in the habits of not only the people who travelled on the Nantes city transport network but also those who had not previously used public transport. A survey carried out by the SEMITAN after the tramway came into service divided journeys into three categories:

-- journeys which would in any case have been made by public transport: 67.1 per cent;

-- journeys representing a higher rate of use (increased mobility): 16.2 per cent;

-- journeys which would have been made by another mode of transport if the tramway had not existed (modal transfer): 16.7 per cent (60 per cent of these being from private cars), and two kinds:

.   journeys by former public transport users: approximately 82 per cent;

.   journeys by new public transport users: approximately 18 per cent (partly from modal transfer, partly from normal turnover in patronage, partly from increased mobility).

The new users of the tramway system[2] may be differentiated from those existing previously by the following:

-- higher proportion of 25-34 and 35-49 age groups

-- higher proportion of car-owners

-- higher socio-occupational category.

Notes

1. The Transport Contribution is a tax introduced by the Act of 12 July 1971 and 11 July 1973 for the purpose of financing (investment and operations) urban public transport. Its base consists of the wages paid -- within the ceiling fixed for ordinary social security contributions -- by all employers of more than nine employees located on the territory of an OA with a population of more than 30 000. The OA decides whether to impose the tax and is free to set its rate within the ceiling fixed under the Act, viz. 1 per cent for OAs with a population of more than 100 000, or 1.5 per cent (raised to 1.75 per cent since early 1989) for OAs that have undertaken projects for dedicated right-of-way public transport and obtained a government grant for that purpose.

2. No agreed technique exists to date for reliably providing quantitative and qualitative data on modal transfers resulting from the introduction of new public transport services. More particularly, there are no before-and-after polls to ascertain the precise nature of the "turnover". The findings given -- obtained from polls carried out after the introduction of the new service -- are therefore purely indicative.

METRO AND TRAMWAY CONSTRUCTION IN FRANCE

1. Tramway lines maintained

The only tramway lines remaining in service after the 1960s were those in Lille, Marseille and Saint-Etienne. Their principal characteristics for 1990 are summarised in the following table:

	Lille	Marseille	Saint-Etienne
Length of line	19 km	3 km	7.1 km
Number of stations	36	8	25
Number of train sets	35	19	35
Average speed	22.4 km/h	12.1 km/h	13.6 km/h
Staff	132	-	80
Kilometres	1 768 000	312 000	1 393 000
Trips	8 652 000	5 500 000	16 777 000

The infrastructure and equipment in Lille is being modernised and the acquisition of new low-floor cars has been decided. The Saint-Etienne tramway has been extended by 2.2 km in December 1991 and 15 new low-floor cars have been put into service.

2. New metro and tramway lines

The first projects to be completed were Lines A and B of the Lyons Metro and Line 1 of the Marseilles Metro.

Next came Line 1 of the Lille VAL, Line 1 of the Nantes tramway service, Line C of the Lyons Metro, Line 2 of the Marseilles Metro, Lines 1 and 2 of the Grenoble tramway system and Line 2 of the Lille VAL.

Under construction are Line D of the Lyons Metro, Line A of the Toulouse VAL, the extension of the Saint-Etienne tramway line and of Line 1 of the Marseilles Metro, and phase one of Line 2 of the Nantes tramway service. In the Ile de France region, a tramway line is being built between the communes of Saint-Denis and Bobigny (to be put into service in 1992), and a dedicated way for buses will shortly come into service in the Val-de-Marne department.

The projects on which work will soon begin include the Strasbourg and Rouen tramway systems, the Bordeaux VAL and extension of the Lyons, Lille (VAL and tramway system modernisation) and Grenoble systems. Further tramway-style projects are likely to be carried out in the Ile de France region.

The completion of these operations received a strong boost when OAs became eligible for special funding, called the "Versement de Transport", or Transport Contribution.

DESCRIPTION OF PROJECTS COMPLETED OR UNDER CONSTRUCTION IN FRANCE

The following table gives details of routing, population served, kilometric capacity and traffic of projects completed or under construction in France.

The figures give an idea of the volume of traffic and performance of each mode of transport.

They reveal that line routing is designed mainly to serve the most heavily populated (in terms of jobs and people) areas, so that priority is given to inner city transit.

Metro, VAL or tramway services are to a large extent interconnected with bus services.

	Metro Lyon (A,B,C)	Metro Marseille (1,2)	Metro Val Lille (line 1)	Tramway Nantes (Line 1)	Tramway Grenoble (Line 1)	Metro Val Toulouse (Line A)	Tramway St Denis Bobigny	Dedicated way for buses Val-de-Marne
Route details								
Line length (km)	14.1	17.9	13.3	12.6	8.9	9.8	9.1	12.5
including underground (%)	96	76	67	0	0	88	0	
Number of stations	24	22	18	24	22	15	22	23
Average distance between stations (m)	640	820	782	547	424	700	433	568
Population served								
Population of catchment area (1982 census)	1 106 055	874 436	1 047 603	464 857	362 518	553 348	--	--
Population and jobs served directly[1]	367 000	413 000	158 000	110 000	93 000	170 000	108 000	87 000
Population and jobs served directly/km of line	26 000	22 900	11 700	9 000	10 500	17 000	11 900	7 000
Capacity								
Number of units (trains, tramcars)	32 (A,B) 9 (C)	36	61	28	21	26	19	19
Unit capacity	388 (A,B)	468	154	168	174	154	174	101
Units x km per year (in thousands)	2 033	2 243	3 124	998	975	2 200	--	--
Performance								
Passenger trips per day	260 000	264 000	120 000	60 000	65 000	125 200	55 000	43 000
Trips per year (millions)	66 271	60 050	29.4	14.5	16.5	30	14.5	11.7
Including trips with bus connection	30	27	18	27	--	46	33	--
Share of network traffic (%)	32.6	37.1	37.8	22.4	31.9	40	--	--
Commercial speed (km/h)	22	24.7	33.9	21.6	17.9	34.5	19	22

1. Figures indicate population and jobs located within a 400-600 metre corridor on either side of the public transport line. They do not include the clientele of public facilities, particularly schoolpupils and students who form a large proportion of public transport users.

Annex C

PERFORMANCE AFTER ENTRY INTO SERVICE

The aim here is to assess the impact of the first lines to go into service, before later additions create a network effect.

The capacity and performance figures given refer to the first lines introduced in Grenoble, Lyons, Marseilles and Nantes.

Percentage changes are given between the year before entry into service and the second year following it, in order to show the increase in patronage.

	Entry into service (year)	Monitoring period	Trips[1] (% change)	Journeys[2] (% change)	Car-kms (% change)
Lille (line 1)	1983	(82/85)	+ 46.8	+ 29.9	+ 45.6
Lyon (lines A and B)	1978	(77/80)	+ 41.1	+ 19.5	+ 23.5
Marseille (line 1)	1977	(76/79)	+ 44.6	+ 25.4	+ 22.2
Nantes (line 1)	1985	(84/87)	+ 31	+ 22.9	+ 5.1
Marseille (line 2)[3]	1986/87	(85/89)	+ 28	+ 10	+ 11
Grenoble (line 1)	1987	(86/89)	+ 30	+ 19.1	+ 15.2

1. A "trip" is a distance travelled on a single public transport line.
2. A "journey" is a distance travelled on the public transport network; it may consist of one or more connected "trips" on different lines of the network.
3. North and South sections of Line 2.

Under the heading "Car-kms", each car forming a Metro train or a tramway set is taken into account.

It will be noted that in Lyons and Marseilles the increase in trips is about the same. In Nantes the increase in trips is much greater than that in "Car-kms".

During the above periods, the estimated transfer rates went up from:

-- 1.15 to 1.30 in Lille
-- 1.22 to 1.44 in Lyons (from 1977 to 1979)
-- 1.11 to 1.28 in Marseilles (from 1977 to 1979)
-- 1.22 to 1.30 in Nantes
-- 1.20 to 1.31 in Grenoble.

This gives some idea of the extent to which the network was reorganised, one of the effects being to increase the transfer rate. (The increases in journeys on all networks after the entry into service of the new lines were calculated using the above transfer rates.)

Annex D

IMPACT ON TRAVEL PATTERNS

The effect of the new services on travel patterns, by mode of transport, was ascertained mainly from household surveys. Before-and-after survey findings for Lille, Lyons, Marseilles and Nantes are now available. The following table shows the number of journeys per person per day by mode of transport.

	On foot	Public transport	Passenger car	Two-wheeled vehicles	Total
Lille 1976 1987	1.07 1.17	0.21 (7.6%) 0.27 (7.8%)	1.15 (41.7%) 1.88 (54.2%)	0.33 0.15	2.76 3.47
Lyon 1976 1985	1.57 1.20	0.39 (11.3%) 0.52 (16%)	1.30 (37.7%) 1.46 (45.1%)	0.19 0.06	3.45 3.24
Marseille 1976 1988	1.79 1.05	0.33 (9.6%) 0.39 (13.3%)	1.13 (42.6%) 1.43 (48.6%)	0.18 0.07	3.43 2.94
Nantes 1980 1989	0.78 0.72	0.38 (14%) 0.44 (13.4%)	1.22 (44.9%) 1.95 (59.5%)	0.34 0.15	2.72 3.28

The Urban Community of Lille is a special case. The conurbation has two poles -- with Lille itself (served by VAL Line 1) in the South-West and Roubaix-Tourcoing in the North-East. Recent findings published in a brochure on the travel patterns of the Lille arrondissement population show that the metro has had a profound impact on the area served (a 67 per cent increase in mobility on public transport and a 50 per cent increase in mobility in passenger cars, for the population of the area, as against 15 and 68 per cent respectively elsewhere).

These overall findings on travel patterns reveal an appreciable increase in public transport use, which may be largely attributed to the new lines, although the actual proportion cannot be identified with any precision. Even so, the increased use of urban public transport must be considered in relation to the much higher increase in the use of passenger cars.

surveys among car and public transport users give an idea of the degree of modal transfer and increased mobility due to the introduction of the new metro, VAL or tramway services.

In interpreting these findings, it should be remembered, however, that the impact of the new lines concerns primarily two-way inner city traffic and that the bulk of urban travel is made up of outer edge-to-outer edge (or suburb to suburb) journeys (74 per cent of total travel in Grenoble, 56 per cent in Lille, 70 per cent in Lyons, 53 per cent in Marseilles and 51 per cent in Nantes). It is unlikely that metro, VAL or tramway services have made much difference to the latter type of travel.

Annex E

THE TRAMWAY AND SAFETY

If the number of accidents causing casualties in which the different modes of transport are involved is set against the number of journeys by people using those modes, public transport has a safety record far superior to that of passenger cars and two-wheeled vehicles.

In Nantes in 1988, urban public transport -- which accounts for over 20 per cent of motorised journeys -- was involved in one collision for every 18 000 km travelled (in the case of the tramway, one collision for 25 000 km). Of these collisions, 91 per cent caused material damage only, mostly slight, while 9 per cent involved casualties. There was only one fatality or serious injury (more than 6 days' incapacity). The figures in the table below show that public transport passengers travel roughly 10 times more safely than car users.

Mode of travel	Distribution per average day (%)	Accident casualties in 1989 (%)
Pedestrians	22	22
Two-wheeled vehicles	5	30
Private car	60	46
Public transport	13	1

The following chart shows the distribution of accident casualties by their mode of travel and change over the period 1982-1989 in the Nantes urban area (population: 465 000 at the 1982 census):

Killed and injured in traffic accidents in Nantes

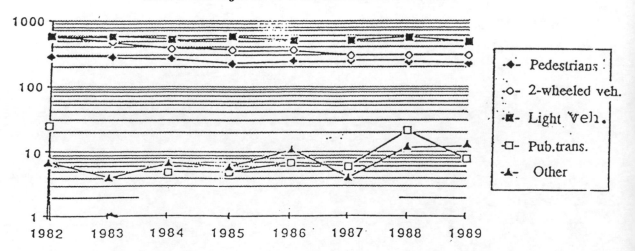

164

The chart below shows the distribution of accidents occurring between public transport (PT) vehicles and other modes of transport. Those involving pedestrians are the most frequent, followed by those involving light vehicles (LV):

Accidents involving PT in Nantes

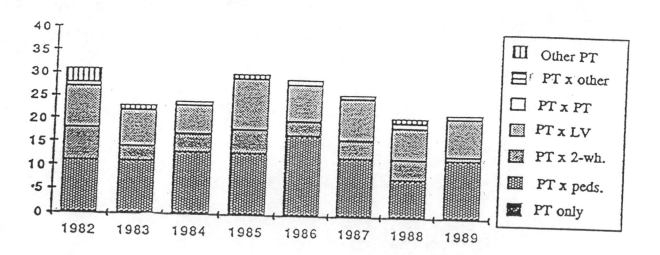

The final chart indicates the severity of accidents involving public transport vehicles:

Severity of accidents involving PT in Nantes

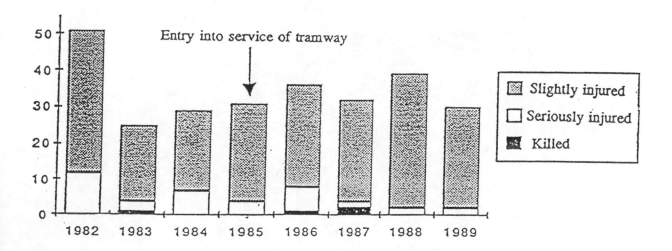

CASE STUDY D.

The Nieuwegein Line: a Case Study in the Netherlands
Francis Cheung
Ministry of Transport and Public Works

Table of Contents

1. OVERVIEW

1.1 Summary

The Nieuwegein line (NGL) was constructed to connect the city of Utrecht with its suburban satellite city Nieuwegein. The first section to Nieuwegein opened in December 1983 and the extension to IJsselstein in December 1985. The Light Rail Transit (LRT) runs on a segregated right-of-way and benefits from a signalling system VETAG which gives priority to the LRT. It offers a frequent, reliable and fast service with a 7.5 minutes headway in the rush hours and a 15 minutes headway in the early morning and late evening periods. The NGL has received favourable comments from the passengers and the operating staff. The LRT carried in 1991 some 25 000 passengers a day. The merit of such a system has led the municipal authority to consider a further extension from the Central Railway Station in Utrecht through the city centre eastward to an employment centre, the Uithof. Good public transport connection(s) which can improve road safety and contribute towards a pleasant urban environment is seen as an important component in an integrated transport strategy now and in the future.

1.2 System origins

In the Netherlands, prior to the 1950's, there were several urban and regional tramways in use. Some of the regional tram networks had similar characteristics as the modern Light Rail Transit (LRT) system. In the 1950's and 60's, all the regional tramways had ceased to operate. The only exception is the tram line operated by the Electric Tramway Company of The Hague (HTM) between the cities of Delft and The Hague. The three largest cities in the Netherlands (Amsterdam, Rotterdam and The Hague), however, continue to operate and improve their urban tram system.

In the 1970's, many municipal authorities were confronted with the task of having to provide good public transport facilities to and from the new satellite towns in their periphery. In 1968, it was decided to combine the villages of Jutphaas, Vreeswijk and IJsselstein (about 15 km to the south east of Utrecht) to form one new town with the name of Nieuwegein. The idea of constructing a new fast tram (LRT) to connect Nieuwegein and Utrecht is born after extensive discussions. The projection was that the new town would have -- in due course -- some 65 000 inhabitants. Historically, LRT had been considered primarily as a transport mode to function and to serve in urban centres. The use of LRT to provide access to a suburban satellite city was a novel idea.

The investment plan was formulated in the period 1968-1974. Construction started in 1977 and the vehicles were ordered in 1979 and the 27th (last) LRT vehicle was delivered in 1983. The first stage of the Nieuwegein line (NGL) opened on 15th December, 1983 and the second stage (an extension to IJsselstein) opened on 14th December, 1985.

169

1.3 Operating environment

In mid-1991, the **population** in Nieuwegein totalled 58 619 while Utrecht itself had 230 175. It is estimated that around 100 000 people live within walking distance (say, 500 metres) from the fixed route service. The **surface area** in Nieuwegein is 3 200 hectares; Utrecht has 5 666 hectares. The **number of jobs** available in Nieuwegein is 21 929 and Utrecht 137 124.

The line has a **segregated right-of-way** with at-grade crossings protected by traffic signals which give priority to the LRT vehicles. The total route length is 19 km with 22 stations. The line is double-tracked in its full length. The **stations sit** on raised platforms. The floor of the LRT vehicle is at the same level so the LRT is also accessible for wheel-chairs and for prams. The stations are equipped with shelters, lighting and an announcing system for passenger information. At present, 13 stations are equipped with "vandal-proof" ticket vending machines for the sale of strip tickets.

The Netherlands has a national **fares system**. It consists of fare zones (not concentric, but grid-like), for which "strip tickets" (one strip for each zone plus one base strip) or season tickets are used. It applies to all buses, trams and metros in the whole country and to limited sections of the Netherlands Railways in specific urban areas. The tickets are normally bought off-vehicle; for those bought on-board, a premium fare applies. This system is also in place at the Nieuwegein line. However, a change is being envisaged. To speed up boarding time and to improve security for the LRT driver, the owner-operator Westnederland (WN) is planning to abandon the practice of ticket sale on board the LRT; passengers must have valid tickets before boarding. New automatic ticket vending machines which sell strip tickets will be installed at all stations. Boarding is through all doors; fares control is done by roving inspectors.

1.4 Objectives

The **strategic transport objectives** in the Netherlands for public transport planning in urban areas at the time when the Nieuwegein line was under consideration were:

-- to increase the proportion of traffic carried by public transport, especially at peak hours;

-- to provide co-ordinated networks of high quality (characterized by reliability and speed) to serve inter-urban commuter traffic to and from the main employment centres in urban areas;

-- to create new links and to improve and adapt the existing public transport facilities to accommodate changing patterns of travel demand.

There has been a shift in emphasis under the Central Government's Second Transport Structure Plan (1990). The stated aim of transport strategy is to strike a balance between accessibility, safety and environmental amenity. The objectives of public transport planning can be stated as:

-- to reduce traffic congestion in urban areas;

-- to promote road safety;

-- to preserve a pleasant physical surrounding;

-- to mitigate the damages caused by environmental degradation;

170

-- to create an attractive alternative to the private car (both for those who have access to a car and for those who do not).

The **corporate aim** of Westnederland as an operating company is to carry as many passenger journeys as possible within socially acceptable financial and community costs. Since the new legislation on public transport came into force on 1st January 1988, municipalities have gained more freedom and responsibilities to determine the local transport services within their administrative areas, (although this is limited when compared with other countries). By the same legislation, the operating companies have gained more control in the planning of inter-regional transport. WN seeks to achieve optimal utilisation of its resources to maximum effects under the new operating environment.

Since the opening in 1983, the Nieuwegein line had been under the responsibility of the Netherlands' Railways (NS) but the actual exploitation was in the hand of WN. As from 1st January 1991, WN has taken over the financial and managerial responsibility from NS; the NGL is now completely managed by WN with full control to make decisions on its own. It sets itself the target to achieve more efficient management of the LRT system. The overall corporate aim is to secure growth in passenger patronage and to put costs under control. It is also explicitly stated that an efficient operating environment would mean taking the interests of the work force into full consideration. The basic **operating philosophy** is to provide quality services which are customer-orientated and to tailor the service frequency to meet the requirements of passengers. The staff and the organisational structure would be attuned to the changing patterns of travel demand as expressed in the market place. Faster and more reliable connection -- such as new LRT line -- is being regarded as an important component in a strategy to develop better services to compete with the private car. Such is the aspiration of the new style WN.

1.5 Alternatives considered

In the beginning, the Netherlands' Railways proposed to build a **normal (heavy) railway line** as a branch of the Utrecht-Den Bosch-Eindhoven main railway line. The Ministry of Transport and Public Works which would provide most of the investment funds discarded the proposal as being too expensive. After extensive studies of different alternatives including a **fast-bus system**, the Minister finally decided in 1974 that a fast tram (LRT) line should be built between Utrecht and Nieuwegein. Costs and the expected ridership were the most important considerations. The initial investment costs for the LRT (track at grade level, level crossing, simple station layout, etc.) and the operating costs would be substantially lower when compared with heavy rail.

2. ECONOMIC PARAMETERS

2.1 Ownership

The Netherlands' Railways was the **owner** of the Nieuwegein line. Up until 1991, NS had the financial responsibility to oversee the funding of its operation and the financing of investment. The **operation** and the day-to-day management was in the hand of the regional public transport company WN under contract to NS. The two companies worked closely together and had a good working relation. As from 1991, WN is the owner of the LRT system with the exception of the rail infrastructure. WN has taken over full operating and financial responsibility. Under the purchase agreement signed in December 1990, specific tasks such as track repairs and major maintenance of the rolling stock will continue to be carried out by NS against payment.

2.2 Funding sources

The Ministry of Transport and Public Works determines the fares policy and covers all operating deficits of the public transport companies whose budgets have to be approved by the Minister. For capital projects, the Central Government normally provides grants for 80 per cent of the investment costs for urban infrastructure. But, because the Nieuwegein line serves beyond the boundary of one municipality, it received 100 per cent grant for its construction and it was financed on a fond perdu basis which means effectively that NS does not have to pay back to the Central Government for the capital costs of the infrastructural investment.

In the financing of operational deficit, up until 1991, NS paid directly to WN for the costs of operating and managing the NGL on its behalf. NS in turn received financial payments in a lump sum from the Central Government for passenger transport services rendered on the basis of services provided, performance achieved and costs laid out. The NGL was considered as an integral part of NS's productions and no separate payment was made. As from 1 January 1991, WN ceased to deal with NS and has to make direct approach to the Ministry of Transport. To finance the overtaking of the NGL, a one time loan (about 50 million Dutch guilders (f)) has been secured with a guarantee from the Central Government against default. WN will receive an annual financial contribution from the Transport Minister for the estimated shortfall in fares receipt to pay for the operating expenses. For the financial year 1991, the estimated sum is f 9.9 million (m).

2.3 Private sector involvement

For political reasons then prevailing, this option was not considered at the decision stage.

3. SYSTEM DESCRIPTION AND OPERATING ENVIRONMENT

3.1 Operational objectives (speed, headway, capacity)

The operational objective is to provide a frequent, fast and reliable service between the two cities. A signalling system giving **priority to the LRT** is regarded as an important element in the operating strategy. This is achieved by the use of the VETAG system (Vehicle Tagging system) developed by the Dutch electronic firm Philips. Each vehicle is equipped with a transmitter whilst receivers are located between the rails at appropriate locations. The system gives the vehicles priority at level crossings. It can also give real time information to the LRT driver and the traffic control centre. On the NGL, all but one level crossing give absolute priority to the LRT vehicle. This is achieved by traffic lights and, at five pedestrians crossings, barriers are used. At the level crossing near the Central Railway Station in Utrecht, where the LRT crosses a taxi-and-bus lane, the priority is pre-programmed, giving priority to the LRT. Such a measure does not mean that the vehicle can proceed at full operating speed but the delay is reduced to a minimum.

As a result of signal prioritization and provision of exclusive right-of-way, the **commercial speed** is high by LRT standards (29 km per hour). The normal LRT schedule provides a 10 minutes

headway. In the rush hours, trams run every 7.5 minutes and in the busiest morning peak it offers a 5 minutes headway. In the early morning and late evening periods, the frequency is 1 tram every 15 minutes. The LRT operates throughout the year. It has an extensive **service period** by any standard. It operates between 6 a.m. and 1 a.m. (the following day) during the working week, between 7.15 a.m. and 1.30 a.m. on Saturday and 7 a.m. to 1 a.m. on Sunday. The in-vehicle **journey times** between the following pairs of stations are:

Utrecht -- Nieuwegein Centre	21 min	(10.6 km)
Nieuwegein centre -- Zuid	6 min	(2.6 km)
Nieuwegein centre -- IJsselstein	10 min	(4.5 km)

In the peak periods, coupled twin-units are put to service. This means that in the morning peak 24 of the 27 vehicles are put to active service. At present some 25 000 passengers a day use the NGL.

3.2 Rail network (see Figure 1)

The Nieuwegein line connects the Central Railway Station of Utrecht with the centre of Nieuwegein and at Nieuwegein centre the LRT line splits into two branches: one going to Nieuwegein Zuid and the other to IJsselstein. At Utrecht Central Station and at Nieuwegein centre, there are good interchange facilities with buses and taxis.

3.3 Rolling stock (see Figure 2)

The **vehicles** are built by the Swiss manufacturer SIG (Schweizerische Industrie Gesellschaft) from Neuhausen am Rheinfall, with components from Dutch manufacturers e.g. Holec. They are based on proven technology and are designed to operate in two directions. They can be coupled together by automatic couplings to enable the vehicles to operate as linked units. Every single unit LRT vehicle is made of two articulated bodies, riding on six axles in three bogies. Each unit is 29.8 metres long. The total **capacity** is 240 passengers (80 sitting passengers plus another 18 on tip-up seats and 142 standing). The vehicle weighs 37.4 tonnes. The **track** is made of steel rails which weigh 46 kg/m and sit on concrete sleepers. The gauge is 1 435 mm wide.

3.4 Control and operating systems

The maximum **speed** is 80 km/hour. The electricity for the two motors in each LRT is delivered by overhead catenary (750 volts D.C.). NS and WN have reached agreement that major repair, maintenance and technical support will be provided by NS. The planning of large scale overhaul remains to be a problem because there is no previous experience. There has been extensive discussion with the NS workshops at Tilburg to make contingency plans. Several modifications to the vehicles took place in 1989.

The level of maintenance in 1988 was the same as in 1987. The amount and kind of work to be carried out depend on the weather conditions in the winter months. For example, as a result of severe wintry conditions in 1988, work on the tracks was inhabited so (more) indoor work (e.g. change of the motors) was undertaken instead.

3.5 Integration with other transport modes

In December 1983, when the NGL was commissioned into service, the bus network in the area was drastically changed. The aim in restructuring the bus routes was to provide an integrated service and to avoid wasteful duplication. The regional bus network was rerouted to provide better **feeding services** to the LRT route. In the inter-city service (to or from Utrecht), several of the original bus lines remained in service because there were local needs for such inter-connecting services.

Today, the NGL is well integrated with the local bus services. At the stations Utrecht and Nieuwegein Centre, passengers have direct and easy access to taxis. Journey to work is the main journey purpose, accounting for more than 50 per cent of the LRT ridership; the equivalent figure for bus use is 24 per cent.

There is no recent survey of the profile of LRT passengers. According to a passenger survey carried out in 1984 as part of an evaluation study, 26 per cent of the LRT users had a car available yet chose to use the LRT. Among the LRT users, 5 per cent used bicycles and 8 per cent used the car for similar journeys in the before situation.

3.6 Expansion plans

The municipal authority in Utrecht has decided in principle to construct a new LRT line from the Central Station of Utrecht through the city centre to an employment centre, the Uithof (east of the city centre). The proposal is to extend the existing NGL to Uithof at ground level. This would present serious traffic problems to the congested city centre. An alternative option is to build an underground section in the city centre and this is the preferred option of WN because any conflict with road traffic will be avoided in the tunnel section. A more recent proposal is to construct a low cost tunnel under the city centre which will be used initially for buses but can be converted at a later stage for LRT operation. This option has also been rejected by the majority parties of the municipal authority because the construction costs of the tunnel are still considered to be high and the required construction work could cause disruption in the city centre.

4. CAPITAL EXPENSES

The total cost for the infrastructure at 1983 prices was f 240 m including the costs for garages and a workshop. This also covered the cost for the construction of a brand new bridge for the LRT over the Amsterdam-Rhine Canal with a length of 380 metres. The purchase cost of the 27 trams from SIC was f 60 million. The total costs for the right of way were f 13.5 million per km, double track at 1983 prices. These costs included the purchase of ground for the right of way, groundwork, cables, road reconstruction, permanent way and power supply.

5. OPERATING EXPENSES (Florins)

	1990	1989	1988
A. Costs			
1 Capacity costs	805 001	692 074	668 519
2 Kilometre costs	1 280 230	1 609 124	1 331 284
3 Operating staff	3 896 851	3 902 625	4 268 698
4 Infrastructure costs	314 323	230 945	256 216
5 Miscellaneous cost	987 193	829 864	697 257
6 General costs	459 419	441 583	380 061
Total Operating costs	7 743 017	7 706 215	7 602 035
7 Early retirement	31 455	27 482	31 073
8 Payment to Previous Employees	168 062	176 257	173 158
9 Interest Payment	129 116		
Total costs	8 071 651	7 909 954	7 806 266

As a result of the transfer of ownership, the NS buildings, premises, spare parts, reserve equipments etc. were handed over to WN. According to the company account of 1990, investment in the LRT rolling stock and the associated equipments, building etc. amounted to f 47 m. The normal lifetime for vehicle equipemnt is 30 years. For the NGL buy-out, the LRT vehicles and other equipments have an assumed lifetime of 20 years. Because the transfer took place on 21st December 1990, the total costs for depreciation and financing were not apparent in the 1990 account; but, it would be fully recorded in the 1991 account. The 1990 acccount has an additional post for depreciation to an amount of f 55 342. Depreciation and interest payment for a full year would be about f 5.6 m and other costs would be increased by some f 6.6 million as a result of the new financial arrangement. The total costs for the LRT operation would be about f 17.5 m. Income from ticket sales would be f 7.5 m and contribution from the Central Government would be about f 9.9 m.

6. REVENUES AND FINANCE (Florins)

B. Revenues	1990	1989	1987
Contribution from NS	8 071 651	7 909 954	7 806 266

Source: Financial Statements -- Profits and Loss accounts of Westnederland.

Since the introduction of the national fares system in 1980, there is (generally speaking) no accurate record of passenger ridership and the type of ticket used. Revenues from the ticket sales are collected centrally and distribution of the share of revenue to the operating companies is calculated on the basis of estimated ridership and production costs. The NS contribution is (necessarily) the same as total expenditure.

7. OPERATIONS -- SERVICE OUTPUT

Westnederland is a regional public transport operator. To illustrate the extent of the company's scale of operation and the passenger market it serves, data on its urban and regional bus services are also given in the tables below. Such background information will help to understand the nature of WN's operation and the difficulty to apportion costs purely related to LRT operation. For example, a group of the operating staff receive extra training to be able to drive the LRT and the bus. They work in day shifts in a rotating system. According to the work schedule, the NGL requires a staff of 50 drivers for direct operation, 24 for repair and maintenance, 21 for control and guidance, making a total of 95.

Table 1. Background Information on Westnederland

	1989	1988	1987	1986	1985	1984
Operating Staff	1 268	1 264	1 241	1 249	1 230	1 147
Technical Staff	126	131	132	130	133	130
Indirect Personnel	264	249	254	250	246	239
Total	**1 658**	**1 644**	**1 627**	**1 629**	**1 609**	**1 516**
Bus Km (x 1000)						
Regional	33 169	33 202	32 801	31 884	31 741	31 605
Urban	3 115	2 721	2 692	2 705	2 707	2 741
Coach and Contract	967	884	1 185	1 196	1 337	1 329
Total	**37 251**	**36 807**	**36 678**	**35 785**	**35 785**	**36 675**
Tram Km (x 1000)	1 746	1 768	1 792	1 711	1 515	1 443
Network Size (Km)						
Regional	2 566	2 370	2 156	2 037	2 122	2 170
Urban	160	143	115	110	118	110.5
Tram	29	29	29	29	14.5	14.5
Share of Peak (as % of Total Ridership on Workday)						
Regional	56.6	56.2	56.5	55.6	55.4	
Urban	45.6	45.1	46.0	45.5	44.4	
Tram	52.2	51.6	51.8	52.3	49.1	

Source: Annual Company Reports of Westnederland.

In 1990, WN operated 3 741 000 bus kilometres in the urban area, 34 575 000 bus kilometres in the regional area and 1 767 000 tram kilometres for the NGL. From the total LRT vehicle km operated per annum, about 88 per cent is the vehicle revenue km.

8. PATRONAGE -- RIDERSHIP

	1990	1989	1988	1987	1986	1985
Passengers Carried (x 1000)						
Regional	46 162	44 368	45 487	45 982	43 887	43 402
Urban	9 121	8 717	8 760	9 253	8 770	8 480
Tram	8 899	8 685	9 310	9 485	8 763	6 342
P.Km Carried (x 1000)						
Regional	448 595	433 920	443 095	451 280	429 095	422 848
Urban	32 797	31 312	31 499	33 174	31 351	31 280
Tram (old)		76 796	82 282	83 854	77 469	56 057
(new)	**60 502**	**59 053**	**63 295**			

Source: Annual Company Reports of Westnederland

The NGL is responsible for about 15 per cent of the total ridership of WN. This is an estimate because in the whole of the Netherlands there is no accurate record of ridership after the introduction of the national fares and ticketing systems in 1980. It is known where tickets are being purchased but there are no reliable data on when and where the tickets are being used. Passenger ridership figures are normally based on occasional passenger counts or surveys carried out by the staff of the operating companies. Since the summer of 1990, the public transport information system (VIS) provides an additional source of data to give a general indication of ridership at line level.

Independent source of data collected by parties other than the operating companies is rare and infrequent. In 1984, a special survey was undertaken by a transport consultant as part of an evaluation study. It was based on passenger counts and questionnaire amongst the passengers using the NGL. The results showed that, since the start of the service, there had been an increase of about 30 per cent in public transport ridership between Nieuwegein and Utrecht and within Nieuwegein itself. This increase was caused not only by an increase in population in the Nieuwegein area but also a result of modal shift. About 23 per cent of the LRT passengers didn't use public transport before.

As a means of determining ridership, the bridge over the Amsterdam - Rhine Canal is used as a cordon to count the number of inter-city riders. In 1988, at that point, some 15 550 passengers were counted using the NGL in two directions per day. If local trips not crossing the cordon were included, the estimated ridership was 21 500 passengers carried per day. The annual ridership was estimated to be 60 m passenger kilometre (pkm).

Because of widespread doubts about the reliability of the passenger counting method, WN carried out a study to investigate the accuracy of the measurement method. The tentative conclusion is that the method used in the past to calculate ridership would underestimate the number of passengers carried. Unrevised method of calculation would produce a figure of 7.1 m passengers in 1988 and 7.4 m in 1987. The argument in support of the claims is that the opening of the new shopping centre City Plaza in Nieuwegein and the extension of the line to IJsselstein had led to an increase in intra-local ridership which did not pass through the cordon (counting) point. The study maintains that there had been a slight increase in the number of passengers but a high proportion of the passengers used the LRT for short distances. The argument put forward is that the two municipalities Nieuwegein and IJsselstein had developed their commercial activities and become less dependent on Utrecht. There were more work and shopping facilities locally hence less need to ride futher afield.

This finding was also supported by the data recently made available by the VIS system. The passenger kilometre (pkm) factor which is responsible for the grossing up had to be revised downward. For this reason, the total passenger kilometre figures in the annual reports had to be revised. Because the existing method of deficit financing is not based on pkm, this revision has no consequence for the calculation of subsidy payment. A new method of deficit financing is under study at present and it is expected to be introduced soon.

9. PERFORMANCE EVALUATION

In the evaluation, it is important to distinguish between the underlying trends and fluctuations round the trend as a result of extraneous factors. In the absence of good data on ridership and on costs allocation, evaluation is difficult.

A set of indicators has been constructed and presented below to give a very rough guide to show developments in the last three financial years. The number of passengers and pkm carried given in the table are based on the new revised figures.

A comparison of performance with other LRT systems will require more detailed break-down of costs and transformation of the cost components based on common definitions and unified discounting method. Recalculation is necessary before any valid comparative analysis can be undertaken.

9.1 Productivity measures

	1990	1989	1988
Passengers carried / V.Km	5.04	4.98	5.27
P.Km carried / Km	34.2	33.8	35.8
Revenue (f) V.Km	4.568	4.414	4.300
Revenue (f) Passenger	0.907	0.911	0.839
Revenue (f) P.Km	0.133	0.134	0.123
Operating Cost / V.Km	4.382	4.414	4.300
Operating Cost / Passenger	0.870	0.887	0.817
Operating Cost / P.Km	0.128	0.131	0.120
Total Cost / V.Km	4.568	4.530	4.415
Total Cost / Passenger	0.907	0.911	0.839
Total Cost / P.Km	0.133	0.134	0.123
Revenue / Personnel	0.085	0.083	0.082
V. Km / Personnel	18.6	18.4	18.6
Passenger / Personnel	93.7	91.4	98.0
P. Km / Personnel	637	622	666

9.2 Analysis of current and historical performance

At the decision stage, a fast bus service with separate busways was evaluated to determine the relative costs and performance. The construction cost of a LRT system was estimated at f 106 million (at price level of 1971). In 1980, halfway in the construction period, the construction cost was f 240 million at 1980 prices. The final (actual) cost in 1988 was f 250 m. The operating cost of the LRT was estimated to be f 8.7 m per annum; the actual in 1988 was f 21.2 m. The investment cost for the fast bus service was f 33 m (price level 1973) and, adjusted for inflation by price index, it would be f 75 m in 1988. The operating costs for the fast-bus option was estimated f 6.6 m per annum in 1971 and f 18 m in 1988.

Patronage was calculated on the basis of carrying a minium of 16 800 passengers per day and a maximum of 25 800. The actual figure in 1988 was 17 500 and was expected to grow yearly. For the fast bus option, 13 500 passengers a day was expected in the Nieuwegein/IJsselstein -- Utrecht region in the beginning increasing to 15 500 passengers.

9.3 Projected compared to actual performance

A before-and-after survey (taken one year after the opening of the Nieuwegein line) showed that the total ridership that passed the boundary of Utrecht had increased by 2.5 per cent. In the section Utrecht-Nieuwegein, the extra traffic was more marked 10 per cent. Where direct accessibility had been improved, the ridership showed an increase of 12-14 per cent. However, in the section Utrecht-Vianen where there was a frequent fast-bus service, the increase rate was only 5 per cent. In the section Utrecht-IJsselstein, there was a direct (unbroken) bus service in the before situation. In the after

180

situation under phase 1, the passengers had to transfer from LRT to a bus at Nieuwegein centre for the remaining journey. As a result, there was a fall of ridership by 16 per cent.

These results should be interpreted with care, bearing in mind that, in the same period, there was a 2 per cent increase in the population and 5 per cent increase in employment. Moreover, Westnederland expected a drop of 2 per cent in ridership as a direct result of general fares increases that were introduced on 1 April 1984.

An appraisal of the NGL within the Ministry of Transport held in 1988 came to the conclusion that the realized travel demand with the LRT had been 15-20 per cent higher than the forecast whereas the operating cost had also risen faster than the original forecast.

9.4 Managerial, policy and technological innovations

The improvement in the operating speed is achieved by extensive **priority measures** using the VETAG system. It is not possible to compare a situation without such facilities because such an option had never been considered. A coarse indication of speed enhancement through signal priorization can be given by way of comparison with situations in other cities. The Nieuwegein line (100 per cent segregated with at-grade crossing) achieves 30 vkm per vehicle hour (vhr). In Amsterdam, the tram (with 55 per cent of the total route length segregated) scores 11.6 vkm/vhr whereas the metro (100 per cent segregated without at-grade crossing) scores 27.7. In Rotterdam the scores are 14.6 for the tram (with 70 per cent of route length segregated), 36.5 for the North-South line of the metro and 28.5 for the light rail East-West line (both 100 per cent segregated).

Another important innovation is the provision of **passenger information** which is developed for the whole public transport system but will obviously benefit Nieuwegein line passengers. The plan is the provision of a telephone network to offer travel information e.g. time table, connection to NS trains and connection to urban or regional services. There will be eight information centres in the whole country providing a full passenger information service. It is envisaged that in 1992 an automatic, fully-integrated passenger information system for the whole country would be in operation with information on all public transport services.

9.5 Social policy

Sick leave for the operating staff is on a slight increase. Since 1989, a sick registration system has been in use to provide continuous management information. In 1988 sick leave accounted for 9.5 per cebt of the workforce, in 1989 9.7 per cent and in 1990 10.2 per cent. A study is underway to examine the underlying cause of sick leave and to identify ways and means to reduce this wastage. A two year study began on 1 January 1990. The study is carried out together with another regional transport company Central Nederland. The aim is to put forward proposals to have a coherent and comprehensive package to reduce sick leave, a problem which is common to most operating companies in the Netherlands. Preliminary findings based on small scale application of a "decentralised" management model suggest that close working relationships between the operating staff and a small management team at local level improve performance. The new organisation structure has generated unity and harmony because the work unit has a common identity; a sense of loyalty to the team has supposedly reduced sick leave.

Vandalism is a problem which is on an increase. It accounted in 1988 for some 40 per cent of the costs spent on materials and man-hours spent on repairs and maintenance. The total cost amounted to f 0.5 m and about half is attributed to the LRT system. The main complaints are destruction of seat covers, damage to exterior of the LRT vehicles. Platform furniture is another target e.g. destruction of lighting, glass panels and safety barriers. It has been estimated that the replacement costs for scratched and vandalized windows of the LRT vehicles would cost f 500,000. Since 1985, the municipalities have introduced the "VIC" system by which young unemployed are recruited on short term contracts to ensure safety, to provide passenger information, to control fraudulent travel and to combat vandalism. The NGL employs 13 VICs in addition to the normal teams of inspectors who control fraudulent travel for the whole of the WN network. Evidence from the VICs experiment suggested that the system is a moderate success at relatively low cost.

10. CONCLUSION

10.1 Innovations

The Nieuwegein line is based on proven technology and there are technical refinements here and there but nothing radical to be regarded as technological innovation.

The concept to construct a LRT system to **connect the city centre with the suburban satellite city** is a novelty and it has worked successfully in the Utrecht region. The concept has subsequently been applied to the planning and the construction of the East-West route in Rotterdam and the Amstelveen line in the Amsterdam region. More recently, there is the proposal to construct a public transport link to the Uithof in the eastern suburb of Utrecht.

The possibility for **bus drivers to learn to drive the LRT** proves to be an attractive option for many because it breaks the monotony (job diversification) and widens the skill (job satisfaction). The drivers receive no extra payment for the dual function so it does not increase the operating cost.

10.2 Insights gained

Experience gained in comparing the estimated costs and the forecasted patronage with the actual shows that estimation of costs and revenues is no easy matter. There are many uncertainties and the **forecast** can only be used **as a planning instrument** to give some rough indications of possible patronage and likely costs and revenues. Professional judgements have to be made; however, the decision-making process can be helped by intelligent use of forecasting models. Because forecasting is based on predicted travel behaviour on the basis of given assumptions, a change in the land use or in the behavioural relationships will lead to other patterns of journey. A case in point in the Nieuwegein example is that an increased volume of inter-regional travel was forecast whereas in the actual situation there is an increase in the number of intra-local trips, many of which are at the expense of inter-regional travel. The number of passenger trips carried is purported to have increased but the average distance travelled per passenger trip has decreased. The implication for revenue will depend on the fares system and structure used.

The importance of having an **effective monitoring system** is also demonstrated here. Marketing means using accurate and up-to-date data to identify passengers' travel needs. Knowledge of changing travel demands would enable the time-table and the service frequency to be altered to suit changing circumstances. In the absence of reliable data, it is difficult to respond promptly to the needs of passengers.

The absence of a passenger monitoring system on ticket use in the Netherlands is partly related to the lack of **incentive or penalty**. Under the existing system of deficit financing, the operator is not rewarded for carrying more passengers (or pkm) nor penalized if the service is not used sufficiently. The operating company is simply required to produce an agreed level of service and any operating deficit is covered by the Central Government. However, the Transport Ministry is currently studying ways and means to overcome this situation and proposals will be made in the near future.

The historical background to the NGL, with NS overseeing the construction of the infrastructure and having the financial control, and WN being responsible for the day-to-day management is based on the concepts of **specialisation** and division of labour. NS has expert knowledge of the railway technology whereas WN the operating flair and the organisation. When the operator has gained sufficient experience and expertise, the financial responsibility can then be transferred. NS remains to be the owner of the infrastructure because NS has the technical know-how and a team of experienced engineers. It would be wasteful if WN also develops the capability. This process can serve as an example for the "build and lease" concept under consideration at present as a possible route to future financing of new infrastructure.

10.3   Retrospection

The proposal to construct a public transport link (in principle, a LRT line) to Uithof is itself an indication that a fast, frequent and reliable service is regarded as an important component in an integrated transport strategy. The actual ridership figures and the patterns of travel support the original decision **not to build a normal (heavy) rail** on the ground that the generated demand and the accrued revenues would not support the operating expenses nor justify the vast investment outlay required by the heavy rail option. The question whether a **fast bus system** would do equally well is hard to prove. A fast bus service has flexibility and involves lower infrastructure costs. But it is doubtful whether a fast bus system will generate the same number of ridership. Marketing studies suggest that passengers, in particular car-owners, regard the LRT as a **new** public transport product whereas a fast bus line is not regarded as a new system. If the objective is to divert car users to the public transport system, a LRT system is more likely to be successful. Whether LRT passengers are prepared to pay premium fares for the faster and more reliable service of the LRT in preference to a fast bus service is not being studied. However, a research carried out recently in the context of the Netherlands' Value of Travel Time Study suggests that many passengers are willing and prepared to pay extra for a fast, frequent and reliable service. The extra amount would depend on the journey purpose, the distance travelled and the personal characteristics of the traveller.

The **land use effect** on the economic development in the Nieuwegein and IJsselstein region is also difficult to assess. There are indications that the NGL has functioned as a catalyst to bring about economic growth in the area, possibly accelerating the pace of development. However, it is difficult to claim that the effect would not have taken place if the NGL had not been there. The presence of a LRT system gives the municipalities a good public image of being served by a modern and reliable public transport connection. Good accessibility will in turn increase the attractiveness of the municipality; it is part of the assets that will appeal to some potential clientele in the choice of location.

Figure 1. Nieuwegein Line

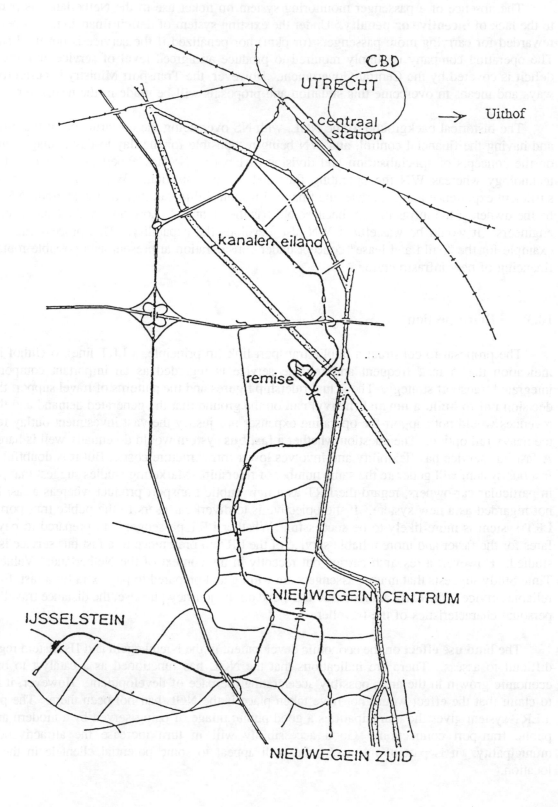

Figure 2. Characteristics of the Nieuwegein line
rolling stock

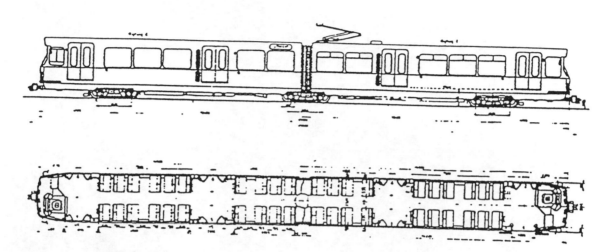

builder : S.I.G. (Switzerland)
number of car sets: 27 (articulated)
maximum speed: 80 km/hour
capacity: 80 seated (+ 18 on tip-up seats)
          142 standing
width: 2.65 meters

CASE STUDY E.

The Hannover and Stuttgart Light Rail Systems
by Dipl.-Ing. Marion Bergen
Dipl.-Geogr. Frank Steinwede
TransTeC

Table of Contents

189

I. GERMAN OVERVIEW

This paper is the German contribution to the international case studies for the Urban Transport Coordinating Group of the European Conference of Ministers of Transport (ECMT).

The Urban Transport Coordinating Group's aim in bringing these case studies together is to help system planners and operators to introduce improvements in the technical, traffic management and economic fields.

The light rail systems of the Stuttgarter Straßenbahnen AG (SSB) and the ÜSTRA Hannoversche Verkehrsbetriebe AG are analysed in line with the proposed framework for the international examples, with their particular traffic, planning, technical and economic aspects, so that the present report fits into the general pattern of the case studies.

In the comparison and evaluation of the two light rail systems it should be borne in mind that the Stuttgart and Hannover systems are both in the course of being developed and grew out of existing tramways. There can thus be no clear distinction between the LRT and tramway systems with respect to operating costs.

As compared with the new LRT in American cities the operating costs in Stuttgart and Hannover are significantly higher, mainly due to the higher maintenance costs for the relatively old tramcars still in use.

This report begins with a chapter on the different types of urban rail system and then a brief survey of all West and East German light railways and tramways. Then come the two case studies of Hannover and Stuttgart and finally a comparative presentation of their economic performance.

1. Classification of urban rail systems

The general concept of "urban railway" is used in the Federal Republic of Germany for all rail-based systems used in major towns, where they run on:

-- on-street rails;
-- segregated infrastructures;
-- completely independent infrastructures.

Depending on the standard to which they are built, urban rail systems in Europe can be split into four main groups:

Group I:

Systems that have been developed through the extension of existing tramway systems:

-- through building segregated and independent infrastructures and through giving railcars priority at traffic signals.
  Examples: Hannover, Karlsruhe, Stuttgart, Köln, Rhein-Ruhr conurbation, Basel, Zürich.

Group II:

Newly-built urban railway systems:

-- on-street, segregated and completely independent infrastructures:
  examples: Nantes, Grenoble, Utrecht, Lausanne, Manchester;

-- essentially independent infrastructures:
  examples: Newcastle, Docklands Light Rail.

Group III:

Systems that have been developed on the basis of existing railway lines:

-- adaptation of the vehicles to "railway standard" as regards power supply and track.
  Example: Karlsruhe (Albtalbahn).

Group IV:

Systems that have been developed through the extension of existing conventional metros:

-- reduction from "railway standard" as regards:
  • vehicle design;
  • train control philosophy, with partial "driving by sight";
  • right of way (crossings with other transport modes).

Examples: Rotterdam, Amsterdam, Stockholm.

In the case of Germany, the present LRT systems are for the most part of the tramway-based Group I type, while the completely new systems of Group II have been considered for only very few West German cities.

The use of existing railway lines characteristic of Group III has also been considered in certain West German conurbations as a cheap method of extending the light rail system into the more outlying areas.

Group IV systems are not being considered at all in Germany at present, simply because there are only four conventional metro systems that could in theory be involved.

Tunnel sections of more than one kilometre are found in fourteen West German urban rail and tramway systems, while there are no underground sections for the tramways in the East German cities.

191

2.   Overview of West and East German light rail and tramway undertakings

As a result of the reunification of the two parts of Germany there are now, in 1991, a total of 51 urban railway and tramway systems in the Federal Republic of Germany. Of these, 23 undertakings are in East Germany, the former GDR, and 28 in West Germany, the former FRG.

In addition, there are in East Germany four comparatively small and in West Germany four comparatively large regional tramway undertakings.

The track lengths of the individual undertakings can be seen in Tables 1 and 2 and Figures 1 and 2.

At present it is not possible to say whether and to what extent the individual tramway undertakings in East Germany, because of their size and ridership, will be economic in the future once the State subsidies for urban public transport paid by the former GDR have been removed. Substantial modification efforts were introduced in 1990 in the large and medium urban rail systems, so that at least their continued existence can be considered assured.

Table 1 lists the West German urban rail and tramway undertakings together with the population figures for the transport areas and cities in each case. The track length is shown as the sum of both systems, as it is not possible to make a systematic distinction because of the constant changes. The importance of the LRT or tramway system in the total transport output of the urban public transport system concerned can also be clearly seen in Table 1. The highest values here are in Frankfurt, Karlsruhe and Hannover. The utilisation of the rail transport supply can be seen in Figure 1, which shows trip frequency per inhabitant per year, in comparison with the total length of the transport undertaking concerned. It is clear from the graph that there is no direct relationship between trip frequency per inhabitant and network length. It is the rail proportion of total public transport output (see Table 1) that shows the relative importance of the LRT or tramway in the system as a whole. The examples of Freiburg, Würzburg and Karlsruhe show that high trip frequencies can be achieved even with a relatively small network (see Figure 1).

In 1989, the average number of tramway trips per inhabitant was 282 in the East and 78 in the West German undertakings. There are no data available for the number of passengers carried by the individual East German undertakings.

The main reason for the big difference is the great importance of tramways in the East German cities, where they carry the bulk of the traffic in all cases except Berlin. The second factor is the low level of car ownership in East Germany, with an average of 220 cars per 1 000 inhabitants as against 530 in West Germany, which obviously leads to greater use of the public transport supply.

II. CASE STUDY OF THE HANNOVER LRT

1. Overview

1.1 Summary

In the Hannover conurbation in 1991 there are eight light rail and three tram lines run by the ÜSTRA Hannoversche Verkehrsbetriebe AG. The remaining tram lines are also to be converted into modern, comfortable light rail operation by the year 2000.

The construction of the Hannover light rail system began in 1965 and since 1975 newly completed stretches have regularly come into operation.

The Hannover system was one of the first urban transport systems to successfully combine the construction and operating components of the metro with those of the tramway and thus showed the way to present day urban light rail.

The Hannover light rail system has been godfather to many other systems in Germany and abroad, for example Tunis and Guadalajara.

1.2 Development of the system

The existing light rail network has been developed out of the former tramway network over the past 25 years.

Electric trams first ran in Hannover in 1893 and the network was subsequently extended to cover a large area. By about 1910 there were 290 kilometres of track, making it the biggest tramway network with goods traffic in Germany at that time.

With growing private car ownership and the resulting decline in ridership and increasing problems with traffic, the entire city and suburban network with the exception of the line to Sarstedt was converted to bus operation in the 50s.

At the beginning of the 60s, a four-line metro network was planned for the town of Hannover, but because of the very long construction period and the associated high costs for the town the project was finally abandoned as infeasible.

In 1965 the Hannover council decided to build an underground system to metro standards in the central area only, the existing surface tramway networks being linked to the tunnel network by ramps.

This established the basic concept for the Hannover light rail system.

The aim of upgrading the former tramway system to a light rail system was to as far as possible separate public transport from private transport, this being the most important requirement for efficient, punctual and regular operation. In order to achieve this it is not always necessary to build a large proportion of the rail network on a second level. The desired traffic effect can also be achieved with the construction of segregated tracks at street level.

1.3 Characteristics of the service area

Hannover is the capital of the Land of Lower Saxony, the third largest Land in the northern part of the Federal Republic of Germany.

With just 500 000 inhabitants, Hannover is one of the twelve biggest cities in Germany. It has an area of 204 square kilometres.

The monocentric conurbation (Greater Hannover) extends over the Land capital and some 20 municipalities around it. A total of 1.05 million people live in this region which covers an area of 2 275 square kilometres.

The industrial structure of the Hannover region is very varied, the biggest enterprises including for example:

-- Volkswagenwerk
-- Continental
-- Varta
-- Bahlsen
-- Geha
-- Pelikan.

The conurbation has a total of 540 000 jobs, about 350 000 of them in the town of Hannover itself.

Another important economic activity for the town and region of Hannover is the exhibition area (Messegelände) to the south of the city. In addition to many specialised fairs and exhibitions there is once a year the biggest industrial exhibition in the world and the CeBIT-Messe (office automation, information and telecommunications technology fair), which are of importance as indicators of the national and international economic situation.

1.4 Objectives

Road traffic problems had greatly increased in Hannover's densely built-up city centre, notably during the 60s. The growing number of traffic conflicts between motor vehicles and public transport lead to considerably reduced mobility and problems in reaching the city centre.

The construction of the light rail system was intended in particular to solve Hannover's traffic problem in a socially and environmentally acceptable way. What is more, a good transport service to the city centre would reduce the area used by motor transport and return these public spaces to their traditional urban functions such as trade and communication.

The light rail system, as the backbone of the urban transport provision, was therefore to be extended through the former tramway system to make it possible to create pedestrian zones and traffic free areas in the city centre and district centres.

1.5 System alternatives

The basis for the decision in favour of the future urban transport system in Hannover lay in the various requirements as perceived in the 60s, which were to be met as satisfactorily as possible.

The most important of these requirements were:

-- low investment cost;
-- low operating costs;
-- high degree of cost coverage;
-- high performance;
-- high degree of adaptability to changing demand;
-- equal service quality over a broad area;
-- good compatibility with urban environment.

The only type of transport that could meet all these requirements in Hannover was a rail-based urban transport system.

After thorough examination, the construction of a conventional metro was rejected because of the high construction cost, so that the decision was in favour of upgrading the existing tramway system to an efficient and rapid LRT system.

This meant that even relatively short sections of the network could come into operation immediately on completion, so that it was possible to aim at early benefits from the traffic management and urban planning standpoints.

2. Economic parameters

2.1 Urban transport organisation

"Großraum Verkehr Hannover (GVH)" (Greater Hannover Transport) was constituted in March 1970 as the second multi-modal transport association in the Federal Republic of Germany. This brought the different public transport operators in the Hannover conurbation together to coordinate their transport supply.

Six partners, including ÜSTRA, Hannoversche Verkehrsbetriebe AG and the Deutsche Bundesbahn, have been in this transport association since 4th March 1970.

An important precondition for founding Großraum Verkehr Hannover was the takeover of ÜSTRA by the local authority in 1970, the greater part of the share capital of ÜSTRA being inherited by the present Zweckverband Großraum Hannover (ZGH). The Zweckverband is a special regional authority with the function of operating public transport in Greater Hannover.

The ZGH has sole responsibility for urban public transport and in its regional transport planning function takes particular account of land use policy goals in order to achieve an integrated settlement and transport concept for the Hannover conurbation.

Cooperation between the ZGH, the Federal government and the Deutsche Bundesbahn is governed by a cooperation agreement and that between ZGH and the five transport undertakings (GVH) by a general agreement.

2.2 Financing

The construction of the Hannover light rail network was financed by the Federal government, the Land of lower Saxony, the Land capital Hannover, the Zweckverband Großraum Hannover and ÜSTRA, Hannoversche Verkehrsbetriebe AG.

With the exception of the vehicles (until 1991) all urban public transport qualifying for central government aid received a 60 per cent subsidy under the law on municipal transport financing (Gemeindeverkehrsfinanzierungsgesetz - GVFG). This law governs financial aid for the improvement for urban transport conditions in the municipalities and is financed through the fuel tax.

In accordance with the agreements on the separate financing of the LRT, the Land of lower Saxony contributes a further 25 per cent of the investment cost, though until 1976 only subsidies for the crossing-free tunnel sections were paid.

The remaining 15 per cent is paid by the local authorities (Land capital, Zweckverband and ÜSTRA).

2.3 Private funding

There has been no private funding of the Hannover light rail system and none is envisaged for the future.

3. System and operation

3.1 Operating data

On the individual light railway lines there is an 8-minute headway between trains in peak periods, 10-minute in normal traffic periods (08.00-14.00 and 18.00-20.00) and 20-minute in the evening low-traffic period (after 20.00), as shown in Table 3.

Since the form of the network is such in Hannover that two lines frequently use the same track, there are correspondingly more trains on the shared stretches.

The average transport speed over the entire rail network is 24 kmh.

The capacity of a stretch with a 2-minute headway and 2-car trainsets is 9 000 places per hour in each direction. The maximum capacity that can be achieved is 18 000 places per hour in each direction with 3-car trainsets.

On the surface stretches, such 3-car trains run only on the occasion of the Hannover Fair with a special dispensation from the technical monitoring authorities, as the length of the train exceeds the authorised maximum for public roads of 75 metres.

The performance of the existing LRT network is largely determined by the tunnel sections, where the safety system allows a maximum of 40 trains per hour in each direction. Under practical operating conditions in Hannover there is a maximum of 35 trains per hour in each direction, in order to allow all trains to reach the maximum permissible speed for these sections.

3.2 Rail network

The Hannover light rail network consists of four core stretches (A to D), that branch to the different parts of the city and to the main dormitory suburbs.

The total line length in 1990 amounted to 76.7 km of which 22.8 km (30 per cent) on-street rails 39.3 km (51 per cent) segregated infrastructure and 14.5 km (19 per cent) in tunnels.

19.8 km of the tracks are used for service purposes only: sidings for train formation and rails in the workshops and yards.

The remaining tramway network had a total length of 15.4 km in 1989.

Thus 83 per cent of the Hannover rail network is used by the light rail system. The entire network, both surface and underground, is double-track. Hannover is ahead of all other West German cities as regards the proportion of completed track.

The gauge of 1 435 mm has remained the same in Hannover ever since the introduction of the first horse-drawn railway in 1872.

All tunnel sections are so arranged that safe, efficient operation at high speed is possible. This means in particular no crossings, broad curves and the fitting of safety devices and automatic train control.

In the light rail system there are 125 stations, including 16 underground stations and 19 stations with high platforms (platform edge 82 cm above the rail surface).

There are many interchange points between rail and bus in the network, but the 13 most important interchange points are so arranged that passengers are protected from the weather and have only a short walk with no changes of level between the light rail vehicle and the bus (see Figure 5).

3.3 Rolling stock

Over all the LRT stretches the vehicles used are exclusively 8-axle railcars 28 m long and 2.40 m wide. Each of the lime green cars has a capacity of 46 sitting and 104 standing passengers, allowing 0.25 m² for the standing places.

Except in low-traffic periods operation is with 2-car trains with a total capacity of 300 passengers.

The Hannover cars are two-directional with a driving cab at each end and five double folding doors along each side. These are fitted with retractable steps that allow low-platform stations to be used. At high platforms the steps remain at the level of the coach floor so passengers have no change of level.

197

The maximum speed is 80 kmh, but operation in the tunnel stretches does not exceed 70 kmh and the permissible maximum on the surface in public streets is 60 kmh.

The cars have direct current electronic control (thyristor control) which makes it possible to have smooth acceleration and braking and regenerative braking which permits an energy saving of up to 20 per cent.

In 1991, ÜSTRA has a total stock of 240 light railcars, made up as shown in Table 4. The technical specifications of the Hannover light railcar are shown in Figure 4.

The last series to No. 6 260 is expected to be delivered by autumn 1993.

The introduction of a second generation of light railcars is planned for the year 2000. The new cars will have a coach width of 2.65 metres, and with six axles and only one articulation will be about 25 metres long.

3.4 Operations monitoring and control

The desired performance and service speed of the light rail system can be achieved only with a punctual and regular train headway time.

Since the rail system on the surface has to share the road with motor traffic in places, special operating strategies have been developed in order to reduce the disruption of rail operation and to a large extent meet the requirements with regard to punctuality and regularity. For this purpose a computer-controlled operating system for public transport (BON) was developed and tested by ÜSTRA.

The BON system consists of the following components:

-- the central installation;
-- on-board equipment;
-- track-side equipment.

The constant data transmission between the control centre and all vehicles improves communications between drivers and the dispatchers in the centre. This on-line communication provides:

-- detailed information for the control centre personnel concerning the present operating situation i.e. the space and time situation of the vehicles as with respect to the timetable (planned and actual situation);

-- targeted indications for the control centre staff concerning any abnormalities and the provision of despatching aid to eliminate them;

-- information for the drivers with respect to the timetable (advance/delay) and the transmission of coded instructions to the driver, notably with regard to ensuring connections.

Other important on-line functions are:

-- passenger information about the present operating situation;

198

-- improvement of operations through the influencing of light signal installations where components of the BON are used in conjunction with the requirements of tunnel section operation.

3.5 *Connections with other transport modes*

The public transport concept for Hannover is that of an integrated, multi-modal system achieved by linking the networks of the DB-City-Bahn, light rail and bus. The precondition for linking the systems is the provision of efficient and convenient interchange facilities where passengers have only a short walk and are protected from the weather (see Figure 5).

The transport systems of the different carriers in the transport association are responsible for the following functions:

City-Bahn: serves the region as rapid link between the city centre and the surrounding area, with long distances between stations and a high service speed.

Light-rail: links the city centre with the rest of the town and the main suburbs along major axes. The light rail system is thus the backbone of the public transport service.

Bus: complements the rail systems and performs the function of a feeder and distribution network. In addition the bus provides the radial and tangential links where it is more economic and more effective than rail-based systems.

The systematic division of tasks makes it possible to provide an attractive and above all economic overall supply in the form of a multi-stage system.

The Hannover public transport system is thus able to offer the passenger clear advantages in the form of an unified tariff and timetable for all carriers and short journey times through appropriate connections where it is necessary to change modes or lines. Over 60 bus lines run by different operators are linked with the Hannover light rail system.

At the terminals and a few other important stations on the light rail network there are Park and Ride -- as well as Bike and Ride -- facilities giving motorists and cyclists the opportunity to switch to the train.

3.6 *Extension plans*

In September 1991, the surface light rail line B-Nord from Berliner Platz will be extended to the centre of Langenhagen. This stretch is 2.4 km long, of which about 0.5 km runs between grass embankments.

The light rail extension programme includes the completion of the C-Nord tunnel stretch (1.7 km) and the surface link to Nordhafen and Haltenhoffstraße in 1993.

Also under construction is the surface stretch of the D-West from Limmer to Ahlem (about 1.6 km) whose opening is also planned for 1993.

199

In the concrete planning stage are surface extensions to Garbsen (about 6 km), Hemmingen (about 3 km) and Anderten (about 1 km).

In addition a plan is being drawn up for a LRT link to the EXPO 2000 World Exhibition to be held in Hannover (near the exhibition area) which involves essentially the construction of tunnel stretch D in the city centre and surface continuation. The planned line from the city centre to EXPO 2 000 totals 12.5 km. This line is planned to come into operation at the end of 1999 to be in time for the World Exhibition.

The planned extensions to the LRT network are shown in Diagram 2.

4.   Investment

Investment expenditure for the Hannover light rail system began in 1965.

Table 5 shows all the funding for each of the core lines to the end of 1989.

Up to 1990, a total of DM 407 million had been spent on the 230 railcars.

This gives a total investment volume for constructing and equipping the light railway (Including vehicles) of DM 1 826 million, which does not include the conversion and modernisation of yards and workshops.

In 1989 the total volume of investment of USTRA was DM 72 million. The main elements included further line extensions and the modernisation of the workshop at Glocksee as well as the purchase of new wagons. For 1987 and 1988, DM 64 million and DM 59 million respectively were invested.

5.   Operating costs

The ÜSTRA rail operating costs cannot be split between light railway and tramway operations. The breakdown of costs for 1989 detailed in Table 6 therefore covers the entire ÜSTRA rail network, not just the LRT.

Each of the cost items in Table 6 includes the labour costs, thus for example, the maintenance and repair costs include the relevant wages.

Labour costs alone amounted to 60.4 per cent of the total operating costs for ÜSTRA rail operation in 1989.

The rail share of 21.7 per cent of ÜSTRA's general operating costs include:

-- operation, repair and maintenance of shared installations;
-- general administration;
-- work clothes;
-- obligatory social insurance contributions.

6. Cost coverage

Table 7 shows operating costs and farebox revenue for the ÜSTRA rail network from 1985 to 1989. The (gross) cost coverage rate is fare revenue as a percentage of operating costs. Taking into account the relevant depreciation costs gives the net cost coverage, which has been very close to 70 per cent in rail operation in recent years.

Table 8 shows the operating costs per passenger for the years 1985 to 1989. The figure for 1989 is DM 1.44 for each individual passenger.

7. Operating figures

ÜSTRA rail operating figures for 1985 to 1989 are shown in Table 9.

The (gross) vehicle kilometres include all rail movements, while to determine the revenue car-kilometres all non-commercial movements and journeys to and from sheds and yards have been deducted. An area of 0.25 m² per passenger was taken as the basis for calculating place kilometres.

There are no data available on vehicle operating hours.

8. Transport output

Table 10 shows the number of passengers carried on the ÜSTRA light railway and tramway network from 1985 to 1989. The number of passengers includes some who transfer from other transport modes.

In 1970, when the Greater Hannover transport authority was founded, the ÜSTRA rail network carried over 81 million passengers. The 1989 figure corresponds to an increase of 19 per cent over 1970. The main reasons for the increase are the establishment of the multi-modal authority and the introduction of the LRT lines as from 1975. The number of passengers rose a further 5 per cent in 1990 as compared with 1989 due to the improved supply.

The increase in the Hannover rail network passenger figures was achieved despite the negative influence of growing unemployment, increasing car ownership and falling total population and school population figures in the late 80s.

Various passenger counts on individual sections show a very clear increase in the maximum transit figures before and after the introduction of new light rail sections, as shown in Table 11.

The sharp increase in the number of passengers is partly due to a shift from other public transport modes and partly due to new traffic. The proportion of new traffic, i.e. passengers who did not use public transport before the LRT came into service, is between 10 and 20 per cent in Hannover.

A study of the mobility of the Hannoverians commissioned by ÜSTRA in 1990 found that the average mobile person made 3.5 trips a day, while the average for all Hannoverians was just under 3 trips a day, the modal split was as follows:

-- 22 per cent public transport (average journey length 5 km);

201

--   23 per cent on foot;
--   16 per cent by cycle;
--   9 per cent as car passenger;
--   30 per cent as car driver (average vehicle occupancy 1.3 person).

The Hannoverians use public transport for 61 per cent of all city centre shopping trips and cars, as driver or passenger, for only 26 per cent. Residents use public transport for 22 per cent of all trips within the city area.

In a comparison of 10 major West German cities, Hannover is in third place as regards the public transport share of total trips while its private car share is the lowest with 30 per cent and the cycle trip share is second highest.

It is thus clear that thanks to the very well developed urban transport network, notably the light railway, the Hannoverians make good use of public transport, but also are encouraged to use the bicycle, and thus travel in a more environmentally friendly manor than the inhabitants of most other comparable cities.

III. CASE STUDY OF THE STUTTGART LRT

1.   Overview

1.1 Summary

The Stuttgarter Straßenbahnen AG has since November 1990 been running a total of six LRT and five tramway lines. The conversion of further tramway lines to operation with modern light railcars is planned for the next few years.

The basic decision to upgrade the tramway system to an "underground tramway", the present light rail system, was taken by the Stuttgart Council in April 1961. In May 1962 Stuttgart became the first German city since the Second World War to start building a tramway tunnel in the city centre. The first line was opened in May 1966, using trams in "Pre-LRT" operation. Since April 1985, modern light railcars only have been used on the converted lines.

1.2 Development of the system

In almost 30 years of light railway construction, two-thirds of the basic tramway network have been upgraded to LRT standard. The most important measures were concerned with:

--   rail infrastructure (tracks segregated from private traffic);
--   operations (centralised monitoring and control);
--   vehicles (comfortable railcars of modern design).

These measures were implemented to guarantee punctual, regular and safe operation in comfortable vehicles.

202

After the first underground tramway line came into operation, the planned basic network was simplified during the 70s. The idea of expensive underground weaving of the network and turntables for the one-way tramcars was abandoned in favour of the construction of a conventional metro. However this plan subsequently ran into substantial implementation and financing problems which led to further rethinking and eventually to the present light rail system.

In June 1976 the Stuttgart Council decided to implement an LRT system with a basic network to which the present extension of the SSB rail network is now oriented. This is part of the integrated urban public transport concept for Greater Stuttgart of the basic contract for the Stuttgart Transport and Tariff Association (Verkehrs- und Tarifverbund Stuttgart - VVS).

Construction of the basic LRT Network is continuing in stages and will be completed by about the year 2000, though further extensions are planned for subsequent years (see Diagram 4).

The introduction of modern DT 8 light railcars, 2.65 metres wide, required the 1 000 mm gauge tram tracks existing since 1868 to be converted to 1 435 mm. standard gauge for LRT operation. Since the conversion of the rail network is an operation taking many years, three-rail tracks make it possible to run the existing trams and the modern rail cars over the same lines. Both types of vehicle use the right hand rail in the direction of travel so that they all arrive at the edge of the platform at stops.

1.3 Characteristics of the service area

As the capital of the land Baden-Württemberg and nucleus of a polycentric industrial region, Stuttgart has a number of central functions. In the region covered by the transport association (VVS) there is a population of 1.6 million people (1989) in 48 towns and communes, among them Böblingen and Esslingen which each have 100 000 inhabitants.

There are some 564 000 inhabitants in Stuttgart itself, which covers an area of about 207 km².

The economic structure of the Stuttgart region is mainly determined by manufacturing industry, which includes the following major firms:

-- Daimler-Benz AG
-- Porsche AG
-- Robert Bosch GmbH
-- IBM Germany (Headquarters)
-- Nixdorf Computer AG
-- Siemens AG
-- Kodak AG
-- BASF AG.

There is a total of about 1 million jobs in the area served by the VVS, of which about 440 000 are in Stuttgart itself.

1.4 Objectives

The objectives aimed at with the construction of the light rail system were similar to those of other conurbations.

The growing number of cars led in the 60s to substantial traffic problems, which began to increasingly affect public transport operation, because buses and trams had no separate right of way. This led to unpunctual buses and trams, falling passenger numbers and a further increase in car use.

This made it increasingly difficult for all road users to reach the city centre, so that the attractiveness of the inner city constantly declined. Service sector enterprises and big shopping complexes sought locations outside the city centre that offered optimal traffic links. In order to counter this trend, plans to step up the economic activity of the inner city were drawn up. The construction of the light rail system was an important precondition for the renovation of the city centre, as the construction of the tunnel sections made it possible to convert a substantial part of the densely built-up centre into attractive pedestrian zones. As the backbone of the city's transport system, the LRT made it possible to reduce car traffic and return the city centre to its residents and visitors.

1.5 System alternatives

The concrete planning for the construction of a conventional metro began in 1969 in Stuttgart, mainly inspired by the success of new metro systems in other cities. After an intensive planning and investigation phase, the Stuttgart Council came to the conclusion in 1976 that the construction of a metro was after all not the right solution for Greater Stuttgart because of the long construction period and in particular the associated very heavy investment cost. It was also apparent that the forecast figure of 800 000 inhabitants by 1980 was not going to be reached.

Instead, it was decided that the "underground tramway" concept of the 60s would be substantially extended in line with the new "urban light rail" concept. The requirements for the future LRT system as perceived in 1976 were as follows:

-- to separate the railcars from other traffic through the construction of segregated infrastructures on the surface;

-- to build tunnels only where strictly necessary because of topographic, traffic management or architectural considerations;

-- priority for railcars at traffic light controlled intersections;

-- standard 1 435 mm gauge for the use of 2.65 m wide vehicles;

-- mixed operation with standard gauge light railcars and 1m gauge tramcars with 2.20 m wide bodies;

-- realisation of a level entry situation with high platforms for the railcars, and on mixed operation sections (in the transitional phase to an all LRT system) high and low level platforms at each stop;

-- construction of tunnel stretches with a clearance gauge for 2.90 m wide metro vehicles (as a later option).

This concept was further developed in agreement with the International Public Transport Union to achieve a qualitative improvement in the system components: track, vehicles and operation.

204

2. Economic parameters

2.1 Urban transport organisation

On 1st October 1978, the Stuttgart Transport and Tariff Association (VVS) was created for the 48 towns and communes of the Stuttgart conurbation. It was the fifth such multi-modal public transport association to be created in Germany after Hamburg (1965), Hannover (1970), München (1972) and Frankfurt (1974).

The VVS service area extends about 55 km around the centre of Stuttgart and includes the Land capital and the four neighbouring administrative districts: Böblingen, Esslingen, Ludwigsburg and Rems-Murr-Kreis (see Figure 6). Within this area the VVS fulfils the following tasks for its members, Deutsche Bundesbahn (DB) and Stuttgarter Straßenbahnen AG (SSB):

-- the planning of further development of the transport network;

-- determination of the service supply (coordinated timetable programme, production of the overall time table, agreed services and capacities);

-- development of the tariff system;

-- distribution of revenue.

There has been tariff cooperation since 1978 with the regional bus undertaking (Regionalbus Stuttgart) and since 1982 with 40 private and municipal undertakings active in the four administrative districts bordering on Stuttgart.

The DB and SSB reimburse the VVS for expenditure arising through their activities. They or their owners (Federal Government and Land capital) bear the deficit arising from the different services provided by the VVS (S-Bahn, tramway, LRT and bus). The Land of Baden-Württemberg and the four administrative districts surrounding Stuttgart make special payments to reduce the burden borne by the Land capital in providing the VVS services. The expenditure arising through regional cooperation is borne by the four administrative districts, the Land capital and the Land of Baden-Württemberg.

The next step in developing regional cooperation between the members of the VVS is the extension of the multi-modal tariff system to the limit of the service area.

2.2 Financing

The investment expenditure for the extension and improvement of the public transport supply cannot be funded by the transport undertakings out of their own resources.

The Federal Government therefore makes a contribution for the funding of municipal transport under the Gemeindeverkehrsfinanzierungsgesetz (GVFG) of 1972. Expenditure qualifying under this law is subsidised to 60 per cent by the Federal Government. In addition, the Land of Baden-Württemberg contributes 25 per cent, i.e. 15 per cent of expenditure is to be borne by the land capital itself which in Stuttgart comes through SSB.

2.3 Private funding

Private investors have so far not participated in the funding of the light railway and no such participation is envisaged for future extensions.

3. System and operation

3.1 Operating data

The headways on the SSB LRT and tramway services vary between 6 and 15 minutes depending on the time of day. In peak traffic periods the headways are generally 6, 7.5 or 10 minutes depending on the line, in normal traffic periods (08.00-14.00 and 18.00-20.00) 12 minutes, and in the late traffic period (after 20:00) 15 minutes.

Because of the form of the network, several lines often coincide, notably in the city centre, so that headways are shorter on the heavily trafficked sections.

The average commercial speed over the 4 LRT lines in service in 1989 was 24.7 kmh, for tramway 20.5 km/h and for the entire tramway network 21.9 km/h.

The performance of the light rail system is determined mainly by the tunnel sections, where the train safety system allows a maximum of 40 trains per hour in each direction. In SSB experience, a maximum of 30-35 trains per hour in each direction is to be considered as realistic, depending on the passenger stop times.

At present the doubled-ended railcars are run as single units, so that with a 2-minute headway the capacity is 6 000 passenger places per hour in each direction. With the use of 2-car trains 78 m long planned for the long term on the Talquer lines the capacity will be doubled to 12 000 places per hour in each direction (allowing standing room of 0.25m^2 per person).

3.2 Rail network

The Stuttgart LRT basic network consists of 3 core sections (Tallängs -, Talquer-/Filderquer and Diagonal lines) that branch into different parts of the city.

The total length of the SSB lines, LRT and tramway together, amounted to 110.4 km in 1989, of which 44.1 km (39.9 per cent) in LRT regular service. Of these LRT lines, 1.9 km (4.3 per cent) were unsegregated on-street lines, 30.6 km (69.4 per cent) segregated infrastructures and 11.6 km. (26.3 per cent) independent infrastructures (tunnel). There is a total of 26.6 km of track in the workshops and yards.

In November 1990 the Talquer line was converted to LRT operation, this additional 27.9 km meaning that 65 per cent of the rail network was in LRT operation by the end of 1990 (see Diagram 3).

The track gauge for the railcars is 1 435 mm (standard gauge) and for the trams 1 000 mm. Over stretches in mixed operation a three-rail track is used in Stuttgart, the length in 1989 being 38.6 km in LRT operation and 46.6 km in tram operation (in both directions). The high figure for tram operation was due to the fact the Talquer LRT line was to be opened in the following year.

There are 186 stops served on the SSB network, of which 17 underground stations in 1990. There are high platforms suitable for use by handicapped people at 95 of the LRT stops.

There are connections between the SSB rail network and the urban and regional bus lines in the city area and at various LRT stations.

3.3 Rolling stock

The railcars used on the standard gauge Stuttgart light railway are 8-axle, double-ended DT 8 cars. The comfort provided by this type of railcar very much projects the "LRT" image.

The requirement laid down for the railcars introduced as from 1985 included the following main criteria:

-- seating with the appropriate degree of comfort;

-- all-axle drive for long up and down gradients;

-- length of 38 m (corresponding to the length of a double-traction tram);

-- the use of modern technologies to minimise costs and save on energy and maintenance expenditure.

The composition of the rolling stock is shown in Table 13.

Thus since 1990, the SSB has 81 modern railcars with a driving cab at each end for 2-way operation and 4 double doors on each side.

Of the 81 cars, the first 49 were fitted with folding steps for use at low platforms. The latest 32 cars for Talquer lines U5 and U6 have no folding steps as all the stations on these lines have high platforms. The technical data for the DT 8 cars can be seen in Figure 4.

Other features of these railcars are: outward swinging doors, rubber-tyred wheels, compact air conditioning unit on the roof, passenger information through digital voice and indication of the next stop on an electronic display.

3.4 Operations monitoring and control

In addition to a new rail network and the use of modern rolling stock, the quality of the light rail system depends very much on the way it is operated. Transport supply has to be regular, punctual, and above all safe.

The requirement for unpeturbed operation presupposes many technical and organisational measures. An important factor in operations monitoring is the use of a computerised operations control system (rechnergestützt Betriebsleitsystem -- RBL) in a control centre. The RBL is now (1991) operational on 6 LRT lines. The system requires equipment to be fitted in the railcars, on the track and in the control centre.

Current operating information is continuously transmitted to the control centre, to which the cars in operation send "data telegrams" at frequent intervals. The control centre receives and processes this information, showing the location of each individual car and at the same time the extent to which it is ahead of or behind timetable. The timetable situation is also transmitted to the driver through the integrated on-board information system (IBIS) on a display, so that he or the dispatcher in the control centre can take action very quickly in the case of any deviation from timetable.

In addition to this basic information, the RBL system provides many other possibilities, such as the handling of radio traffic, ensuring connections between train and bus, passenger information at stops and in the vehicle and the situation that is going to arise in case of any disruption of operations.

In the case of any incident, an important component of the LRT design in Stuttgart is track switching possibilities so that trains can change direction before the terminus, thus maintaining operations and saving expensive bussing over long distances.

3.5 Connections with other transport modes

The urban transport network of S-Bahn, LRT, tram and bus agreed in the VVS statute is the basis for the linking of the networks of the individual carriers. The aim is to coordinate the operations of the different networks and attribute to each mode a service area where it can best fulfil its function at the lowest cost to the community as a whole.

The VVS network is so designed that the S-Bahn, with its high speed and long distances between stations, links the region with the centre of Stuttgart, the LRT serves mainly the major traffic axes in Stuttgart itself and the bus lines fulfil feeder, terminal and complementary functions to the S-Bahn and LRT and handle traffic flows within the broad mesh of the rail networks. There are major transfer points in all parts of the city.

Within the Stuttgart transport area there are 7 500 park and ride parking spaces which enable motorists to switch to VVS rail and bus services. There are also parking facilities for cyclists at various stops to facilitate access to public transport for them too.

3.6 Extension plans

The extension of the Talquer line U6 from Feuerbach to Giebel is planned to enter service in Autumn 1992. This 3.7 km stretch includes a tunnel section of about 1 km. through Weilimdorf. The conversion of the remaining stretch from Giebel to Gerlingen is planned for a later date, as a short tunnel section has to be built in Gerlingen.

The LRT line from Eckarthaldenweg to Killesberg is planned to open in April 1993. This roughly 1 km section will serve a housing, green and trade-fair centre area in 1993.

The extension of the west-bound Diagonal line from Vogelsang to Botnang is at present under construction and is planned to open for LRT service in 1994. Conversion of the east-bound Diagonal line to standard gauge to the future terminus at Untertürkheim station is also planned to be completed in 1994.

It is also planned to build a branch from the tunnel section of the Talquer line to Ruhbank and from there a surface line -- with the exception of an underground section through Sillenbuch -- to the terminus at Heumaden. Longer-term plans include surface extensions from the present terminals in the outlying areas, for example from Freiberg to Mönchfeld (about 0.8 km), from Mühlhausen to Remseck (about 4.9 km), from Heumaden through Ruit to Nellingen (about 5.7 km) and from Obere Ziegelei to Neugereut (about 3 km).

Diagram 4 shows the planned extensions to the Stuttgart LRT network.

4.   Investment

Investment in the Stuttgart light rail system has proceeded in stages ever since 1962.

The total investment cost includes all expenditure on the individual lines in the year concerned.

An overview of the investment cost since LRT construction began until the end of 1989, together with the corresponding subsidies, is shown in Table 14.

Under the Federal law on the financing of municipal transport (GVFG) there are no subsidies for rail vehicles. The acquisition of new, standard gauge vehicles in large numbers was nevertheless urgently necessary, so after negotiations between the transport undertakings and the city of Stuttgart, the later agreed to subsidise the cost of the 81 DT 8 railcars to the extent of 50 per cent (meaning a total of DM 268.1 million).

The total investment cost of building the LRT system,including the cost of the railcars, amounted to DM 2 182.40 million by the end of 1989, which was funded as follows:

	DM million	(percentage)
Bund/Land	1 517.70	70
Stadt Stuttgart	229.30	10
SSB	435.40	20
TOTAL	2 182.40	100.00

Note: In 1989, investment in the light rail system (vehicles + track) was DM 219 million. In earlier years, the investment was as shown above.

5.   Operating costs

It is not possible to show the operating costs for light rail and tramway operation separately. Table 15 thus shows the breakdown of operating costs in 1989 for the entire SSB rail network, and the subsequent tables show total operating costs for the entire network for the years 1985 to 1989. The individual cost items virtually all include the relevant labour costs, which amount to 64 per cent of total rail operating costs.

209

It is clear from Table 15 that the biggest cost items are the rail share of general costs (24.3 per cent) and operating and maintenance work.

The general costs to be shared between all modes are:

-- operation, repair and maintenance of shared facilities;
-- general administration;
-- work clothes;
-- obligatory social insurance contributions;

6. Cost coverage

Table 16 shows the operating costs and fares revenue for the SSB rail network. It also shows the farebox return ratio with and without depreciation. Over the period covered the degree of cost coverage including depreciation was roughly 65 per cent.

Table 17 shows the operating costs per passenger for the years 1985 to 1989. In 1989 operating costs per passenger amounted to DM 1.92.

7. Operating figures

Table 18 shows the operating figures for the SSB rail network for the years 1985 to 1989: vehicle kilometres, vehicle hours and capacity kilometres.

The vehicle and capacity kilometres are for two-car operation for the tramway, which doubles the vehicle kilometres in this calculation, and single car LRT operation.

Capacity kilometres were calculated on the basis of 0.15 m^2 per passenger, meaning a capacity of 329 passengers per railcar and 152 per tramcar.

There are at present no data available on vehicle operating hours.

The light railway accounted for 28.2 per cent of total rail vehicle kilometres in 1989, but with the coming into service of the Talquer lines in November 1990, the percentage for 1991 will be significantly higher.

8. Transport output

The operational performance of the SSB rail network is shown in Table 19.

Total boardings cover all rail passengers, including those transferring from other modes. There are no data available for LRT passengers only.

The framework conditions for the development of urban public transport in Stuttgart have become increasingly favourable in recent years:

-- the number of inhabitants increased with the growing industrial structure of the region;

210

-- the number of jobs increased with falling unemployment.

However, the number of schoolpupils fell.

In addition, the founding of the VVS in 1978 and the opening of successive stretches of the light rail network since 1985 have had positive affects on the number of passengers carried on the SSB rail network.

Before and after figures for the individual light rail stretches show increases of ridership of between 10 and 20 per cent, due solely to the improved LRT supply.

In 1990, the Stuttgart Transport and Tariff Association (VVS) commissioned a mobility study, which found that the Stuttgarters' modal choice for all trips was as follows:

-- 23 per cent public transport (with an average trip length of 5.4 km);
-- 28 per cent on foot;
-- 6 per cent by cycle;
-- 35 per cent as car driver;
-- 8 per cent as car passenger.

As compared with a study of modal choice carried out in 1976, the public transport share had risen by 7 percentage points, though mainly at the expense of the proportion of trips made on foot. The proportion of trips made as car driver did not change between 1976 and 1990, but the proportion made as car passenger fell by 5 percentage points. Average car occupancy is now 1.2 person.

The comparison of 1976 and 1990 modal choice clearly shows that the greater use of urban public transport is due to the improved quality of the network.

Here it should be noted that the use of very modern light railcars did not begin until 1985. The 27.9 km long Talquer line was opened in November 1990 and was thus not taken into account in the modal split study. It can be assumed however that this most important transport axis will have had a substantial influence in favour of public transport in the Stuttgarters' modal choice.

9. Economic performance of the two light rail systems

9.1 Economic performance criteria

The case studies of the Hannover and Stuttgart light rail systems were compared with 29 other West German rail transit and tramway undertakings. Since the costs and other data for the 29 individual undertakings are not available for publication, the average values were determined and our two systems compared with these averages. In 1989 there were no urban transport undertakings in the Federal Republic of Germany with LRT traffic only. The larger undertakings have a residual tramway system in addition to the LRT. For this reason, all the data for the larger undertakings cover both systems.

In the case of Hannover and Stuttgart it should be taken into account that both LRT systems are still under construction. The tramway sections not yet converted to LRT operation are included in the calculations below, which means that the economic performance is at present lower than in the case of a newly-built pure LRT system.

211

This applies in particular for the Stuttgart data, as for the greater part of 1989 only 3 of the LRT lines were in operation.

In Figure 8, the operating costs per revenue car-kilometre are compared. The average for the 29 other rail systems amount to DM 10.54 per car-kilometre as compared with only DM 6.30 for Hannover and DM 8.50 for Stuttgart. The relatively high figure for Stuttgart as compared with Hannover is due to the small number of light railcars in 1989 and the still very high number of relatively old tramcars, which require substantially higher maintenance expenditure then the newer vehicles (see Figure 9).

Figure 9 shows vehicle maintenance costs per revenue car-kilometre. While the figure for Hannover is very good as compared with the average for the reference group of 29 undertakings, the figure for Stuttgart is considerably higher than that for Hannover due to the high proportion of old vehicles.

Figure 10 shows operating costs per boarding. Since this does not take into account the average trip length per passenger, it is also useful to compare operating costs per passenger-kilometre. This is shown in Figure 11. The figures for both Hannover and Stuttgart lie substantially below the average value of the reference group.

On the whole, the Hannover and Stuttgart rail systems come out rather well in this comparison of economic performance.

As shown in Section VI of each of the two case studies, farebox revenue on the Hannover and Stuttgart LRT/tram networks cover 83.3 and 74.8 per cent respectively of operating costs. Taking into account the associated depreciation, the cost coverage in 1989 was 69.9 per cent in Hannover and 64.4 per cent in Stuttgart as compared with the average for the 29 other undertakings of 53.7 per cent.

Figure 12 shows the load factor for Hannover, Stuttgart and the 29 other undertakings.

The load factor (passenger-kilometres per revenue car-kilometre) is a good indicator of the extent to which the urban transport supply is used. The values for both Hannover and Stuttgart are substantially higher than the average for the other undertakings.

An indication of the extent of urban transport supply can be seen in the number of car-kilometres per inhabitant per year. Hannover -- with 37 car-kilometres per inhabitant -- has a somewhat higher value than Stuttgart with 33.5.

The average trip length per boarding is 5.0 km in Hannover, 5.4 km in Stuttgart and averages 3.4 km in the reference group (see Figure 13).

In considering the average commercial speed (Figure 14) various influencing factors have to be taken into account, such as the proportion of segregated infrastructure, priority at traffic lights and distance between stops. The average distance between stops in Hannover and Stuttgart is almost identical at 550 m while the average for the 29 other undertakings is 500 m. The rail vehicles also have priority at many crossings in both cities, but this does not apply to the whole of any line, only sections of individual lines.

The relatively low average speed of 21.9 km/h for the LRT and tramway in Stuttgart is mainly due to the fact that the LRT system consisted of only 3 lines in 1989. If we take the LRT only, the average speed is 24.7 km/h.

Table 20 shows the economic performance of the ÜSTRA and SSB LRT and tramways as compared with the respective bus systems in 1989.

This comparison of the two transport modes is of somewhat limited value to the extent that the bus systems in both cities perform essentially feeder and distributor functions for the rail systems. This means that the majority of urban transport passengers use the rail system, so that the number of bus boardings and hence the economic performance depending on it is lower than that of the rail network.

The operating cost per revenue vehicle kilometre is lower than that of the rail vehicles, but bus performs significantly worse than rail according to all other criteria.

9.2 Analysis of present and past performance data

Operating costs in Hannover increased by about 15 per cent between 1985 and 1989, mainly due to the improved supply (shorter train headways) and the general increase in prices. Over the same period the farebox revenue increased by only about 1 per cent, so that there was an overall decline in the degree of cost coverage by 1989.

The increase in operating costs in Stuttgart between 1985 and 1989 remained relatively low at 5 per cent, while farebox revenue increased by 8 per cent. The degree of cost coverage thus improved by 3 per cent.

9.3 Comparison of forecast and actual performance data

There was a substantial increase in passenger numbers in Hannover thanks to the construction and bringing into operation the LRT system. This made it possible to reduce operating costs as compared with the former tramway system while providing an equal supply. One reason for this is the use of modern vehicles which enable maintenance expenditure to be kept to a minimum.

Stuttgart too saw a substantial increase in passenger numbers after the opening of the LRT, again with lower operating costs mainly thanks to the use of modern, low-maintenance vehicles. There was also a reduction in vehicle use thanks to measures to accelerate operations (segregated infrastructures, the characteristics of the DT 8 railcar, high platforms, priority at traffic lights).

9.4 Concepts and measures in management, policy and technique -- Results

In addition to the systematic extension of the LRT system in Hannover, the ÜSTRA as operator plays an active research and development role both within the Hannover undertaking and in many other public transport undertakings in Germany and abroad. ÜSTRA has been a leader in the use of modern technology:

-- the urban public transport control system (BON), developed and tested by ÜSTRA, has been installed under license by a number of other undertakings;

-- the operations planning system (EPON) for the computerised production and optimisation of timetables and schedules is used in more than 16 transport undertakings in Germany and abroad.

In its strategy paper published in 1989, "Nahverkehr in Hannover, das Konzept der ÜSTRA", ÜSTRA stresses the importance of public transport, notably LRT, in efforts to reduce traffic in the city centre (see Point 10.2 below).

Stuttgart

As in Hannover, the accent in future activities will be on extending the LRT network and its infrastructures. In addition the SSB is making efforts to become more user-friendly, in order to attract a greater share of the potential passengers among the population. Measures include the extension and improvement of passenger information (plans to provide dynamic indication of actual departure times) and assured connections between LRT and bus. Further components of the SSB marketing approach are:

-- additional customer information points;
-- electronic timetable information ("personalised timetable");
-- improvement and simplification of the tariff system;
-- media packages for employee training (internal marketing);
-- aggressive publicity campaigns.

9.5 Socio-economic policy -- Analysis of the possibilities for achieving local objectives

Hannover

With the construction of the underground railway, the opportunity was given in the 60s to design and implement many urban renewal measures in the centre of Hannover. On completion of the tunnelling work the inner city was improved by the creation of many pedestrian zones.

The general urban improvement measures had their effects on the LRT, notably a marked increased in commercial speeds and passenger numbers and a reduction in journey times (see Figure 14).

The effects of the urban renewal measures introduced in the course of LRT construction on the whole of the Hannover city centre can be seen in particular in an improved shopping environment, reduction of noise and exhaust gas emissions and less use of the private car for journeys to the city centre.

In Hannover these successes are attributed to the LRT which has greatly improved the accessibility of the city centre for all user groups and at all times of day. Thus the LRT system has made a very positive contribution to a more environmentally friendly urban transport system fully compatible with the improvement of the urban environment.

Stuttgart

A comparable involvement can be seen in Stuttgart. The construction of the LRT made urban public transport faster and more attractive, increasing passenger numbers on the new stretches by between 10 and 20 per cent.

It was possible to achieve the aim of effectively relieving the city centre of car traffic and improving retail trade, mainly due to the construction of the LRT. After the completion of the tunnelling work in the city centre, broad areas were converted to pedestrian zones, thus substantially improving the attractiveness of the city as a whole.

Supporting measures in favour of urban public transport are also required however, on the one hand to improve the quality of urban life and on the other to increase urban transport supply. It is possible to envisage measures affecting private cars, for example:

-- charging for car parking (systematic charging for parking in the city centre);

-- guaranteed parking for residents;

-- reduction in the number of parking places that have to be provided for new building within the LRT line catchment areas (in accordance with the Land building ordinance).

10. Conclusions

10.1   General

Light rail systems as in Hannover and Stuttgart are ideally suited for the demanding tasks of urban public transport. Important characteristics common to both these systems are:

-- high acceptance by the public;
-- development out of an existing tramway system;
-- high level of punctuality, regularity and safety;
-- high transport capacity (through forming trains);
-- low-cost implementation;
-- low operating costs per passenger.

The choice of the construction standards for the LRT lines determines the investment costs to a very large extent. In addition, LRT stretches can be brought into operation in stages and thus provide a useful transport supply at an early stage.

The operating costs of the two LRT systems examined are on the whole lower per passenger carried than in the case of conventional metro or bus systems.

Light rail transit benefits the community as a whole, improves the quality of urban life and enhances the image of a town, because the flexible way in which such a system can be organised enable it to be incorporated very well into a mature city.

10.2   Future development goals

Hannover

The possibilities for continuing to further improve public transport in Hannover are described by ÜSTRA in terms of the following future measures:

215

-- extension of the LRT system to Ahlem, Garbsen, Anderten, Wettbergen, Hemmingen;

-- development of an environmentally-friendly city bus line for Hannover city centre;

-- planning for a 2.65m wide railcar and low-floor buses;

-- new locations and standards for park-and-ride and bike-and-ride facilities;

-- further acceleration programmes for buses and trains;

-- new services such as the ÜSTRA parcels service and the ÜSTRA taxi service;

-- extension of the ticket sales network;

-- ticket sales without the use of cash;

-- timetable information system and issue of personalised timetables.

Stuttgart

The urban public transport supply is to be systematically improved and extended in the Stuttgart conurbation too, with particular emphasis on the LRT system for which the following measures are to be implemented over the next few years:

-- conversion of the remaining tramway stretches to LRT operation and use of modern railcars;

-- acceleration of all LRT and major bus line operation through priority switching at traffic lights;

-- LRT extensions to Mönchfeld, Remseck, Ruit/Nellingen and Neugereut;

-- extension of the park and ride supply through new facilities at LRT stations;

-- the use of electronic payment for non-cash ticket sales;

-- extension of customer service and marketing;

-- coordinated planning of public transport supply in the case of construction or renewal of residential and industrial areas. Provision of the capacity required for future passenger numbers (80 m long LRT trainsets).

ANNEXES

List of Tables

Table 1. **West German urban railways and tramways with number of inhabitants, line length and rail proportion of total urban public transport output (1989)**

Town	Inhabitants in town	Inhabitants in town	Total line length (km)	LRT/tramway share of total ridership in per cent
Augsburg	346 000	250 100	25.0	42
Bielefeld	312 000	312 000	25.7	53
Braunschweig	349 600	257 600	31.7	40
Bremen	586 000	539 800	56.9	51
Bochum-Gelsenkirchen	961 300	685 800	102.8	36
Bonn	359 800	296 800	102.8	34
Darmstadt	221 400	135 600	36.2	63
Dortmund	659 000	576 600	71.4	61
Düsseldorf	597 000	532 000	145.4	52
Essen	1 146 000	571 000	74.4	58
Frankfurt/Main	664 400	623 500	121.2	51
Freiburg	977 200	626 200	20.1	88
Hannover	206 300	177 000	92.1	58
Heidelberg	780 000	500 000	21.1	75
Karlsruhe (ohne Albtalbahn)	263 300	132 400	51.2	46
Kassel	311 200	266 200	40.1	76
Köln	234 800	191 600	138.8	66
Krefeld	1 095 000	988 800	37.6	74
Ludwigshafen	503 000	237 500	30.2	39
Mainz	163 000	163 000	21.6	34
Mannheim	244 700	184 900	47.2	21
Mulheim	340 000	253 000	37.9	67
München	1 343 500	1 264 400	85.3	50
Nürnberg	676 100	480 000	39.8	23
Stuttgart	863 400	564 000	112.9	29
Ulm	110 000	108 000	5.5	68
Würburg	125 500	125 500	14.4	30
Regional Services				
Albtalbahn (Karls-ruhe)	125 00	--	51.0	
Köln-Bonner-Eisenbahn (KBE)	213 000	--	55.5	
Oberrheinische Eisenbahn-Ges. (OEG), Mannheim	260 000	--	49.0	77
Rhein-Haardtbahn (RHB/Ludwigshafen)			16.3	

Source: VOV statistics

Table 2. East German urban railways and tramways with number of inhabitants (1988) and line length (1989)

Town	Inhabitants in town	Total line length (km)
Berlin/East	1 285 000	171.5
Brandenburg	95 000	22.4
Cottbus	129 000	22.8
Chemnitz	312 000	22.3
Dessau	104 000	10.1
Dresden	518 000	137.4
Erfurt	220 000	49.2
Frankfurt/Oder	88 000	18.5
Gera	135 000	14.0
Görlitz	78 000	12.7
Gotha (including Thüringerwaldbahn)	57 000	25.3
Halberstadt	47 000	14.8
Halle	236 000	77.1
Jena	108 000	12.4
Leipzig	530 000	162.8
Magdeburg	291 000	55.7
Naumburg	32 000	5.2
Nordhausen	49 000	6.2
Plauen	78 000	17.3
Potsdam	143 000	25.8
Rostock	254 000	18.4
Schwerin	131 000	42.4
Zwickau	122 000	12.6
Überlandbetriebe rural tramway		
Bad Schandau	5 000	8.0
Schöneiche (near Berlin)	10 000	14.1
Strausberg (near Berlin)	28 000	5.0
Woltersdorf (near Berlin)	7 000	5.6

Source: VDV-Statistics

Table 3. Hannover train and tram headways according to traffic period

| | Mondays to Fridays | | | Saturdays | | Sundays | |
	PTP	NTP	LTP	NTP	LTP	NTP	LTP
Light Railway	8	8/10	20	15	20	15	20
Tram	12	12/15	20	15	20	15	20

PTP Peak traffic period (06.00-08.00; 14.00-18.00)
NTP Normal traffic period (08.00-14.00; 18.00-20.00)
LTP Late traffic period (from 20.00)

Table 4. Hannover rail car stock

Manufacturer	Delivery	No. of Cars	Car Numbers
DÜWAG	1975 - 1978	100	6001 - 6100
LHB(Linke Hofmann-Busch)	1980 - 1989	130	6101 - 6230
LHB	1990 -	30	6231 - (6260)

Table 5. Infrastructure investment for the individual core stretches of Hannover LRT to the end of 1989 (excluding vehicles)

(DM million)

Measure	Gross investment	GVFV subsidy	Land and local authority subsidy	USTRA investment
Line A (1)	500 61	263 83	231 8	4 98
Line B (2)	463 59	276 14	179 40	8 05
Line C	454 8	272 88	174 0	7 92
Total	1 419 0	812 85	585 2	20 95

1. The construction costs of the Kröpcke-Hauptbahnhof section of Line B are included here.
2. The construction costs of the Kröpcke-Aegdientorplatz section of Line C are included here.

Source: U-Bahnbauamt Hannover, brochures on Lines A, B and C.

Table 6. Operating costs (excluding depreciation) of the ÜSTRA rail network in 1989

Cost category	HANNOVER (USTRA)	Per cent
Drivers and operating staff (total)	29 428	25.4
Sales expenses (total)	5 667	4.9
Power supply	11 687	10.1
Maintenance and repair of installations (total)	10 590	9.1
Track and safety equipment	7 618	6.6
Maintenance and repair of vehicles (total	21 974	19.0
Maintenance and repair of land and buildings	3 601	3.2
Share of total USTRA costs	25 048	21.7
TOTAL	115 613	100.00
Depreciation (without capital repayments)	23 219	

Table 7. Cost coverage of the ÜSTRA rail network, 1985-89

Year	Operating Costs (general) (DM '000)	Farebox revenue (DM '000)	Cost coverage (gross) (%)	Operating costs plus depreciation (DM '000)	Cost coverage including depreciation (%)
1985	100 080	95 321	95.2	122 350	77.9
1986	107 037	92 185	86.1	127 831	72.1
1987	113 575	96 157	84.6	133 832	71.8
1988	113 476	94 146	82.9	134 595	69.9
1989	115 613	96 337	83.3	138 832	69.3

Table 8. **Operating costs of the ÜSTRA rail network per passenger per year, 1985-89**

Year	Operating Costs (general) (DM '000)	Number of Passengers Boarding (DM '000)	Operating costs per passenger (gross) (DM)	Operating costs plus depreciation (DM '000)	Operating costs incl. depreciation per passenger (net) (DM)
1985	100 080	98 236	1.02	122 350	1.25
1986	107 037	97 163	1.10	127 831	1.32
1987	113 575	96 309	1.18	133 832	1.39
1988	113 476	94 622	1.20	134 595	1.42
1989	115 613	96 501	1.20	138 832	1.44

Table 9. **ÜSTRA rail network operating statistics, 1985-89**

Year	Vehicle km (gross) ('000)	Revenue vehicle km (net) ('000)	Revenue vehicle hours (gross) (per train)	Revenue vehicle hours (net) (per train)	Place km (million)
1985	18 400	18 019	-	-	3 504.4
1986	18 300	18 241	-	-	3 622.0
1987	18 219	17 855	-	-	3 552.9
1988	17 919	17 561	-	-	3 546.8
1989	18 490	18 336	-	752 000	3 706.7

Table 10. **Total boardings and boardings per revenue car-kilometre on the ÜSTRA rail network, 1985-89**

Year	Boardings ('000)	Revenue car-km ('000)	Boardings per revenue car-km
1985	98 236	18 019	5.5
1986	97 163	18 241	5.3
1987	96 309	17 855	5.4
1988	94 622	17 561	5.4
1989	96 501	18 336	5.3

Table 11. **Increase in the number of passengers after the opening of the Hannover LRT (trips per day in each direction on the most heavily trafficked sections)**

Line	Opening date	Number of passengers per day in both directions		Percentage change
		Before (1)	After (2)	
A-Nord	April 1976	40 300	60 200	+ 49.5
B-Nord	May 1979	32 700	43 700	+ 34
C-West	June 1985	21 800	32 500	+ 49
C-Ost	September 1989	29 100	35 900	+ 23

1. "Before" survey about nine months before opening.
2. "After" survey about three months after opening.

Table 12. **SSB light rail and tram headways according to traffic period**

	Monday to Fridays			Saturdays		Sundays	
	PTP	NTP	LTP	NTP	LTP	NTP	LTP
Light rail	7.5/10	12	15	12	15	12	15
Tram	6/7.5/10	12	15	12	15	12	15

PTP Peak traffic period (0600-0800; 1400-1800)
NTP Normal traffic period (0800-1400; 1800-2000)
LTP Late traffic period (from 2000)

Table 13. **Stuttgart rail car stock**

Manufacturer	Delivery	Number of cars	Car numbers
DUEWAG	1985-1986	40	3007/3008-3085/3086
ABB/AEG/SIEMENS	1989	9	3087/3088-3103/3104
	1990	32	3105/3106-3167/3168

Table 14. Investment costs and subsidies to 1989 for the individual Stuttgart LRT core sections
(DM million)

Line	Gross Investment	Federal and Land subsidies	Other subsidies	Net investment
Tallängs	548.9	451	--	97.9
Talquer	1 048.1	868.9	--	179.2
Diagonal	80.4	62.9	--	17.5
Other	236.9	134.9	31.5	70.5
Total	1 914.3	1 517.7	31.5	365.1

Table 15. Operating costs (excluding depreciation) of the SSB rail network in 1989

Cost category	DM '000	Per cent
Drivers and operating staff (total)	35 345	22.6
Sales expenses (total)	5 347	3.4
Power supply	14 822	9.5
Maintenance and repair of installations (total)	18 903	12.2
Track and safety equipment	7 653	4.9
Maintenance and repair of vehicles (total)	28 618	18.3
Maintenance and repair of land and buildings	7 471	4.8
Share of total SSB costs	37 894	24.3
TOTAL	156 053	100.00
Depreciation (without capital repayments)	25 302	

Table 16. Cost coverage of the SSB rail network, 1985-89

Year	Operating Costs (general) (DM'000)	Farebox revenue (DM'000)	Operating costs per passenger (gross)(DM) %	Operating costs plus depreciation	Cost coverage including depreciation (%)
1985	148 780	107 698	72.4	164 128	65.6
1986	--	110 362	--	--	--
1987	166 689	114 030	68.4	183 645	62.0
1988	157 812	118 077	74.8	179 141	65.9
1989	156 053	116 796	74.8	181 355	64.4

Table 17. Operating costs of the SSB rail network per passenger per year, 1985-89

Year	Operating costs (general) (DM'000)	Number of passengers (boardings) ('000)	Operating costs per passenger (gross) (DM) %	Operating costs plus depreciation	Operating costs incl. depreciation per passenger (net) (DM)
1985	148 780	93 356	1.59	164 128	1.75
1986	--	92 099	--	--	--
1987	166 689	93 990	1.77	183 645	1.95
1988	157 812	95 679	1.65	179 141	1.87
1989	156 053	94 383	1.65	181 355	1.92

Table 18. SSB rail network operating statistics, 1985-89

Year	Vehicle km	Revenue	Vehicle hours	Revenue vehicle hours (net)(per train)	Place km (million)
1985	22 076	21 749	n.a.	n.a.	3 346 5
1986	20 332	19 739	n.a.	n.a.	3 343 2
1987	19 311	18 748	n.a.	n.a.	3 363 9
1988	19 154	18 596	n.a.	n.a.	3 333 9
1989	18 914	18 363	n.a.	726 898	3 341 7

Table 19. Total boardings and boardings per revenue car-kilometre on the SSB rail network, 1985-89

Year	Boardings	Revenue car-km	Boardings per revenue car-km
1985	93 356	21 749	4.3
1986	92 099	19 739	4.7
1987	93 990	18 748	5.0
1988	95 679	18 596	5.1
1989	94 383	18 363	5.1

Table 20. Comparison of the economic performance of the LRT/tramway and bus systems in Hannover and Stuttgart (1989)

	Hannover USTRA		Stuttgart SSB	
	RailBus		RailBus	
Operating costs per vehicle-km (DM)	6.30	5.55	8.50	6.02
Operating costs per boarding (DM)	1.19	2.04	1.65	1.95
Operating costs per passenger-km (DM)	0.24	0.41	0.30	0.36
Vehicle maintenance costs per revenue vehicle-km (DM)	1.19	0.73	1.55	1.04
Average commercial speed (kmh)	24	23.7	21.9*	22.7

* For the LRT system alone the average speed was 24.7 kmh in 1989.

Table 21. **Staff categories employed by Hannover and Stuttgart LR (1989)**

	Technicians	Maintenance staff	Administrative staff	Total
HANNOVER	1 135	727	552	2 414
STUTTGART	1 448	1 250	458	3 156

228

LIST OF FIGURES

229

Figure 1. Annual trip frequency per inhabitant and total line length for West German urban railway and tramway systems (in ascending order of trip frequency)

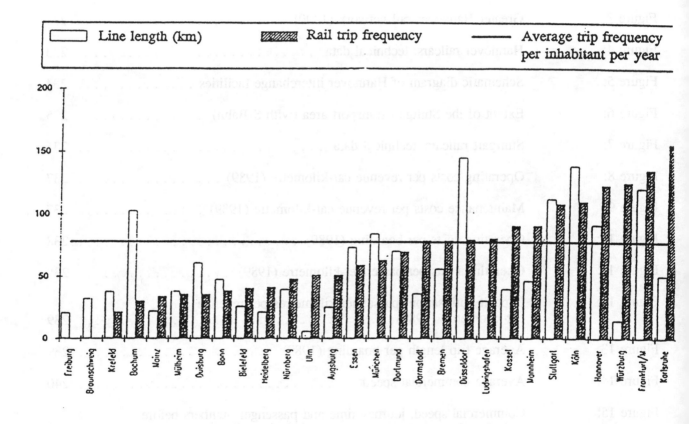

Figure 2. **East German light rail and tramway operations classified by length of line**

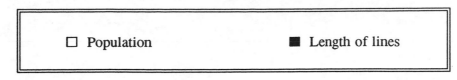

Inhabitants (000)

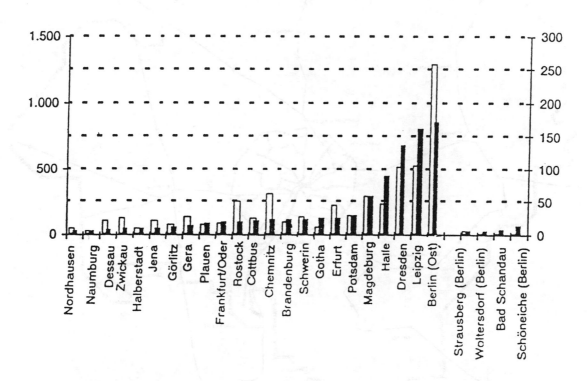

Figure 3. Greater Hannover rail network (1990)

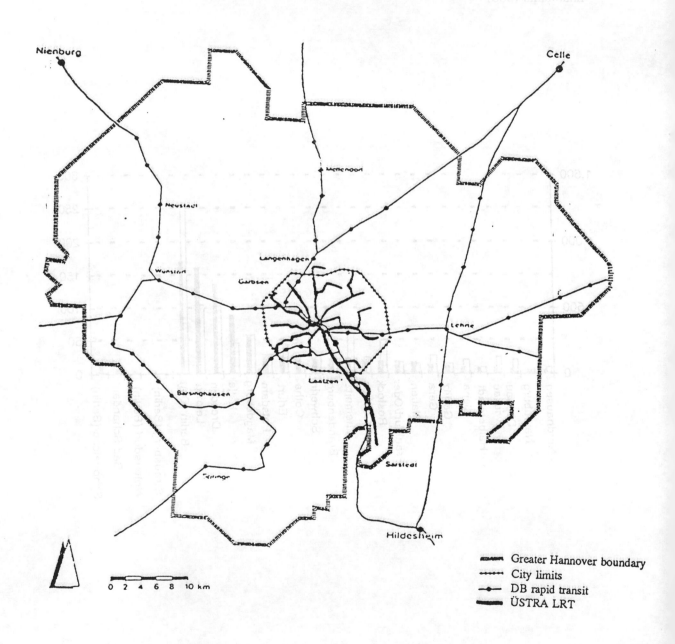

Nienburg
Celle
Mellendorf
Neustadt
Langenhagen
Garbsen
Wunstorf
Lehrte
Barsinghausen
Laatzen
Sarstedt
Springe
Hildesheim

Greater Hannover boundary
City limits
DB rapid transit
ÜSTRA LRT

0 2 4 6 8 10 km

Figure 4. Hannover railcars: technical data

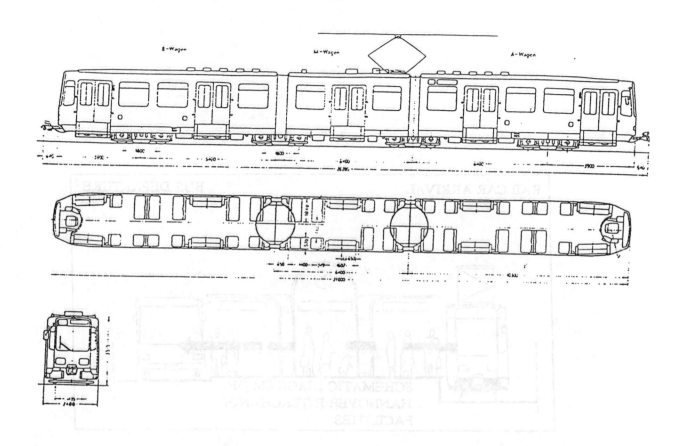

Type	8-axle light motor car for two-way operation with thyristor control and electronics.	Width	2 400 mm.
		Height over roof	3 310 mm.
		Floor height	943 mm.
		Step heights	388/294/261mm with folding steps for high/low platforms.
Axles	4 driving axles, 2 braked, 2 unbraked running axles.		
Gauge	1 435 mm.	Unladen weight	38 800 kg.
Bogies	Two-axle drive; Primary suspension: megi-suspension (axle); secondary suspension: Rubber roll suspension (cradle).	Adhesion weight	approx. 60% of actual weight.
		Capacity	46 seated passengers and 104 standing with 0.25m^2 per person.
Wheel diameter	730 mm.	Minimum curve radius	17.5 m.
Motor power	2 x 217 = 434kWh at 600V DC.	Acceleration	1 m/s^2.
		Emergency braking	3 m/s^2.
Maximum speed	80kmh.	Train set	Maximum 4 cars.
Length over couplings	28 280 mm.	Design	In accordance with BOStrab, VÖV and VDE regulations.

Figure 5.

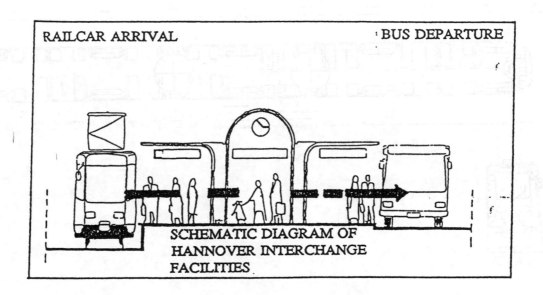

RAILCAR ARRIVAL

BUS DEPARTURE

SCHEMATIC DIAGRAM OF
HANNOVER INTERCHANGE
FACILITIES

Figure 6. **Extent of the Stuttgart transport area (with S-Bahn)**

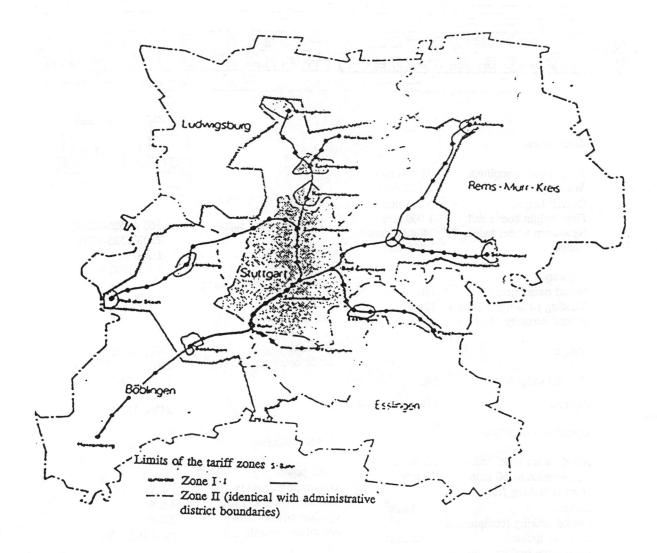

Limits of the tariff zones
━━━ Zone I
━·━ Zone II (identical with administrative district boundaries)

Figure 7. **Stuttgart railcars: technical data**

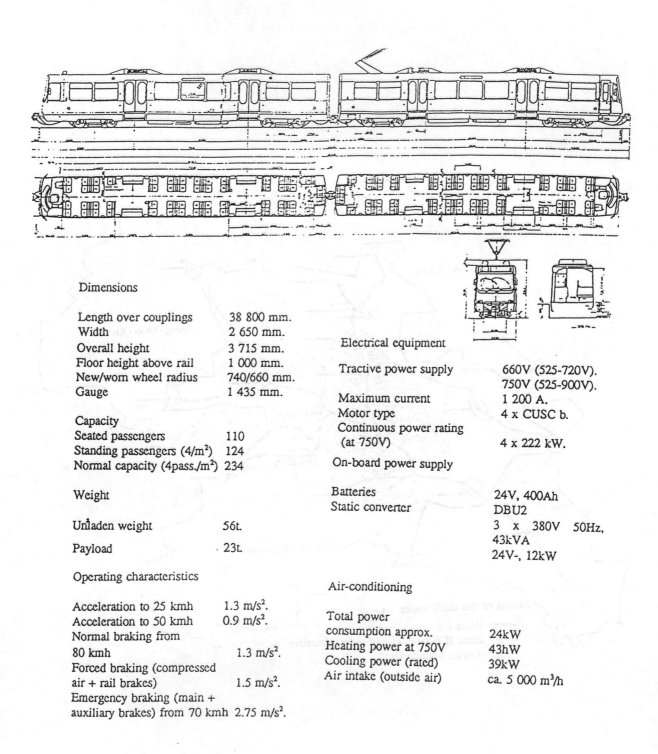

Dimensions

Length over couplings	38 800 mm.
Width	2 650 mm.
Overall height	3 715 mm.
Floor height above rail	1 000 mm.
New/worn wheel radius	740/660 mm.
Gauge	1 435 mm.

Capacity

Seated passengers	110
Standing passengers (4/m^2)	124
Normal capacity (4pass./m^2)	234

Weight

Unladen weight	56t.
Payload	23t.

Operating characteristics

Acceleration to 25 kmh	1.3 m/s^2.
Acceleration to 50 kmh	0.9 m/s^2.
Normal braking from 80 kmh	1.3 m/s^2.
Forced braking (compressed air + rail brakes)	1.5 m/s^2.
Emergency braking (main + auxiliary brakes) from 70 kmh	2.75 m/s^2.

Electrical equipment

Tractive power supply	660V (525-720V).
	750V (525-900V).
Maximum current	1 200 A.
Motor type	4 x CUSC b.
Continuous power rating (at 750V)	4 x 222 kW.

On-board power supply

Batteries	24V, 400Ah
Static converter	DBU2
	3 x 380V 50Hz, 43kVA
	24V-, 12kW

Air-conditioning

Total power consumption approx.	24kW
Heating power at 750V	43hW
Cooling power (rated)	39kW
Air intake (outside air)	ca. 5 000 m^3/h

Figure 8. **Operating costs per revenue car-kilometre (1989)**

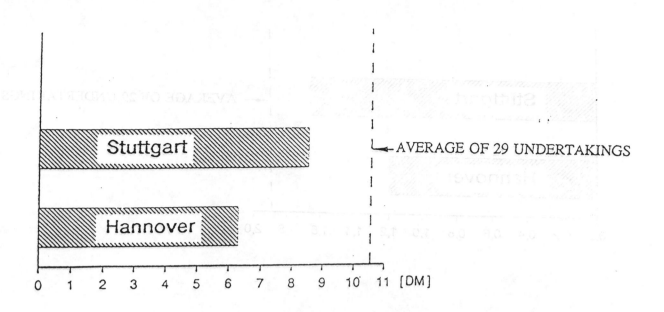

Figure 9. **Maintenance costs per revenue car-kilometre (1989)**

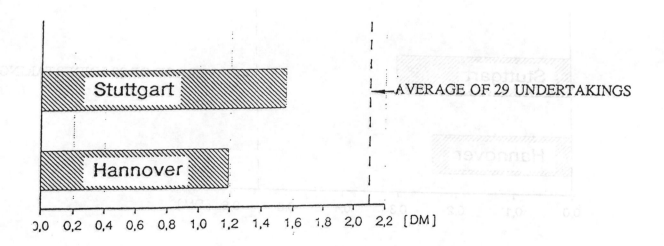

Figure 10. **Operating costs per boarding (1989)**

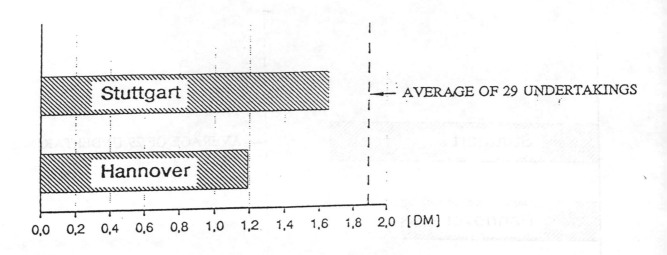

Figure 11. **Operating costs per passenger-kilometre (1989)**

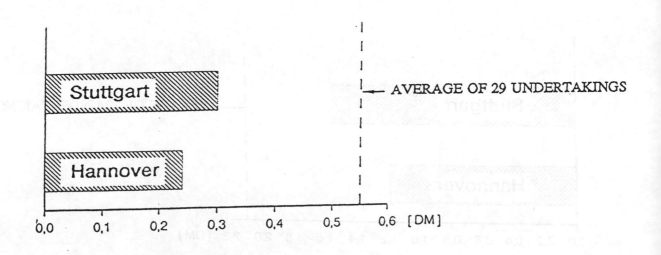

Figure 12. **Capacity utilisation (passenger-kilometres per revenue car-kilometre) (1989)**

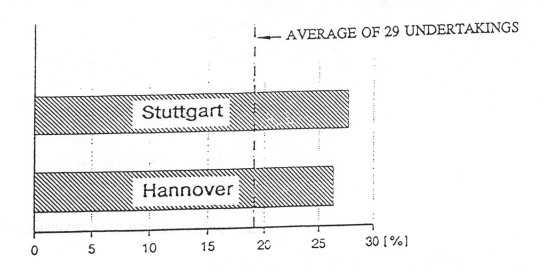

Figure 13. **Average trip length (1989)**

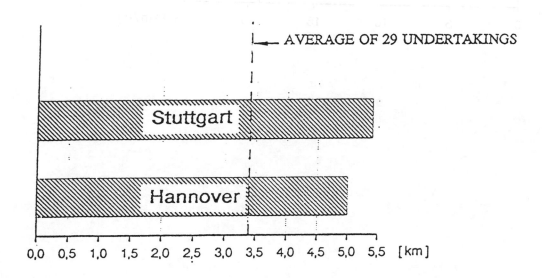

Figure 14. **Average commercial speed (1989)**

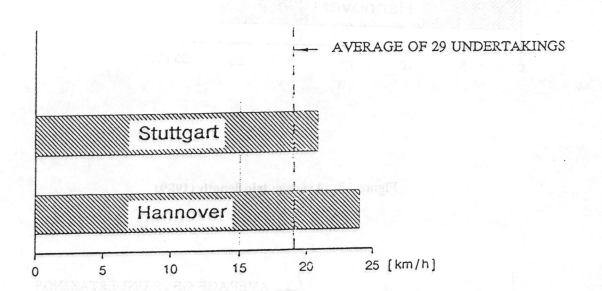

Figure 15. **Commercial speed, journey time and passenger numbers before and after the introduction of the Hannover light rail system (data for selected sections)**

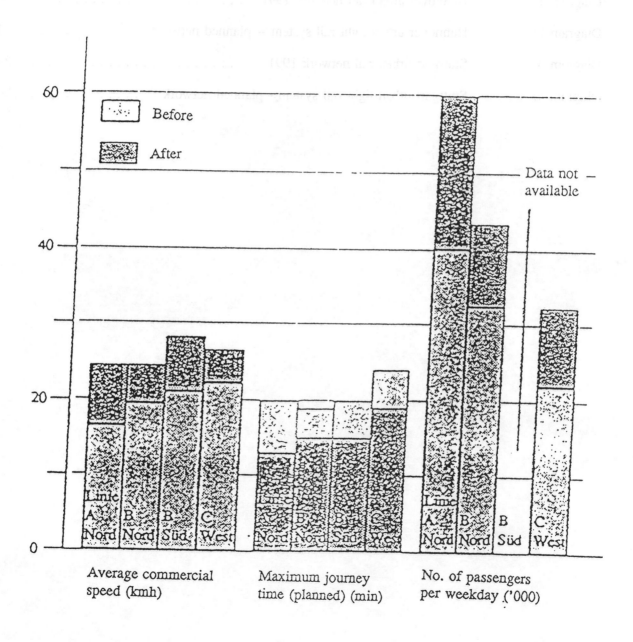

LIST OF DIAGRAMS

Diagram 1. **Hannover urban rail network 1991**

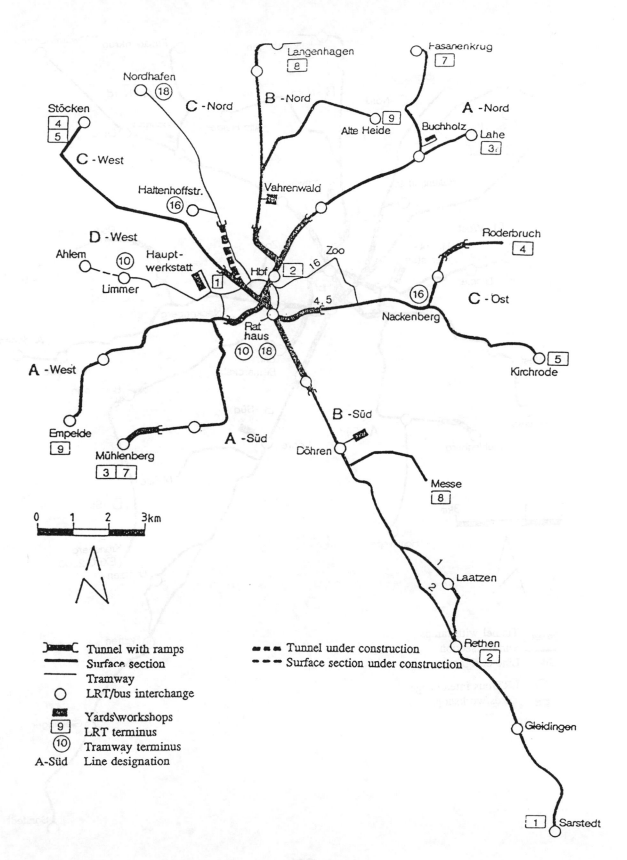

Tunnel with ramps
Surface section
Tramway
LRT/bus interchange
Yards\workshops
⑨ LRT terminus
⑩ Tramway terminus
A-Süd Line designation

Tunnel under construction
Surface section under construction

Diagram 2. **Hannover urban light rail system -- planned network**

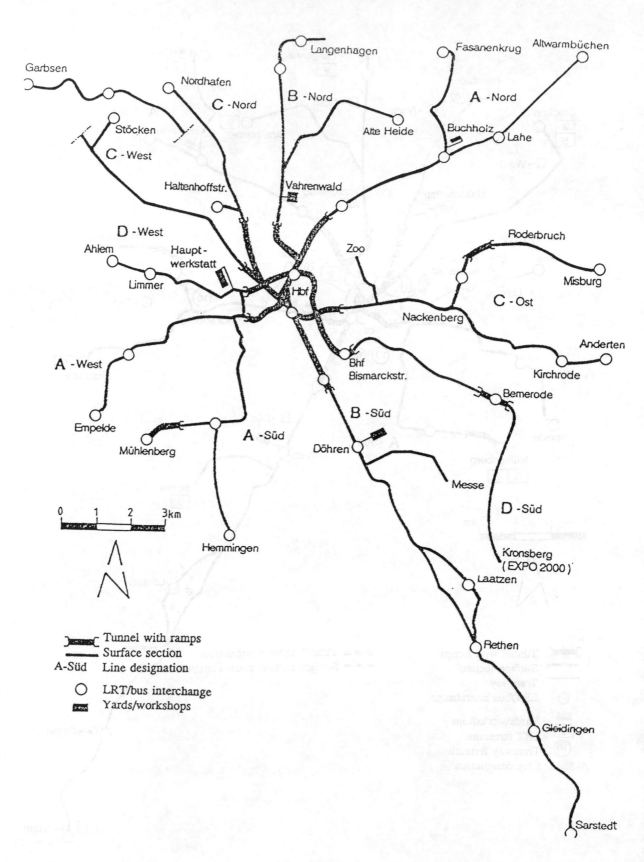

Garbsen

Nordhafen

C - Nord

Langenhagen

B - Nord

Fasanenkrug   Altwarmbüchen

A - Nord

Stöcken

C - West

Alte Heide

Buchholz   Lahe

Haltenhoffstr.

Vahrenwald

D - West

Ahlem

Haupt-
werkstatt

Zoo

Roderbruch

Limmer

Hbf

Misburg

C - Ost

A - West

Nackenberg

Anderten

Bhf
Bismarckstr.

Kirchrode

Empelde

Bemerode

Mühlenberg

B - Süd

A - Süd

Döhren

Messe

Hemmingen

D - Süd

0   1   2   3km

Kronsberg
(EXPO 2000)

Laatzen

Rethen

Tunnel with ramps

Surface section

A-Süd   Line designation

○   LRT/bus interchange

▦   Yards/workshops

Gleidingen

Sarstedt

Diagram 3. **Stuttgart urban rail network 1991**

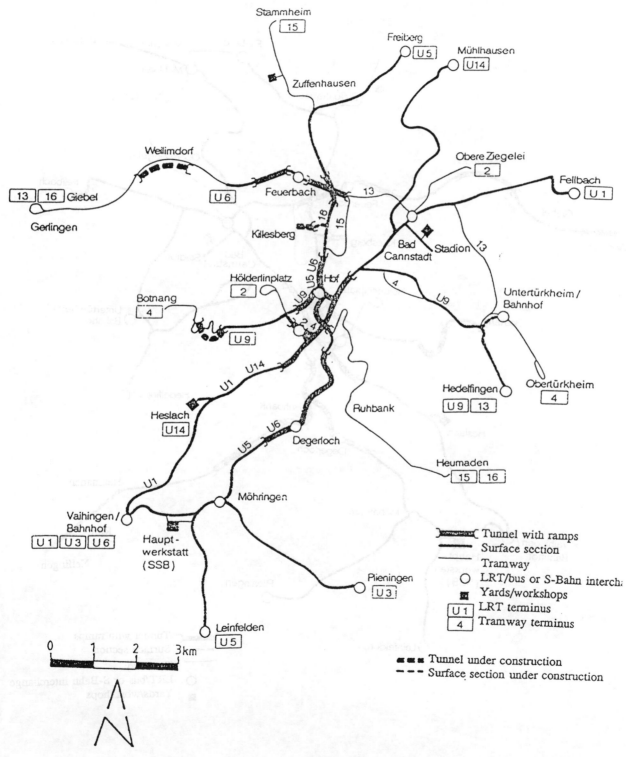

Stammheim
15

Freiberg
U5

Mühlhausen
U14

Zuffenhausen

Weilimdorf

Obere Ziegelei
2

Fellbach
U1

13 16 Giebel

U6

Feuerbach

13

Gerlingen

Killesberg

16

15

Bad
Cannstadt

Stadion

13

Hölderlinplatz
2

U5 U6

Hof

Untertürkheim/
Bahnhof

Botnang
4

U9 U5 U6

4

U9

U9

Obertürkheim
4

Hedelfingen
U9 13

Ruhbank

U14

U1

Heslach
U14

U6

Degerloch

Heumaden
15 16

U5

U1

Vaihingen/
Bahnhof
U1 U3 U6

Möhringen

Haupt-
werkstatt
(SSB)

Pieningen
U3

Leinfelden
U5

0 1 2 3km

N

⊏▬▬▬⊐ Tunnel with ramps
━━━ Surface section
─── Tramway
○ LRT/bus or S-Bahn intercha
▪ Yards/workshops
U1 LRT terminus
4 Tramway terminus

▬ ▬ ▬ Tunnel under construction
─ ─ ─ Surface section under construction

Diagram 4. Stuttgart urban light rail system -- planned network

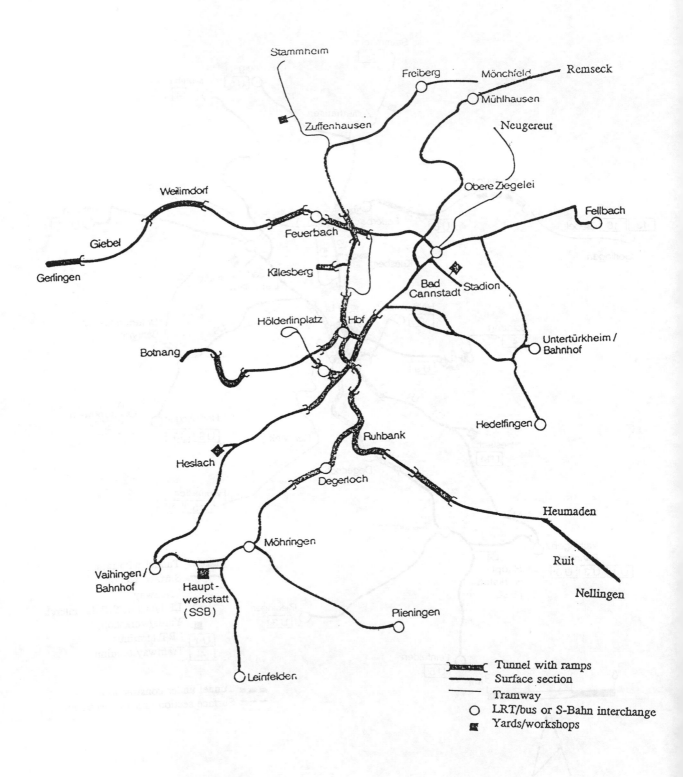

Legend:
- Tunnel with ramps
- Surface section
- Tramway
- ○ LRT/bus or S-Bahn interchange
- ■ Yards/workshops

II. AN OVERVIEW OF

LIGHT RAIL TRANSIT SYSTEMS IN THE UNITED STATES

Prepared by

William M. Lyons
U.S. Department of Transportation
Research and Special Programs Administration
Volpe National Transportation Systems Center
Cambridge, Massachusetts

Jonathan Belcher and Paul Shadle
EG & G Dynatrend Inc.

NOTICE

Table of Contents

1. INTRODUCTION

This overview summarizes the current status of light rail transit in the United States and describes the major systems. The definition of light rail used in this overview is as follows:

a mode of urban transportation utilizing predominantly reserved but not necessarily grade-separated rights-of-way; service utilizes electrically propelled rail vehicles operated singularly or in trains.

This definition allows older tram systems, even those operating primarily in mixed-traffic with no grade separation, to be included in this overview.

Light rail is distinguished from metro systems (also called rapid rail), which can be defined as follows:

-- transit service using rail cars with motive capability, driven by electric power usually drawn from a third rail, configured for passenger traffic and usually operated on exclusive rights-of-way; service generally utilizes longer trains and station spacing than light rail;

-- also not covered by this report are automated guideway systems which are defined as follows:

-- one or more automatically controlled vehicles operating over an exclusive guideway.

The lines of definition between these three modes can sometimes be cloudy. Both light rail and heavy rail can use high platform stations, but only light rail generally uses low platforms. Some metro systems use overhead wire to supply power instead of contact (third) rail, but it is very unusual for light rail to use contact (third) rail. Both metros and light rail systems can use automated technology. Most metro systems are completely grade separated, but there are several metro lines in Chicago, Illinois which contain grade crossings. Conversely, there is a light rail line in Boston, Massachusetts which is completely free of grade crossings, and St.Louis, Missouri is constructing a light rail line which will use high platforms and be grade free.

As of the end of 1991, there were 13 light rail or tram systems operating in the United States. These systems can be divided into two categories:

a) **older systems**, that can be traced back at least to the 1930's, and usually to the horse-tram days of the 1880's. Older systems are in the following cities (listed geographically from east to west): Boston, Massachusetts; Newark, New Jersey; Philadelphia, Pennsylvania; Pittsburgh, Pennsylvania; Cleveland, Ohio; New Orleans, Louisiana and San Francisco, California;

b) **new start systems**, built in their entirety after 1980.

Newer systems can be found in the following cities (from east to west): Baltimore, Maryland; Buffalo, New York; Portland, Oregon; Sacramento, California; San Jose, California; Los Angeles, California and San Diego, California. Construction is proceeding on three more new systems: St.Louis, Missouri; Dallas, Texas and Denver, Colorado. Numerous other U.S. cities have discussed light rail construction, but as of this writing, no others have actually started construction.

Several other U.S. cities have tram lines which operate primarily as tourist lines. These cities include: Seattle, Washington; Detroit, Michigan; Dallas, Texas; Galveston, Texas; Lowell, Massachussetts and under-construction in Memphis, Tennessee. In Fort Worth, Texas, a department store has operated a short tram line in tunnel since 1963, connecting its store to its main parking lot. These tourist lines will not be discussed in this overview.

2. OLDER OPERATIONS

A brief description is provided below of the seven light rail systems now operating which were also operating prior to 1980. With two exceptions, all of these systems have two things in common, which help to explain their survival into the present day. The first is equipment. With the exception of the entire New Orleans system, and several rush-hour supplemental cars on a Philadelphia suburban line, all light rail systems in the United States, prior to 1976, used Presidents' Conference Committee (PCC) trams. The PCC was a standardized design, developed by a voluntary committee of tram operators and builders, built between 1936 and 1951. All American PCC cars were built as non-articulated, four axle cars. Most were single-ended. From the construction of the last PCC car in 1951 until the delivery of light rail vehicles to Boston in 1976, no new trams or light rail cars were built for a United States transit system, and no trams were built by any U.S.manufacturer. The durable design of the PCC car allowed for these vehicles to continue in operation for a long period of time, even with the very poor maintenance practices which characterized some U.S. operators during the 1951-1976 period. Had the PCC fleets of U.S. operators worn out earlier than they did, bus replacement would likely have occurred.

The second factor characterizing U.S.tram/light rail lines that survived from the mid 60's into the present is limited access rights of way. With the exception of several routes in northern Philadelphia, all surviving older U.S.tram systems contained either tunnels, elevated structures, reserved street medians, or private at grade rights of way for a portion of their routes. These characteristics made these operations difficult to replace with bus substitution providing an equal level of service; trams operating on limited access rights of way allow faster travel times or more direct routes, compared to busses traveling in mixed traffic on local streets.

The majority of tram systems in the United States which were operating following the end of World War II either did not modernize their systems with PCC cars, switching to less costly busses, or operated systems that contained a large amount of track operating directly in the street, competing with the ever growing number of automobiles. For these systems, even those that acquired PCC cars, conversion to busses was the only logical step for dealing with declining ridership and escalating costs. Thus, by 1966 the seven older systems mentioned above (as well as a mixed street operation in El Paso, Texas, which was converted to bus in 1974) were the only tram operations left in the United States.

The following section addresses a number of issues related to older light rail systems and makes a number of general observations.

Vehicle Procurement

Equipment operated by the older systems comes from varied sources. Boston, Philadelphia, and Pittsburgh still operate small rebuilt portions of their 40 to 45 year old PCC tram car fleets. Newark's system is run exclusively with rebuilt PCC cars. San Francisco plans to reactivate a small number of PCC cars for use on a tourist tram line. New Orleans still uses pre-PCC era equipment built in 1923, and has started a program to completely reconstruct these vehicles to like-new condition.

Boston and San Francisco were the first older U.S. systems to purchase new light rail vehicles (LRVs) to replace PCC cars, which they ordered in 1973 and received between 1976 and 1978. The cars, built by the Boeing company, were intended to be the standard U.S. light rail design used by all U.S. systems. The design proved to be unsuccessful; no additional cities beyond Boston and San Francisco purchased the design, and Boeing ultimately left the light rail car business.

With no domestic supplier of light rail cars available, Philadelphia purchased its modern LRVs from Kawasaki of Japan in 1980/1, while Cleveland purchased its fleet from Breda of Italy in 1982. Boston purchased new LRVs in 1986/7 from Kinki-Sharyo of Japan, to replace a portion of the problematic Boeing fleet. San Francisco has recently ordered 35 cars from Breda of Italy which will ultimately be used to replace the Boeing cars in that city.

All of the above mentioned vehicles were, with the exception of the unsuccessful Boeing cars, designed and built to specifications developed by the purchasing transit agency. No "off the shelf" designs have been used by older U.S. light rail operators with the exception of Pittsburgh. When Pittsburgh needed new light rail vehicles to modernize its system and replace most of its PCC fleet, it purchased (in 1985) 55 cars from Duewag/Siemens. These cars are of a design similar to that already used in Frankfurt, Germany; Edmonton and Calgary, Canada and by several new U.S. systems (these will be covered in the "New Starts" section).

When Boeing left the rail car manufacturing business, the remaining U.S. passenger rail car manufactures (Pullman-Standard and Budd) showed no interest in manufacturing light rail vehicles (both of these companies later left the passenger rail car business, leaving no U.S.manufacturers, until the recent entry of Morrison-Knudson into the passenger car market). The Federal government agency which provides capital money to U.S.transit operating agencies requires that all vehicles purchased using Federal funds have 50 per cent of their components produced in the United States. With no domestic supplier available until recently, but a need to meet domestic content laws, foreign suppliers of LRVs have performed final assembly work of their vehicles in the United States, and have primarily used sub-components from U.S. suppliers.

Capital expenditures and system expansion policies

From 1976 to the present, most of the older light rail/tram operators in the United States have spent the limited available capital funds on repairing and rebuilding existing services, rather than expanding into new areas. Most of the remaining operating older U.S. systems fell into disrepair during the 1960-1976 period for several reasons:

-- several of the systems were owned by private operators until the late 1960's (New Orleans until 1983). Private operators with declining revenues often lacked the capital to maintain facilities. Even public ownership did not ensure upkeep, because public agencies frequently had to scramble for money just to continue operations;

251

--   federal support for mass transit began in 1964 for capital grants and 1973 for operating subsidies, but the funding fluctuated because urban transit policies have changed with different U.S. administrations;

--   some systems did not decide on whether to maintain tram service or convert to bus or full metro until the 1970's. Uncertainty about the permanence of tram/light rail operations resulted in a reluctance to spend scarce dollars on major capital repairs and purchases. The lack of a domestic manufacturer of light rail vehicles also made the replacement of ageing PCC cars difficult.

Of the seven older systems, only one, New Orleans, has built an entirely new line. However, this is a short tourist oriented service. San Francisco is the only older system to have extended an existing line into previously unserved (by light rail) territory. Pittsburgh did realign all of its downtown light rail/tram traffic from above ground street tracks into a new tunnel segment and rebuilt a tram line into a full light-rail route. This improved rather than expanded existing service.

Fare integration with other modes

In Boston, Philadelphia, Cleveland, and San Francisco, light rail systems are operated in addition to metro systems. The Boston and Cleveland light rail routes are considered a part of the metro network, and free transfers are allowed between light rail and metro. In Philadelphia, free transfers are allowed between light rail routes operating in a downtown tunnel and the metro network. Tram routes operating in the northern part of the city, however, which operate exclusively in mixed-traffic, are not considered part of the "high-speed" network and are treated in the Philadelphia fare scheme as related to busses. Transfers between "high-speed rail"[1] and "surface lines" must be purchased. The light rail and metro systems in San Francisco are operated by two separate agencies, but free transfers are allowed between the underground portion of the light rail system and the metro system for travel within the city of San Francisco itself.

In New Orleans, Pittsburgh, and Newark, the light rail systems, which in all three cities comprise only a small portion of total transit route kilometres operated (bus making up the remainder), are treated as additional parts of the bus system. The same fares are charged for busses and light rail. In Newark, a portion of the bus system feeds into light rail stops. In New Orleans and Pittsburgh, the light rail lines connect with busses primarily in the downtown areas, and limited feeder service is provided from outlying areas to light rail stops.

In San Francisco and Cleveland, transfers between light rail and connecting bus routes are free. In Philadelphia, Pittsburgh, and New Orleans, transfers from bus to bus and between bus and light rail must be purchased. In Boston and Newark, no free or reduced rate transfers are available. In all of these cities, regular riders can purchase reduced rate monthly passes, which are also valid on both bus and rail[2]. In San Francisco, Boston and New Orleans, multi-day tourist passes are available.

None of the older light rail systems uses the honor-based, random check, proof of payment method of collecting fares. In New Orleans and Newark fares are collected by the operator as passengers board the car. In Philadelphia and San Francisco, operators collect fares as passengers board except in underground stations, where passengers pay to enter the station, and then board the car.

In Cleveland, passengers pay getting on when heading away from downtown, and pay on exiting when traveling to the city. In Pittsburgh, the opposite is followed, passengers pay getting on when

252

going to the city and getting off when traveling from the city. No fare is charged to enter or exit underground stations in Pittsburgh, and any passengers traveling exclusively between downtown underground stations can do so for free. In Boston, passengers pay when entering underground stations, and when boarding cars above ground heading towards the downtown. When boarding or exiting cars above ground heading away from the city, no fare is charged.

Accessibility to the disabled

Of the older light rail systems, only the portions of the San Francisco and Pittsburgh systems containing high-platforms are accessible to the disabled. San Francisco is considering the construction of additional high platforms while Boston and Philadelphia are considering the purchase of low-floor cars and the construction of elevators at underground stops to make the system accessible. New Orleans operates a tourist tram line that is accessible, but its regular route is not.

In 1990 a Federal regulation, known as the Americans with Disabilities Act was passed, requiring that all major transportation facilities be made accessible to people with mobility, sight and sound impairments within three years of the enactment of the legislation. In cases where the cost of accessibility will be extraordinary, however, the Federal Department of Transportation may grant a waiver extending the time available for accessibility changes to be implemented up to thirty years. An exemption is made for systems that are considered national historic landmarks, including the trams in New Orleans.

Specifically, as far as light rail is concerned, the legislation requires one car per train to be accessible by 1995, key stations to be identified and made accessible by 1993, and supplementary para-transit be available to those riders who still cannot make use of an accessible rail line. All light rail lines must prepare Key Station Accessibility Plans by July 26, 1992.

Summary descriptions of older systems

A series of graphs and tables summarizing ridership, route length, operating costs, vehicle information, and performance measure comparisons for all U.S. light rail and tram systems are provided at the end of this overview.

Boston, Massachusetts

The Boston metropolitan area has a population of 2.7 million[3]. Public transportation in several modes (light rail, metro, regional rail, ferry, bus, and trolley bus) is operated by the Massachusetts Bay Transportation Authority (M.B.T.A).

Boston opened a tram tunnel in 1897, giving it the distinction of having the first transit tunnel in the United States. This tunnel still serves as the core of Boston's light rail network, which also includes elevated segments, private rights of way built on former railroad lines, and middle of street private reservations. Only one segment of one line operates in mixed traffic. The last addition to the Boston system was made in 1959, when a former railroad line was converted to a tram/light rail line. This was the last light rail line built by a public agency in the United States until the opening of San Diego's new system in 1980.[4]

A majority of service in Boston is provided by a fleet of 100 LRVs built in 1986-7 by Kinki-Sharyo of Japan, and 85 remaining 1976-8 Boeing LRVs. A small fleet of 12 rebuilt PCC cars continue to serve one short isolated route.

The total length of Boston's five-route light rail system is 44.9 km. Virtually all of the track and overhead wire in the Boston system was replaced in several large projects between 1975 and 1989. The system is currently proposing to construct a short tunnel extension to replace and relocate the short elevated segment remaining. A street running portion of one of Boston's routes has had service suspended (and replaced by busses) since 1985. This service may be restored by 1995.

Currently under development is a three-section, articulated, low-floor car design. One hundred of these cars (to be known as Type 8s) would be purchased to replace the last of the Boeing cars and to make the light-rail system fully accessible.

Newark, New Jersey

Newark, New Jersey is considered part of the New York City metropolitan area. Public transportation in the entire state of New Jersey is the responsibility of one agency, New Jersey Transit (NJT). In addition to an extensive bus system throughout the state, and an extensive regional rail system, which provides commuter service to New York City, NJT also operates one light rail route in Newark.

The line consists of both a downtown tunnel, and a reserved surface right of way that has only one grade crossing. The line was built in 1935 in the bed of an abandoned canal to provide a high speed route for surface tram lines to reach downtown Newark. All of the feeder tram lines have long since been abandoned and converted to bus routes, but the core light rail line remains. The route is serviced by a fleet of 24 rebuilt PCC cars. The Newark light rail line connects at its downtown terminal to a metro route, which operates to New York city. The light rail line is not accessible to the disabled. Track was rebuilt during the 1980's, and there are no immediate plans to replace the PCC cars or expand the line. The need to make the line accessible may change this. Various ideas have been raised through the years to expand the line, including an extension to Newark airport, but no extension plans are currently in full development.

Philadelphia, Pennsylvania

The current population of the metropolitan Philadelphia area is 4.2 million. The Southeastern Pennsylvania Transportation Authority (SEPTA) is the operator of most public transportation in the region. SEPTA operates light rail, metros, electrified regional rail lines, trolley busses, and diesel busses. In addition to SEPTA, interstate commuter service is provided from the state of New Jersey to Philadelphia by two agencies: New Jersey Transit (which provides bus service) and the Port Authority Transit Corporation (which operates an inter-state metro line).

Philadelphia, which operates the largest tram/light-rail system in the U.S., has three types of operations. First are five lines that begin as surface mixed-traffic routes and feed into a single tram tunnel running into downtown. The tram tunnel was first opened in 1905, and was extended in 1954. The surface portion of these routes operates in the western section of the city. The second group of tram lines are three routes that operate primarily in northern Philadelphia. These routes are traditional tram lines, with few light rail features. Four other northern Philadelphia tram lines have been

254

abandoned within the last 12 years and SEPTA considered abandoning the three remaining tram lines, but the current policy is to retain tram service. The third group of routes are two suburban lines, which serve as a feeder to a metro line. Parts of these two suburban lines operate on private rights of way and also include some single-track operations.

The five surface-tunnel routes are served by 112 single ended four-axle LRVs built by Kawasaki in the early 1980's, when they replaced PCC cars. The two suburban lines are served by a fleet of 29 double-ended, four-axle Kawasaki LRV's. The three remaining northern Philadelphia tram lines are served by a fleet of 89 rebuilt (1946-built) PCC cars.

Philadelphia also has two metro lines, and an electrified regional metro line, which feed into center-city tunnels. The regional rail line tunnel, and one of the metro lines run parallel to the light rail tunnel. The remaining metro line intersects with these three parallel rail lines. None of Philadelphia's three groups of light rail lines is accessible to the disabled, and there are no current plans to expand the system.

Philadelphia has started development of a low-floor car design which would replace the 1981 Kawasaki cars on the five surface-tunnel routes. The Kawasaki cars would then be transferred to the northern Philadelphia tram routes.

Pittsburgh, Pennsylvania

The current population of the Pittsburgh metropolitan area is 1.6 million people. Public transportation, both light rail and bus, is operated by Port Authority Transit. The bus system is unusual in that it features segregated right of way busways in two areas of the city.

Pittsburgh had a very large tram system until the early 60's. From that time until 1971, massive abandonments of tram lines (with bus substitutions) occurred. In 1971, the only tram lines remaining were three lines that operated through a hillside tunnel. Consideration was given to converting these routes either to bus lines (with busways), or to people mover lines, using an advanced automated technology promoted by the Westinghouse company as "skytrain". Ultimately, it was decided to retain the existing tram lines and convert a portion of them to full light rail standards. This modernization program included the construction of a downtown tunnel to replace mixed-traffic surface tracks.

Fifty-five six axle, articulated LRV's were ordered from Duewag-Siemens of Germany to service the rebuilt line, while 16 of the system's old PCC cars were rebuilt to service the remaining lines that were not rebuilt.

The modernized segment of the system includes high platforms, which are accessible to the disabled. There has been discussion of plans to modernize the remainder of the tram system, and to extend the downtown tunnel.

Cleveland, Ohio

The current population of the Cleveland metropolitan area is 1.6 million. Public transportation in Cleveland is the responsibility of the Greater Cleveland Regional Transportation Authority (GCRTA). GCRTA operates light rail, a metro line, and an extensive bus system.

Cleveland's light rail system consists of two lines operating on private rights of way, and reservations in the middle of streets, which connect downtown Cleveland with the suburbs of Shaker Heights. The two lines were originally built in 1919 by real estate developers. The lines were served by PCC cars until 1982, when a fleet of 48 six-axle, articulated LRV's were purchased from Breda of Italy. Extensive renovations to the track, power systems, and stations were made during the 1980's to bring the system up to light rail standards. The lines are not accessible to the disabled. Cleveland also has one metro line, which shares a maintenance facility and a small part of its right of way with the light rail lines. Both the light rail and metro lines share a common downtown terminal, which has recently been completely rebuilt. Short downtown extensions to the light rail lines have been proposed.

New Orleans, Louisiana

The current population of the New Orleans metropolitan area is 1.04 million. Public transportation (bus and light rail) is provided by the New Orleans Regional Transportation Authority (RTA).

New Orleans is the only one of the older tram operations that never owned PCC cars. It instead relied, and continues to rely on, a fleet of 35 pre-PCC era cars built in 1923 by the Perley Thomas Company.

The cars serve one original line, which operates primarily on a center reservation, but does have some mixed-traffic tracks in street portions. Reconstruction of the tracks and cars (the second major rebuilding for the vehicles during their almost 70 years of service) is currently underway. While the line has been declared a national monument, it operates as part of the RTA's revenue service, and not as a special tourist tram line.

In 1988, a second line was opened along New Orleans' riverfront primarily as a tourist service. This line operates along former freight railroad switching track, does not connect with the older route, and uses a different track gauge. The tourist line uses two original New Orleans cars that were reclaimed from tram museums, as well as two cars acquired from Melbourne, Australia. The Australian cars have been modified for disabled access, but none of the other cars on the original line is accessible. There are proposals both to extend the riverfront line and to build new lines. If any new lines are constructed, it is possible that they will be served by a fleet of new "1923" tram replicas manufactured in-house by the transit authority.

San Francisco, California

The current population of the San Francisco metropolitan area is 3.6 million. Public transportation within the city is provided by the San Francisco Municipal Railway (MUNI). MUNI operates light rail lines, busses, trolley busses, and the famous cable cars. Metro service in San Francisco, and to far reaching suburban areas (including the city of Oakland) is provided by a different agency, the Bay Area Rapid Transit system (BART). Suburban counties each run their own bus systems, and the California Department of Transportation (CalTrans) operates a regional rail line that connects San Francisco to San Jose.

San Francisco's light rail system consists of five routes from outer areas of the city, which merge together for the final portion of their trips into the downtown area. A portion of the system travels through a tunnel dating to the early 1900's, but until 1981, the majority of the system ran in mixed-traffic at-grade. In 1981, a downtown tunnel (locally referred to as a "light rail metro") was opened.

The light rail tunnel opened with 100 1978 built Boeing LRVs and replaced the old PCC cars. 30 Boeing LRVs rejected by Boston's MBTA were later purchased, raising the total LRV fleet to 130 cars. The LRVs have retractable stairs that allow both high and low platform compatibility, which is needed in the all high platform tunnel stations.

In addition to a conventional light rail system, San Francisco has in recent years operated a "Festival Trolley" using historic museum trams from all over the world (as well as some PCC cars). The trams operate on downtown street trackage, which was made surplus by the opening of the light rail tunnel and its stations in 1981. There are currently plans to construct new track to extend this service, and to purchase 20 rebuilt PCC cars from Philadelphia to serve it.

The underground downtown portion of the BART metro system runs in a separate tunnel directly below the light rail tunnel. Connections for passengers are available at all downtown stations between the two levels and the two systems.

San Francisco has recently extended one of its light rail lines to connect with two other lines (at their outer terminals) and a station on the BART metro, and plans to extend rail for the tourist tram service. The opening of this extension, however, has been delayed because of a shortage of equipment to operate it. Plans are under development to further extend the light rail system. The conversion of a very heavily traveled diesel bus route to a light rail line has been proposed, but there are no active plans to construct this line. Actively under consideration, however, is a plan to extend the underground tunnel segment to a location near the existing regional-rail terminal.

Downtown light rail tunnel stations are accessible to the disabled by use of high platforms. In addition, key surface stops have high platforms.

Thirty-five cars have been ordered from Breda of Italy to provide additional cars to expand service. An option exists to purchase additional cars to replace the Boeing LRVs. The new cars, in addition to having high platform/low platform compatibility, will be wheel-chair lift equipped, which will make all stops accessible.

3. NEWER OPERATIONS

Construction of new light rail systems began in the United States in 1979, when San Diego, California broke ground for a new light rail line. Since then, new light rail systems have opened in five additional cities: Buffalo, New York; Portland, Oregon; Sacramento, California; San Jose, California; Los Angeles, California, and in April 1992, Baltimore, Maryland. Construction has also started on light rail lines in three other cities: St. Louis, Missouri; Dallas, Texas and Denver, Colorado.

Most of the new systems in operation use at-grade rights of way rather than tunnels. The exceptions are Buffalo and a small portion of the new Los Angeles-Long Beach line. All of the new systems have mixed traffic (traditional tram style) track at grade in the downtown areas, with reserved rights of way on the outer portion of the system (the Buffalo system uses a tunnel). Unlike traditional trams, the in-street trackage is in auto restricted transit malls or clearly marked transit lanes, in some cases with barriers. All of the new U.S. light rail systems use the proof-of-payment system with automatic ticket vending machines and roving inspectors checking for proper payment.

There has been a resurgence in light rail in the United States since 1980 for several reasons:

-- light rail systems are potentially cheaper to construct than full metros. There is also greater freedom (and reduced costs) in choosing and constructing rights of way because light rail systems do not have to be completely grade separated;

-- the seven older systems, for which survival was uncertain during the 1960's and early 1970's, were undergoing reconstruction and were available as examples of light rail technology at work;

-- initial openings of new systems both in Canada and the United States served as examples for other U.S. cities to follow;

-- federal money was available in several instances to pay for 80 per cent of the construction costs of new light rail systems. Had local governments been forced to pay more of the costs, the prospects for system construction would have been considerably reduced;

-- in two instances (Sacramento and Portland) decisions to abandon road construction plans released highway money for other transportation projects and already cleared rights of way became available for rail construction;

-- light rail is considered a catalyst to stimulate ridership in some cities served by all bus transit systems, which had declining or flat ridership rates;

-- light rail is considered a more cost-effective means to handle future high passenger load demand projections in cities whose bus systems may not be able to meet increased demand.

The following section addresses a number of issues related to newer light rail systems and makes a number of general observations.

Population factors

New light rail systems have been built both in high-growth, expanding metropolitan areas, and in older urban areas with declining population. The California cities, Sacramento, San Diego, San Jose, and Los Angeles are all high growth areas where light rail construction is viewed as one way to reduce future highway congestion in a rapidly growing metropolitan area.

Conversely, light rail proposals have also been considered by cities with declining populations and employment bases as a tool to increase the attractiveness and living conditions of the urban environment and as a means to reverse negative growth.

Vehicle procurement

Most of the new systems have purchased LRVs with proven designs. Sacramento, San Diego, and the systems under construction in St.Louis and Denver use Duewag/Siemens cars of a design used in Germany since 1968. Portland's cars were built by Bombardier using a design previously used by BN of Belgium. San Jose purchased cars from UTDC of Canada, based on a Toronto LRV design. As is the case with the older U.S. systems, the lack of domestic manufacturers means that all vehicle orders must be filled by foreign manufacturers. The "Buy-America" content requirements have resulted in final assembly taking place in the U.S.and most sub-components (electrical control equipment, brakes, seats, air conditioning, etc.) coming from U.S. manufacturers. Two European manufacturers (ABB and Siemens-Duewag) and one Canadian manufacturer (Bombardier) have constructed permanent final assembly plants in the United States which have produced light rail vehicles. Morrison-Knudsen, a long time U.S remanufacturer of rail cars, has now entered into new car manufacturing, being the first U.S.-owned company to do so since the early 1980s.

Accessibility to the disabled

All of the new light rail systems have been built as accessible to the disabled, using either high platforms, platform mounted lifts, or car mounted lifts. This is in response to federal regulations from the 1970's for the construction of new transit systems which require wheel-chair accessibility. None of the current systems uses low floor technology. The 1990 Americans with Disabilities Act (ADA) (see "older systems section for more details) reemphasizes the requirement that any new systems or extensions to current systems be accessible to the handicapped. While all of the American light rail systems built new since 1978 are accessible, some modifications will still have to be made to comply fully with ADA requirements. This is particularly the case for regulations regarding access to those with sight and sound impairments.

Fare collection methods and multi-modal integration

Integration with existing bus service is common with all of the new U.S. light rail systems. Sacramento, San Jose, San Diego, Portland, and Buffalo all re-routed existing bus routes to LRT stations when the rail service was initiated. Because it is common in most U.S.cities with both bus and urban rail service for a single agency to control both modes, it is institutionally easy to discontinue or reroute bus services that run parallel to new light rail lines. Free transfers are available between all local bus routes and light rail in Sacramento, San Diego, Portland, and Buffalo. In San Jose, riders can buy a one day pass which is valid on both bus and rail. In all of these cities, regular riders can buy discounted monthly passes which are good on both light rail and bus.

All of the newer light rail systems in the United States use the honor-based, random inspection, barrier free, proof-of-payment method for collecting fares. Passengers either buy a ticket from a machine, carry a transfer from a bus, or own a monthly pass. At any time during the trip, inspectors can ask to see one of the above mentioned proofs of payment. A passenger with no proof is fined. None of the seven older U.S.systems currently uses this system. Instead, they rely on fares paid to the vehicle operator, or payment to enter underground stations.

In Buffalo and Portland there is no charge to ride the light rail line exclusively within the at-grade, auto-restricted downtown transit malls found in both of these cities. In Sacramento, a reduced fare is charged for travel exclusively within the downtown area.

Summary descriptions of newer systems

Buffalo, New York

Buffalo, with a metropolitan area population of 900 000, is the smallest U.S. city to have light rail service. Public transportation in Buffalo (light rail and bus) is provided by the Niagara Frontier Transit Metro System (NFTMS).

Buffalo opened a single route light rail system, which extends to the north from the downtown area, in 1985. It is served by 27 four-axle light rail cars built by Tokyu Car Company of Japan. The system is unusual in that it operates downtown above ground, in a transit mall, and operates in a tunnel through the outer section of the line (the inverse of all other United States light rail systems with tunnel sections). The system is 10 kilometres long, with 7.7 kilometres of the route in tunnels.

An extension of the light rail system in its current form to the suburb of Tonawanda has been proposed, but because of the costs of building a light rail tunnel, the system is now considering building an at-grade line using used PCC trams recently purchased from the Greater Cleveland (Ohio) Regional Transit Authority.

Buffalo's entire transit system (427 buses, 27 LRVs) shut down for several days in 1990 due to a shortage of operating funds. The shutdown, caused by a lack of dedicated local funding, resulted in emergency measures to provide local money to restore service.

Portland, Oregon

The current population of the Portland metropolitan area is 1.1 million people. Public transportation (light rail and bus) is the responsibility of the Tri-County Metropolitan District of Oregon (Tri-Met).

Portland's light rail system, which opened in 1986, has one rail line connecting the Downtown area with the suburb of Gresham. The 24.2 kilometre line is totally at grade, and includes street running in a downtown transit mall loop. The suburban portion of the line operates in former railroad rights of way, next to an existing highway, and in a corridor originally planned for highway construction.

The system is served by 26 cars built by Bombardier of Canada. Wheelchair lifts are available at all station platforms to make the system fully accessible to the disabled.

Voters recently approved tax and bond measures to provide money for the construction of light rail extensions. Plans are under development to build a second line to the west of the city. This new line will make use of underground segments, and be partially funded by Federal money. The system currently has several historic tram replicas used on a downtown circular shuttle, which operate on the same tracks as the regular light rail service.

Sacramento, California

The current population of the metropolitan Sacramento area is 1.09 million. Public transportation (light rail and bus) is provided by the Sacramento Regional Transit District (RTD). The development of the Sacramento light rail system began with the abandonment of an interstate highway project in

1979, the need to add capacity for a growing area, and the availability of an already cleared right of way. A 29.5 km light rail route was built, using part of the right of way originally intended for the roadway. The first segments of the line opened in 1987, using a fleet of 26 Siemens/Duewag LRV's. A large portion of the line opened as a single track system. Double tracking was added later to increase the capacity of the line, and ten additional cars were purchased. The system operates primarily on reserved rights of way, but does include mixed-traffic street running through the downtown segment. The system is considering extending the light rail network.

San Jose, California

The current population of the San Jose metropolitan area is 1.4 million people. Public transportation (light rail and bus) in San Jose is provided by the Santa Clara County Transit District (SCCTD). The light rail system consists of a single 32 km line that opened in several segments between 1987 and 1991. A majority of the line operates in segregated reservations in the middle of major avenues and freeways. The downtown portion operates in mixed-traffic through a "transit mall". Lifts for disabled accessibility are provided at all stops. The fleet is made up of 50 articulated LRVs manufactured by Urban Transit Development Corporation (UTDC) of Canada in 1987/88. In addition to normal light rail service, a shuttle route is operated on the downtown segment of the line using several restored historic trams. Extensions to the system are being considered, including one which may connect with the southern portion of the BART system from San Francisco. An existing regional rail line from San Francisco to San Jose has been extended to a new terminal which provides connections to the light rail system.

Los Angeles, California

With a population of 11.4 million people, the greater Los Angeles area is the second largest metropolitan area in the United States. The Clean Air Act Amendments of 1990 induced Los Angeles, which has the worst air quality of any U.S. urbanized area, to place strong emphasis on developing transit as an alternative to auto travel. The primary operator of public transit service in Los Angeles is the Southern California Rapid Transit District (SCRTD). The SCRTD operates an extensive bus system and a light rail line opened in 1990. It will also operate a metro currently under construction. The Los Angeles County Transportation Commission (LACTC) plans and builds new urban rail lines. LACTC and Commissions for the neighboring counties are planning and completing a regional commuter rail network for Los Angeles. Several small to mid-size municipal bus operators, which complement the SCRTD's large bus network, round out the Los Angeles area public transportation network.

Until the opening of the Los Angeles-Long Beach light rail line in 1990, Los Angeles was the largest U.S. city without urban rail transport. Los Angeles's conventional tram system was abandoned by 1963, while a separate interurban tram system that connected Los Angeles with its many suburbs was abandoned by 1961. Much of the right of way used to construct the current Los Angeles-Long Beach light rail line was used by the line abandoned in 1961.

The current line (known as the Blue Line), for which construction began in 1985, is 36 kilometres long. It is served by a fleet of 54 LRVs built by Nippon-Sharyo of Japan. The line is fully equipped with high platform stations, making it completely accessible. The line is planned to be the first of a large network of light rail, metro, busways, and regional commuter rail lines.

A second light rail line (known as the Green Line) is currently under construction. This will be an east-west line, which will intersect the current north-south (Blue) line. The Green line has been the subject of controversy, as some local leaders have pushed for this line to be fully automated. An order was place for 41 automated cars with Sumitomo of Japan. The high cost of this equipment combined with the contract going to a non-domestic supplier over a domestic one (Morrison-Knudsen) caused a political controversy which resulted in national media attention. Ultimately, the contract with Sumitomo was canceled, and the use of automated equipment postponed. It has now been proposed by Los Angeles local government to purchase locally manufactured, non-automated equipment.

San Diego, California

The San Diego Trolley opened in 1980 and was the first of the "new start" light rail systems in the U.S. The system has grown to a 53.4 km network, served by 71 Siemens/Duewag LRVs built between 1979 and 1990. The system currently has 75 additional cars ordered and has additional extensions planned. Please refer to the ECMT case study for more data on the San Diego system.

4. SYSTEMS CURRENTLY UNDER CONSTRUCTION

Baltimore, Maryland

The current population of metropolitan Baltimore is 1.8 million people. The Maryland Mass Transit Administration (MTA) is responsible for providing public transportation in Baltimore, and most of the state of Maryland. The current public transit system includes a large bus network serving the greater Baltimore area, a metro line connecting the suburb of Owens Mills with downtown Baltimore, and contracted private carrier bus operators serving more distant parts of the state. A regional commuter rail carrier, the state-owned Maryland Rail Commuter Service (MARC), provides service between Baltimore and the city of Washington, D.C.

The MTA originally planned to build a full network of metro lines after the completion of the first. Escalating costs of building full metros lead to a decision to use light rail technology to complete the remainder of the proposed Baltimore urban rail corridors. Construction has started on a 36.2 km north-south route, which will intercept the east-northwest metro line in downtown Baltimore. Thirty-five articulated LRVs have been ordered from ABB Traction to service the line, which partially opened in early 1992.

St.Louis, Missouri

The current population of metropolitan St. Louis is 1.9 million people. The Bi-State Development Agency is responsible for public transit in the St. Louis metropolitan area and nearby East St. Louis, Illinois. Bi-State is responsible for the region's river-ports, airports, bridges, and bus system. St.Louis is in the midst of constructing of a 29 km light rail route. The route is being built primarily using abandoned freight railroad rights of way, including a downtown tunnel and a bridge across the Mississippi River. The route will link downtown St.Louis with East St.Louis, Illinois to the east and the St.Louis airport to the west. The area hopes that the light rail system will play a role in revitalizing a blighted portion of the St.Louis metropolitan area.

Dallas, Texas

The current population of metropolitan Dallas is 3.1 million people. Public transportation in the greater Dallas area is the responsibility of the Dallas Area Rapid Transit system (DART). DART operates an extensive bus network, and has plans to construct an extensive network of busways, light rail lines, and commuter rail lines. Construction has started on a 32 km long light rail route, and 45 light rail vehicles will be ordered soon. Part of the proposed initial line may use tunnel segments constructed next to a highway, but plans have not been finalized.

Denver, Colorado

The Regional Transit District (RTD) of Denver, using local money, is now building a short downtown light rail line, which it is hoped will be the nucleus of a future full-scale light rail system. Eight cars have been ordered from Siemens-Duewag to provide the service. The cars are an add-on to vehicles currently on order for the San Diego, California system.

5. PROPOSED NEW SYSTEMS

Seventeen of the 35 U.S. metropolitan areas with populations of 500,000 or more (and some smaller areas as well) which currently have no urban rail service have at various times proposed the construction of light rail lines. The list of cities includes the following (listed from largest metropolitan area to smallest):

New York, New York (42nd St.); Chicago, Illinois (downtown distributor); Detroit, Michigan; Seattle, Washington; Minneapolis, Minnesota; Phoenix, Arizona; Cincinnati, Ohio; Milwaukee, Wisconsin; Kansas City, Missouri; Norfolk, Virginia; Columbus, Ohio; Charlotte, North Carolina; Hartford, Connecticut; Salt Lake City, Utah; Rochester, New York; Memphis, Tennessee; Nashville, Tennessee; Raleigh-Durham, North Carolina; Austin, Texas; Harrisburg, Pennsylvania and Oklahoma City, Oklahoma.

Three cities with the most active current plans are Salt Lake City, Minneapolis, and a light rail downtown distributer for Chicago. Difficulties in securing funding (both local and federal) and in identifying route alignments are the major barriers to construction. Several of these cities have discussed light rail proposals for more than a decade, without taking action. Cities that are able to develop local funding sources, including dedicated sales taxes or bond authority, are the most likely candidates to develop new systems.

The transportation agencies of two smaller cities (Austin, Texas and Oklahoma City, Oklahoma) have been acquiring local railroad right of way for possible light rail alignments, even though the actual construction of light rail lines may be many years away. Another example of long range planning for light rail can be found in Seattle, Washington. Seattle has recently opened an underground tunnel for electric busses through the heart of its downtown area. The tunnel has had rail for use by light rail cars built into its floor to allow future conversion should it be warranted by demand, although there are no immediate plans for light rail in the tunnel.

As can be seen in graphs #1, #2, and #3, the cities proposing light rail systems vary greatly in current transit use and projected growth. Several cities have populations over two million, while several have populations of less than 500,000. Some carry heavy loads on their current bus systems while others carry comparatively light loads. Projected traffic congestion severity[5] for the year 2005 does indicate that some cities which currently have smaller populations and light use of public transport may develop congestion problems in the future because of rapid growth.

6. PERFORMANCE EVALUATION OF U.S. LIGHT RAIL SYSTEMS

Methodology

This section provides a summary evaluation of the performance of U.S.light rail undertakings. The evaluation uses a limited set of indicators selected to provide a brief but balanced view of performance. The methodology applied is based on a framework that considers performance as composed on the following three dimensions[6].

Service Effectiveness -- based on ratios of service consumption (Passengers, Passenger Kilometres, or Operating Revenue) divided by service outputs (Vehicle Hours, Vehicle Kilometres, Capacity Kilometres). Service effectiveness measures the extent to which passengers consume the service produced. This evaluation uses Load Factor (Passenger Kilometres per Revenue Vehicle Kilometres - Graph 4) to determine how successfully the undertaking delivers services that are consumed. The load factor figures presented combine peak and off-peak service.

A comparison of average speeds (Graph 5) is also provided to improve understanding of the operating environments of U.S.undertakings.

Cost Efficiency -- measures how economically the undertaking produces basic outputs of service, using ratios of service inputs (Labor, Capital, Fuel), often monetarized, divided by service outputs (Vehicle Hours, Vehicle Kilometres, Capacity Kilometres). This evaluation uses Operating Expense (US$) per Revenue Vehicle Kilometre (Graph 6) and Hour (Graph 7) to indicate cost efficiency, and adds Maintenance Cost per Revenue Vehicle Hours (Graph 8) to provide a closer look at one aspect of efficiency.

Use of both Revenue Vehicle Hour and Kilometre as outputs provides a more balanced view of performance than would use of one or the other. Because evaluation should emphasize measures that managers can control, it would be unfair to contrast the performance of one operator to that of another based on factors outside a manager's influence. The cost of Revenue Kilometres is affected by speed, which can be influenced by route design and scheduling, but is to a great degree limited by congestion and urban design -- factors out of the control of the undertaking. Vehicle Hours add an important performance dimension, particularly because of its correlation to operators' wages -- the largest component of operating expense.

Cost Effectiveness -- measures how economically the undertaking provides service that is actually consumed by riders. Evaluation of cost effectiveness uses ratios of service inputs divided by service consumption (Passengers, Passenger Kilometres, or Operating Revenue). This evaluation uses Operating Expense per Unlinked Passenger Trip (Graph 9) and Passenger Kilometre (Graph 10) to indicate cost effectiveness. Farebox Return (Passenger Revenue divided by Operating Expense - Graph 11) is also included, although it is provided for all modes combined rather than light rail only because most U.S.operators do not provide the US Department of Transportation with fare revenues by mode.

There are important reasons to use both unlinked trips and passenger kilometres in performance comparisons. Unlinked trips are easier to measure and consequently more accurate than passenger kilometres (the total distance travelled by all passengers), which typically require statistical sampling. However, because average trip lengths vary significantly among operators, use of this indicator alone can bias comparisons in favor of operators with short average trip lengths and large numbers of transfers over operators with long trips and fewer transfers. Passenger kilometres overcome these limitations.

This evaluation also uses average trip length (Passenger Kilometres divided by Unlinked Passenger Trips - Graph 12) to indicate the relationship between these two measures of service usage, and provide additional insight into comparisons.

Capital expenses, which could be annualized, are not included in the evaluation because of lack of comparable data. The resultant focus on operating expenses produces a significant but unavoidable bias in the comparisons. In cost efficiency and effectiveness comparisons the lack of capital expenses make the systems that are capital intense, for example, those with new technology and a minimal reliance on labor, appear more productive than more labor intense systems. This bias can only be reduced by combining operating and annualized capital costs in the performance measures. The detailed case studies in this ECMT project include combined capital and operating costs.

Passenger revenue or fare recovery ratios (Graph 11) are other important measures of economic performance. In a business sense, the value of the undertaking is determined by passengers' willingness to pay for its service outputs instead of alternatives, particularly travel in automobiles. For public transport, which seldom produces a profit, assessment of success involves minimization of deficits and public subsidies. Another, perhaps "public policy", view of public transport might recognize the value of revenue to cost measures, but add other environmental (congestion relief and reduction in energy consumption) or social (mobility for elderly and handicapped) objectives for public transport that are important but difficult to measure and evaluate.

Performance evaluation

The following nine tables indicate the broad range in characteristics and performance of the U.S. light rail systems. The evaluation excludes the Boston MBTA because of data problems.

A key consideration in performance evaluation is speed (Graph 5). Faster speeds allow either shorter headways and a higher level of service with the same equipment and operators, or the ability to maintain headways and levels of service with less equipment and fewer operators than required of systems with slower speeds. Systems with large amounts of segregated rights-of-way, such as Cleveland, Sacramento, Portland and San Diego, have high average speeds (30 to 37 kilometres per hour) when compared to systems with a large amount of mixed-traffic operation (Philadelphia and San Francisco) or historic equipment (New Orleans).

Load factor is an important indicator of service utilization, and ultimately, of productivity -- high loads contribute to lower costs per rider. Graph 4 indicates a significant range in load factors, from 12.64 passengers per kilometre for Newark to 32.85 for Cleveland. However, the importance of local policy decisions on level of service should also be recognized. Load factor is influenced, for example, by local policies on crowding and headways.

San Diego, Pittsburgh, Portland, Cleveland, and Sacramento are characterized by relatively long average trip lengths (Graph 12). At 11.66 kilometres, San Diego has 200-300 per cent longer trips than six of the other ten systems. In the five cities with the longest trips, light rail primarily transports workers from suburbs to the central business district. In San Francisco and Philadelphia service primarily provides urban circulation, and is operated in mixed-traffic, through older urban areas. The length of the Newark line is short compared to the other operations, resulting in relatively low average trip lengths.

As mentioned above, cost efficiency and effectiveness measures are influenced by speed and average trip length, among other factors. High costs per kilometre (Graph 6) for Buffalo and older systems San Francisco and Philadelphia are probably influenced by slower speeds; low costs for newer systems, San Diego and Portland, are probably influenced by their higher speeds.

Other factors besides speed have important influences on cost efficiency. As one would expect, the fastest systems have lower costs per kilometre, as do San Diego and Portland, and relatively slow San Francisco has the second highest cost per kilometre. However, Sacramento and Cleveland, two of the faster systems, are only in the middle of the ten in costs per kilometre.
Graph 7 presents cost per hour, which is unaffected by speed. Operators' wages, typically the most significant single operating cost component, is paid on an hourly basis, independent of speed. In terms of cost per hour, the most economical systems are three older systems -- New Orleans, Philadelphia, and Newark -- and San Diego, a new system that was built economically on existing right-of-way, using existing vehicle technology.

Relatively high maintenance costs per hour for Cleveland, Pittsburgh, and San Francisco are probably important contributors to the high cost per hour and kilometre for these systems. It should be noted that, with the exception of systems with PCC fleets, Cleveland and San Francisco have the oldest fleets (Table 5), which will also contribute to high maintenance costs. New Orleans, despite the age of its equipment, comes in with the lowest costs in this category.

San Diego and Portland perform consistently well in both cost efficiency and effectiveness measures. San Diego is either the first or second best performer and Portland is among the five best performers measured in operating expenses per revenue vehicle kilometre, per passenger kilometre, and per unlinked passenger trip. Detailed analysis of San Diego is provided in the U.S.case study for the ECMT project.

Newark ranks well when comparing operating expenses per revenue vehicle kilometre, and per unlinked passenger trip, but ranks less favorably when comparing costs per passenger kilometre. The short length of passenger trips contributes to these relative positions.

Sacramento and Pittsburgh perform well when comparing costs per passenger kilometre, but have higher costs per passenger trip, an effect of the longer average trip lengths found on these systems. Conversely, San Francisco's relative position improves when comparing operating expenses per passenger trip to operating expenses per passenger kilometre, an effect of its lower average trip length.

In examining the passenger revenues to operating expense indicator (Graph 11), it is important to make two observations. First, as noted, capital costs are excluded, thereby limiting the ability to determine the extent to which total costs of producing service are recovered from passenger revenues.

Second, with the exception of San Diego, which operates light rail as a single mode, the other nine operators provide revenue to cost ratios for light rail combined with one or other mode, usually large urban fixed route services.

San Diego's light rail system is very successful at recovering its costs from revenue --- at 92 per cent it comes very close to recovering all operating costs. The second system, Newark, is over 40 per cent lower, at 53 per cent. Philadelphia also recovers almost half of its costs, while the remaining seven systems recover a third or less of their costs for all modes combined.

A more detailed understanding of cost efficiency and effectiveness would require examination of annualized capital costs and the next level of operating cost detail. Operating costs would have to be disaggregated into major components, for example, operations (primarily operators' wages), administration, labour, or energy. Although this is beyond the scope of this summary evaluation, the maintenance cost per hour indicator (Graph 8) is included as an example of the next level of analysis. Similar analysis could be conducted of other major cost components. Further insights into comparative economic performance might include consideration of work rules and staffing policies, for example, the use of large degrees of automated control, single motormen, conductors, and guards.

Notes

1. In Philadelphia, the metro lines, segregated light rail lines and regional commuter rail lines are collectively referred to as the "high-speed" network.

2. In Boston, riders can purchase a pass valid only on light rail and metro, a pass valid only on bus, or a more expensive "Combo" pass valid on both rail and bus services.

3. 1990 U.S. Census figures.

4. In 1963, a short light rail line was built by a department store in Fort Worth, Texas to connect their outlying parking lot to their main store.

5. Congestion severity index equals total delay divided by million vehicle miles of travel. *Source:* Traffic Congestion Trends, Measures, and Effects: Report to the Chairman, Subcommittee on Transportation and Related agencies, Committee on Appropriations, US Senate, November 1989.

6. Fielding, G.J., Managing Public Transit Strategically, Jossey-Bass, San Francisco, California, 1987.

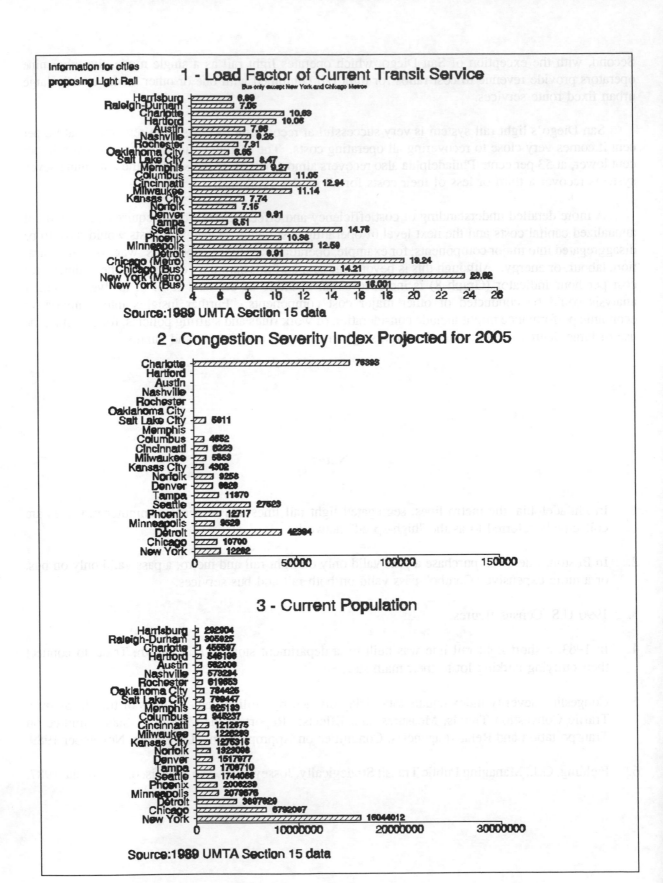

Information for cities proposing Light Rail

1 - Load Factor of Current Transit Service

Bus only except New York and Chicago Metros

Harrisburg	6.89
Raleigh-Durham	7.05
Charlotte	10.69
Hartford	10.06
Austin	7.66
Nashville	6.25
Rochester	7.31
Oklahoma City	6.65
Salt Lake City	6.47
Memphis	6.27
Columbus	11.05
Cincinnatti	12.94
Milwaukee	11.14
Kansas City	7.74
Norfolk	7.15
Denver	6.91
Tampa	6.51
Seattle	14.76
Phoenix	10.38
Minneapolis	12.59
Detroit	6.91
Chicago (Metro)	19.24
Chicago (Bus)	14.21
New York (Metro)	29.62
New York (Bus)	16.001

Source:1989 UMTA Section 15 data

2 - Congestion Severity Index Projected for 2005

Charlotte	76393
Hartford	
Austin	
Nashville	
Rochester	
Oklahoma City	
Salt Lake City	5611
Memphis	
Columbus	4652
Cincinnatti	6223
Milwaukee	5859
Kansas City	4302
Norfolk	9258
Denver	6629
Tampa	11870
Seattle	27623
Phoenix	12717
Minneapolis	9529
Detroit	42394
Chicago	10700
New York	12262

3 - Current Population

Harrisburg	292904
Raleigh-Durham	305025
Charlotte	455597
Hartford	546190
Austin	562008
Nashville	573294
Rochester	619653
Oklahoma City	784425
Salt Lake City	769447
Memphis	825153
Columbus	945237
Cincinnatti	1212675
Milwaukee	1226263
Kansas City	1275315
Norfolk	1323098
Denver	1517977
Tampa	1708710
Seattle	1744066
Phoenix	2006239
Minneapolis	2079676
Detroit	3697029
Chicago	6792087
New York	16044012

Source:1989 UMTA Section 15 data

268

4 - Load Factor
Passenger Kilometres/Vehicle Kilometres

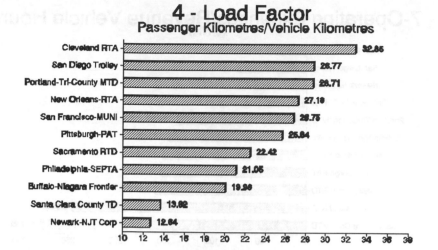

Cleveland RTA	32.85
San Diego Trolley	28.77
Portland-Tri-County MTD	28.71
New Orleans-RTA	27.18
San Francisco-MUNI	26.75
Pittsburgh-PAT	25.84
Sacramento RTD	22.42
Philadelphia-SEPTA	21.05
Buffalo-Niagara Frontier	19.98
Santa Clara County TD	13.82
Newark-NJT Corp	12.64

5 - Speed
Kilometres per Hour

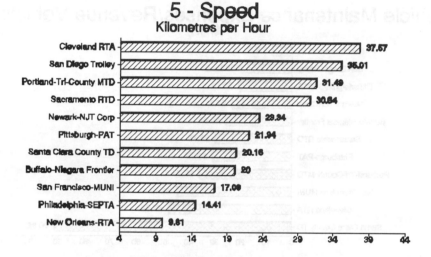

Cleveland RTA	37.57
San Diego Trolley	35.01
Portland-Tri-County MTD	31.49
Sacramento RTD	30.84
Newark-NJT Corp	23.34
Pittsburgh-PAT	21.94
Santa Clara County TD	20.16
Buffalo-Niagara Frontier	20
San Francisco-MUNI	17.06
Philadelphia-SEPTA	14.41
New Orleans-RTA	9.61

6-Operating Expenses/Vehicle Kilometres
($/Kilom)

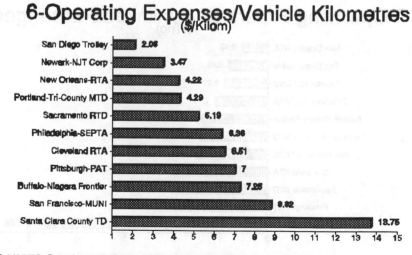

San Diego Trolley	2.06
Newark-NJT Corp	3.47
New Orleans-RTA	4.22
Portland-Tri-County MTD	4.29
Sacramento RTD	5.19
Philadelphia-SEPTA	6.38
Cleveland RTA	6.51
Pittsburgh-PAT	7
Buffalo-Niagara Frontier	7.25
San Francisco-MUNI	9.82
Santa Clara County TD	13.75

Source:1990 UMTA Section 15 Data, Note:Data for Boston excluded because of inconsistent data

7-Operating Expenses/Revenue Vehicle Hours
($/HR)

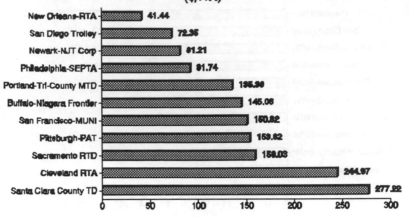

New Orleans-RTA	41.44
San Diego Trolley	72.35
Newark-NJT Corp	81.21
Philadelphia-SEPTA	91.74
Portland-Tri-County MTD	135.98
Buffalo-Niagara Frontier	145.06
San Francisco-MUNI	150.82
Pittsburgh-PAT	159.62
Sacramento RTD	158.03
Cleveland RTA	244.97
Santa Clara County TD	277.22

8-Vehicle Maintenance Expenses/Revenue Vehicle Hours
($/HR)

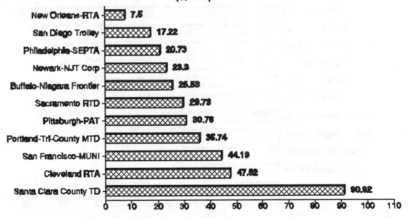

New Orleans-RTA	7.5
San Diego Trolley	17.22
Philadelphia-SEPTA	20.73
Newark-NJT Corp	23.3
Buffalo-Niagara Frontier	25.53
Sacramento RTD	29.73
Pittsburgh-PAT	30.76
Portland-Tri-County MTD	35.74
San Francisco-MUNI	44.19
Cleveland RTA	47.52
Santa Clara County TD	90.92

9-Operating Expenses / Unlinked Passenger Trips
($/Trip)

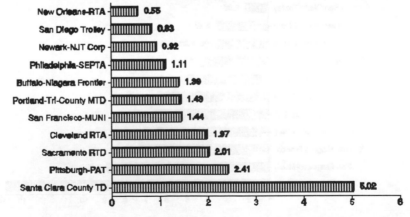

New Orleans-RTA	0.55
San Diego Trolley	0.83
Newark-NJT Corp	0.92
Philadelphia-SEPTA	1.11
Buffalo-Niagara Frontier	1.39
Portland-Tri-County MTD	1.43
San Francisco-MUNI	1.44
Cleveland RTA	1.97
Sacramento RTD	2.01
Pittsburgh-PAT	2.41
Santa Clara County TD	5.02

Source:1990 UMTA Section 15 Data, Note:Data for Boston excluded because of inconsistant data

10-Operating Expenses / Passenger Kilometres
($/Pass Kilom)

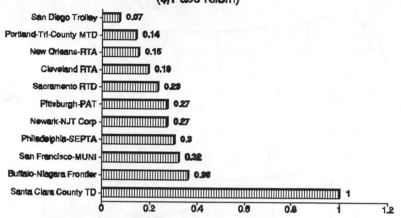

San Diego Trolley	0.07
Portland-Tri-County MTD	0.14
New Orleans-RTA	0.15
Cleveland RTA	0.19
Sacramento RTD	0.23
Pittsburgh-PAT	0.27
Newark-NJT Corp	0.27
Philadelphia-SEPTA	0.3
San Francisco-MUNI	0.32
Buffalo-Niagara Frontier	0.96
Santa Clara County TD	1

11 - Passenger Revenue/Operating Expenses (Ratio)
(For all modes operated by agency)

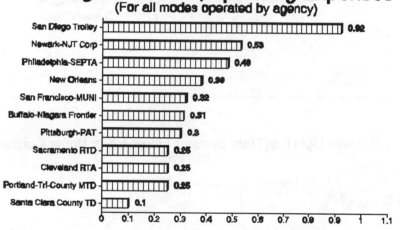

San Diego Trolley	0.92
Newark-NJT Corp	0.53
Philadelphia-SEPTA	0.48
New Orleans	0.38
San Francisco-MUNI	0.32
Buffalo-Niagara Frontier	0.31
Pittsburgh-PAT	0.3
Sacramento RTD	0.25
Cleveland RTA	0.25
Portland-Tri-County MTD	0.25
Santa Clara County TD	0.1

12 - Average Trip Length (Kilometres)

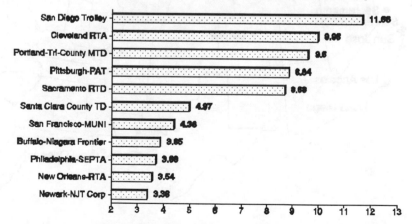

San Diego Trolley	11.56
Cleveland RTA	9.96
Portland-Tri-County MTD	9.6
Pittsburgh-PAT	6.84
Sacramento RTD	5.69
Santa Clara County TD	4.97
San Francisco-MUNI	4.36
Buffalo-Niagara Frontier	3.85
Philadelphia-SEPTA	3.66
New Orleans-RTA	3.54
Newark-NJT Corp	3.36

Source:1990 UMTA Section 15 Data, Note:Data for Boston excluded because of inconsistant data

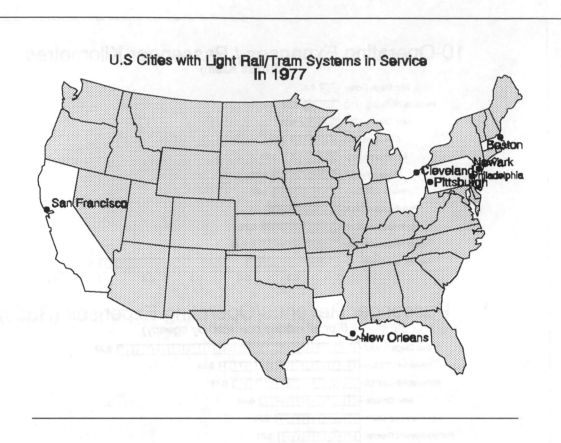

U.S Cities with Light Rail/Tram Systems in Service In 1977

- Boston
- Newark
- Cleveland
- Philadelphia
- Pittsburgh
- San Francisco
- New Orleans

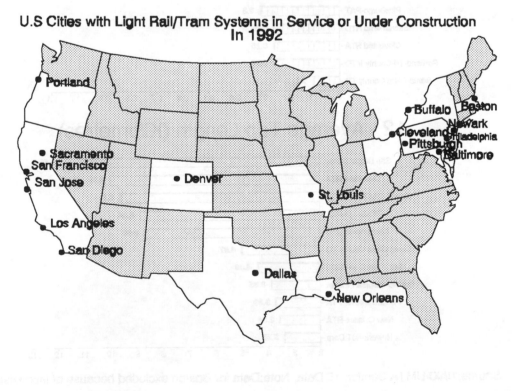

U.S Cities with Light Rail/Tram Systems in Service or Under Construction In 1992

- Portland
- Buffalo
- Boston
- Newark
- Sacramento
- San Francisco
- Cleveland
- Philadelphia
- Pittsburgh
- Baltimore
- San Jose
- Denver
- St. Louis
- Los Angeles
- San Diego
- Dallas
- New Orleans

Table 1

			(000)		Requirement
Boston	1897	1975-89	2 678	1 207	139
Buffalo	1985	new system	1 002	1 455	23
Cleveland	1919	1980s	1 752	1 076	30
New Orleans	1893	currently	1 078	1 077	21
Newark	1935	1980s	15 590	2 144	16
Philadelphia	1892	1981	4 112	1 564	182
Pittsburgh	1891	1985	1 810	980	45
Portland	1986	new system	1 026	1 135	23
Sacramento	1987	new system	796	1 547	45
San Diego	1980	new system	1 704	1 077	101
San Francisco	1897	1981	3 190	1 547	16
San Jose	1988	new system			

	Route Kilometres			
	At Grade	Elevated	Underground	Total
Boston	36.5	1.6	6.8	44.9
Buffalo	2.3		7.7	10.0
Cleveland	19.6	1.4		21.0
New Orleans	13.1			13.1
Newark	4.7		2.0	6.7
Philadelphia	115.3		3.4	118.7
Pittsburgh	28.3	1.7	3.0	33.0
Portland	24.2			24.2
Sacramento	27.9	1.6		29.5
San Diego	53.4			53.4
San Francisco	29.7		10.2	39.9
San Jose	31.6	.4		32.0

	Number of Stations	Number of Staff			
		Total	Operations	Maintenance	Administration
Boston	77	335.0	130	153	52
Buffalo	14	160.1	37.3	102.6	20.2
Cleveland	29	204.8	63.7	99.6	41.5
New Orleans		155.3	59.5	84.2	11.6
Newark	11	57.1	24.2	27.2	5.7
Philadelphia	9	1 185	422.8	582.7	179.5
Pittsburgh	14	466.1	134.3	331.8	
Portland	25	128.7	41	63.1	24.6
Sacramento	15	98	49	41	8
San Diego	22	225	84.5	113.5	27
San Francisco	9	756	345	385	26
San Jose	20	163.5	80.9	72.1	30.7

Source: UMTA 1990 Section 15 data

Table 2

	Operating Costs Total ($000)	Operations ($000)	Administration ($000)	Maintenance ($000)
Boston	27 326.2	10 110.7	6 531.0	10 657.2
Buffalo	11 851.8	2 346.7	3 804.4	5 700.7
Cleveland	10 876.9	2 784.5	2 599.6	5 498.8
New Orleans	4 596.6	2 077.7	1 470.9	1 048.0
Newark	3 548.9	1 604.1	617.5	1 323.7
Philadelphia	48 708.5	22 113.7	8 183.0	18 460.5
Pittsburgh	23 904.0	8 868.4	2 342.6	13 796.6
Portland	9 220.0	2 812.1	2 507.8	3 890.8
Sacramento	11 466.3	3 829.7	4 758.5	2 889.5
San Diego	13 350.3	5 246.7	2 857.0	5 246.7
San Francisco	58 128.5	25 227.8	8 254.2	24 558.4
San Jose	12 225.6	3 227.6	2 848.6	6 149.5

	Operating Costs Per veh. rev. hour	Vehicule Maintenance Costs Per veh. rev. hour
Boston	N/A.	N/A.
Buffalo	$ 145.1	$ 25.53
Cleveland	$ 244.9	$ 47.52
New Orleans	$ 41.4	$ 7.50
Newark	$ 81.1	$ 23.30
Philadelphia	$ 91.7	$ 20.73
Pittsburgh	$ 153.8	$ 30.76
Portland	$ 135.3	$ 35.74
Sacramento	$ 159.1	$ 29.73
San Diego	$ 72.3	$ 17.22
San Francisco	$ 150.8	$ 44.19
San Jose	$ 277.2	$ 90.92

Source: 1990 UMTA/FTA Section 15 Data

Table 3

Revenues (for total system, all modes)

	Fares ($000)	National ($000)	Regional ($000)	Local ($000)	Other ($000)	All other Rev ($000)	Revenue/Op Expense
Boston	127 681.3	18 409.9	323 063.3	103 332.8		21 379.2	
Buffalo	17 447.4	6 261.8	15 520.7	9 205.4		5 084.4	.31
Cleveland	38 021.3	9 236.0	7 542.7	94 360.6		4 771.9	.25
New Orleans	27 583.6	4 774.1	3 713.2	35 692.0		4 016.3	.38
Newark	329 854.0	43 590.2	244 625.5	0.		32 530.0	.53
Philadelphia	267 170.2	18 133.7	244 200.8	64 676.9		10 880.2	.48
Pittsburgh	50 360.7	9 505.2	83 545.5	49 343.9		4 002.2	.30
Portland	22 330.1	5 736.2	1 536.5	66 785.3		5 941.0	.25
Sacramento	10 479.3	3 574.3	0.0	25 142.2		1 421.6	.25
San Diego	12 411.4	0	877.3	1 006.7		86.3	.92
San Francisco	77 881.0	8 021.0	19 146.8	132 734.1	14 489.5	6 468.5	.32
San Jose	13 686.7	6 252.0	43 087.9	90 738.1		15 038.5	.10

Light Rail System Characteristics

	Outputs Avg. Speed km/hr	Annual Rev Capacity km (000)	Annual Total Rev Vehicle km (000)	Annual Total Rev Vehicle Hours (000)	Ridership Passenger Trips Unlinked (000)	Passenger Kilometres (000)
Boston	17.8	364 518.8	2 083.6	116.9	23 354.8	52 608.9
Buffalo	19.9	196 099.8	1 634.1	81.7	8 479.8	32 654.3
Cleveland	37.5	223 559.1	1 668.4	44.4	5 498.3	54 807.3
New Orleans	9.8	85 685.2	1 088.6	110.9	8 346.8	29 594.3
Newark	23.3	127 513.1	1 020.1	43.7	3 837.7	12 895.9
Philadelphia	14.4	619 797.9	7 651.7	530.9	43 747.6	87 479.2
Pittsburgh	21.9	392 231 .2	3 410.7	155.4	9 890.1	61 577.8
Portland	31.5	355 989.0	2 144.4	68.1	6 414.3	49 530.0
Sacramento	30.6	386 599.9	2 209.2	72.1	5 702.5	185 868.8
San Diego	35.0	1 223 564.0	6 459.6	184.5	15 933.5	176 160.4
San Francisco	17.0	895 611.2	6 585.3	385.4	40 213.6	176 160.4
San Jose	21.0	138 594.0	889.1	44.1	2 432.3	12 110.6

Source: 1990 UMTA/FTA Section 15 Data

275

Table 4a

Older Systems City/Route Frequency of Service	Peak	Mid-day	Evening	Saturday	Sunday	Fare Collection and Transfer Policy
Boston						Free transfer to metro, none to bus.
B Boston College-Government Center	5	6	10	7	5	Fares collected in underground stations and
C Cleveland Circle-North Station	6	6	10	5	7	on board cars on surface inbound only.
D Riverside-Government Center	6	6	10	6	7	
H Heath St.-Lechmere	8	8	10	7	7	
M Mattapan-Ashmont (isolated from other routes)	4	8	11	8	11	
Newark						Free transfer to certain bus routes.
7 city subway	2	6	30	8	15	Fares collected on cars, with zones.
						No multiple car trains (single cars only).
Philadelphia						
10 Overbrook-Center City	<10	<10	20/30	12	15	Free transfer to metro in underground stations only.
11 Darby-Center City	<10	<10	20/30	15	15	Purchased transfers to bus and metro stations.
13 Darby & Yeardon-Center City	<10	<10	17	13	15	Fares collected on cars.
34 Angora-Center City	<10	<10	20	12	15	Flat fares for city service, zones for suburban.
36 Eastwick-Center City	<10	<10	20	15	15	Most routes operate 24 hours a day.
56 Tacony-Nicetown	<10	14	40	30	30	No multiple car trains (single cars only).
15 Port Richmond-Haddington	10	12	30	20	20	
23 Chestnut Hill-South Philadelphia	<10	<10	20	12	20	
Suburban division						
101 Media-69th St. (metro) Station	6	20	30	30	30	
102 Sharon Hill - 69th St. metro (Station)	9	20	30	30	30	
Cleveland						
(Green) Shaker	8	20	30	20	40	Free transfer to busses and metro.
(Blue) Van Aken	8	20	30	20	40	Fares collected on cars when boarding outbound, exiting inbound.
Pittsburgh						Purchased transfer to busses.
47 Drake	<10	15	25	30	45	Fares collected on cars when boarding inbound, exiting outbound.
421 Library	<10	30	30	30	30	Free fare zone in Downtown underground segment.
42s South Hills	<10	10	30	10	15	
New Orleans						Purchase transfer to bus.
12 St. Charles	<10	<10	18	<10	<10	Flat fares collected boarding car. Operates 24 hours a day. No multiple car trains (single cars only).
San Francisco						Free transfer to bus and trolley bus.
J Church	5/6	10	20	10/15	15/20	Flat fare collected on cars above ground, in stations underground.
K Ingleside	<10	10	20	10/15	14	
L Taraval	10	10	20	10/15	10/12	Free transfer to local portion of BART metro.
M Ocean View	<10	10	20	10/15	12/16	Operates 24 hours, except replaced by busses 0100-0500.
N Judah	5/6	10	20	6/10	10	

Table 4b

New Start Systems City/Route Frequency of Service	Peak	Mid-day	Evening	Saturday	Sunday	Fare Collection and Transfer Policy
Buffalo Auditorium-South Campus	5	10	20	10	15	Free transfer to busses. Barrier free, proof of purchase system. Fare free downtown transit mall.
Portland Portland-Gresham	7	15	30	15	15	Free transfer to bus, fare zones. Barrier free, proof of purchase system. Free fares in Downtown zone.
Sacramento Watt I-80 - Butterfield	15	15	30	15	15	Free transfer to busses, flat fare. Downtown area reduced fare. Barrier free, proof of purchase system.
San Jose Great America-South Teresa or Almaden	10	10	30	15	15	Flat fare, all day pass good on busses available. Barrier free, proof of purchase system.
Los Angeles L.A. - Long Beach	10	15	15	15	15	Free transfer to bus, flat fare. Barrier free, proof of purchase system.
San Diego (East) El Cajon (South) San Ysidro	15 7-15	15 15	30 30	15 15	15 15	Free transfer to bus, distance based fares. Barrier free, proof of purchase system.

Source: Public timetables

Table 5

U.S. Light Rail Vehicle and Tram fleet

City	Year Built	Manufacturer	Electrical Supplier	Seats	Length	Width	# active	Air conditioned?
Boston	1945	Pullman-Standard (PCC)	Westinghouse	42	14.2 m	2.56 m	12	No
	1976-8	Boeing-Vertol	Garret	50	21.8 m	2.71 m	83	Yes
	1986-7	Kinki-Sharyo	Westinghouse	50	22.1 m	2.71 m	99	Yes
Buffalo	1983-4	Tokyo Car	Westinghouse	51	20.3 m	2.64 m	27	Yes
Cleveland	1981	Breda	Brown Boveri Canada	84	24.6 m	2.84 m	48	Yes
New Orleans	1923	Perley-Thomas	General Electric	52	14.6 m	2.56 m	42	No
	1930	MMTD W-2	General Electric	52	14.7 m	2.76 m	2	No
Newark	1946-9	St. Louis Car Co. (PCC)	General Electric	55	41.2 m	2.76 m	24	No
Philadelphia	1981	Kawasaki	Westinghouse	51	15.3 m	2.61 m	112	Yes
	1981	Kawasaki	Westinghouse	50	16.3 m	2.71 m	29	Yes
	1947-48	St. Louis Car Co. (PCC)	G.E./W.H.	49	14.2 m	2.58 m	89	No
Pittsburgh	1986	Siemens-Duewag (U3)	Siemens	63	26.1 m	2.97 m	55	Yes
	1948	St. Louis Car Co. (PCC)	Westinghouse	50	14.1 m	2.56 m	16	1 only
Portland	1986	Bombardier	Brown Boveri Canada	76	26.7 m	2.66 m	26	No
Sacramento	1985	Siemens-Duewag (UA2)	Siemens	65	24.4 m	2.66 m	26	Yes
	1991	Siemens-Duewag (UA2)	Siemens	65	24.4 m	2.66 m	10	Yes
San Diego	1980	Siemens-Duewag (U2)	Siemens	64	24.4 m	2.66	14	Yes
	1982	Siemens-Duewag (U2)	Siemens	64	24.4 m	m2.66 m	10	Yes
	1985	Siemens-Duewag (U2)	Siemens	64	24.4 m	2.66 m	6	Yes
	1989-90	Siemens-Duewag (U2)	Siemens	64	24.4 m	2.66 m	41	Yes
	1992-3	Siemens-Duewag (U3)					75 on order	
San Francisco	1978	Boeing-Vertol	Garret	58/68	21.8 m	2.71 m	128	No
San Jose	1987-88	UTDC	Brown Boveri Canada	76	27.0 m	2.76 m	50	Yes
								Yes
Los Angeles	1990	Nippon-Sharyo					54	
Baltimore	1991-2	ABB	ABB				34 on order	
Denver	1993	Siemens-Duewag	Siemens				8 on order	
St Louis	1992-3	Siemens-Duewag	Siemens				31 on order	

III. ANNEXES

A. STATISTICAL DATA TABLES

Table of Contents

Table 1. General Information on Systems

	Opened	Modernized	Population (000)	Peak Vehicle Requirement
Bern-RBS	1899		190	60 (for passenger service only)
Grenoble (1988)	1987		362	21
Hannover	1883	1965-1992	1 050	
Manchester	1992		2 600	
Nantes (1988)	1985		464	28
Nieuwegein	1977		230	24
San Diego	1980		1 704	45
Stuttgart	1868	1966-1992	1 600	

All data is 1989 data unless noted

Table 2. Route kilometres

	Total	At Grade	Elevated	Underground	# of Stations
Bern-RBS	63.0	61.1	0.0	1.9	46
Grenoble (1988)	8.9	8.9	0.0	0.0	22
Hannover	191.8	128.2	0.0	31.8	
Manchester					
Nantes (1988)	12.6	12.6	0.0	0.0	24
Nieuwegein	18.0				
San Diego	53.4	53.4	0.0	0.0	22
Stuttgart	110.4	98.8	0.0	11.6	

All data is 1989 data unless noted

Table 3. **Light Rail Staff**

	Total	Operations	Maintenance	Administration
Bern-RBS	353.0	197.0	111.0	45.0
Grenoble (1988)	58.6	38.6	20.0	combined with bus
Hannover	2 414.0	1 135.0	727.0	552.0
Manchester				
Nantes (1988)	81.2	46.3	26.1	combined with bus
Nieuwegein	combined with bus			
San Diego	148.0	63.5	67.5	17.0
Stuttgart	3 156.0	1 448.0	1 250.0	458.0

All data is 1989 data unless noted

Table 4. **Operating Costs of Light Rail Systems**

	Total ($000)	Of Which Operations ($000)	Maintenance ($000)	Administration ($000)
Bern-RBS	27 324.28			
Grenoble (1988)	5 130.65			
Hannover	72 804.16			
Manchester				
Nantes (1988)	6 099.97			
Nieuwegein	4 255.23			
San Diego	9 159.20	3 810.23	2 848.51	2 500.46
Stuttgart	98 270.15			

All data is 1989 data unless noted

Table 5. **System Revenues**

	Fares ($000)	Subsidies Total ($000)	Local ($000)	Regional ($000)	Federal ($000)	Other ($000)	Other Income ($000)
Bern-RBS	17 844.93	10 802.72	0.00	0.00	0.00	0.00	2 833.23
Grenoble (1988)	23 087.92	20 705.83					
Hannover	60 665.62						
Manchester							
Nantes (1988)	22 721.44	20 705.83					
Nieuwegein	National fare system, cannot breakdown						
San Diego	8 732.22	1 786.62	0.00	1 786.62	0.00	0.00	52.86
Stuttgart	73 549.12						

All data is 1989 data unless noted

283

Tableau 6. **Operating Data**

| | Train Intervals (minutes) | | | Total Vehicle Revenue | | | | Passenger Trips | |
	Speed (km/h)	Peak	Off Peak	Capacity Km/p.a. (000)	Kms/p.a. (000)	Hours/p.a. (000)	Unlinked (000)	Passenger-Kms. (000)
Bern-RBS	36.80	15.00	30-60	1 078 460.46	8 418.35		16 500.00	158 600.00
Grenoble (1988)	18.00	4-each seg. 2-comb			1 910.00		16 500.00	
Hannover	24.00	8/12	15.00		18 336.00	752.00	96 501.00	
Manchester								
Nantes (1988)	23.60	5.00			826.00		14 500.00	
Nieuwegein	29.00	>7.50	10.00		1 746.00	45.30	8 685.00	59 053.00
San Diego	30.34	7-15	15.00	816 861.14	3 807.70	125.50	11 216.60	122 181.99
Stuttgart	20.80	6/10	12/15		18 363.00	726.89	94 383.00	

B. ANALYSIS FRAMEWORK

Table of Contents

1. OBJECTIVES OF FRAMEWORK

This framework provides a standardized approach for participants in the Urban Transport Coordinating Group to use in case studies of light rail transit (LRT) systems. The framework is intended to:

a) encourage objectivity, consistency, and clarity in analyses;

b) promote comparability and transferability of experiences;

c) be flexible enough to reflect unique characteristics of each system;

d) focus on economic performance and social policy issues, including environmental considerations and urban development;

e) produce results that can be synthesized into generalizations and conclusions on the conditions under which LRT does and does not "succeed";

f) produce a standardized basic data base that will be a resource for future analyses;

g) minimize the burden for data collection.

2. APPROACH

The framework provides a point of discussion for the Group as it works toward a mutually agreed upon format. The framework defines seven analytical areas with issues and concerns to be addressed. A set of data items and performance ratios are recommended to provide the basic tools for analysis of the issues. The analytical areas, issues, and data items define a minimum foundation for analysis. Participants are encouraged to expand the structure to explain the performance of each light rail system studied.

Participants can modify the framework to adjust for local situations, including data availability. For example, to understand the effects of a new LRT on congestion, it may be necessary to examine the system: as part of urban area-wide transportation (auto and public transport); as part of a multi-mode public transport system; within a specific corridor; or in comparison to bus routes that it replaces.

It also may be necessary to examine LRT performance over several years, as the system becomes established, or as any planned economic development along the corridor occurs. For historical analysis, participants should make adjustments for inflation, and identify assumptions, including the use of discount rates.

The list of basic data items provides a common statistical basis for participants to use in describing LRT systems. Performance measures recommended in the analysis areas will be derived from the basic data items, and will increase consistency and comparability in the case studies. Data items selected are based in part on a study by the U.S. Department of Transportation (US DOT) on applications and availability of international data. Definitions rely heavily on those in the US DOT's Section 15 data base and other international data bases.

The data items are recommendations, and participants are not expected to undertake special collections or estimations if data are not locally available. For example, ridership can be described using passenger boardings, passenger journeys, or passenger kilometres. Ideally, participants will provide all three items. Participants unable to provide all three items can use the definitions to identify precisely those which are available locally.

In another example, the framework suggests an approach to capital expenses that will differentiate it from operating expenses. Ideally, this approach will be used. If participants are unable to provide capital expenses in the suggested categories, they can substitute what is available, with clear definitions.

In most cases distinction of service by time-of-day (morning or evening peak, base period, other) may be important to understand LRT performance. Use of this level of detail is encouraged, but will depend on local system characteristics and the availability of data allocating service, ridership, expenses, and revenues by time period.

3. CRITERIA FOR SELECTION OF CASE STUDIES

Participants should undertake case studies of LRT systems that have been constructed and placed into operation in the last ten years. If new systems are not available for study, an acceptable alternative is to study a substantial extension to an established LRT system. The extension should be a "discrete" operation to which expenses (including overhead), revenues, service, and ridership can be accurately allocated.

Because the case studies are intended to identify both advantages and disadvantages of LRT, participants are encouraged to consider both "successful" and "unsuccessful" systems, and to complete more than one case study. This will extend the range of experience exchanged among the Group.

4. CASE STUDY INTRODUCTION

The case study should begin with a summary overview of the LRT system, its operating environment, modes operated, and description of physical network. The data described in section 5 should be presented to provide readers with a basic understanding of the system.

5. ANALYTICAL CATEGORIES

The following seven analytical categories identify issues and concerns to be addressed in each case study. Participants should use the recommended data items and performance measures whenever possible. If other data items must be substituted, clear definitions should be provided. The categories below deal with LRT only. Information from other modes can be added to extend the analysis, as background, in comparisons, or to understand LRT as part of a multi-modal system.

Expenses

It is crucial that both operating and capital expenses be considered in the case studies to allow comparisons among systems with different levels of capital or labour intensity, including comparisons among LRT systems or between LRT and other modes. The approach to capital and operating expenses is partially derived from the US DOT's Section 15 program, the work of the ECMT Urban Transport Coordinating Group, the UITP/Jane's data base, and the UITP comparative study of metro productivity.

Identify the currency used. For historical data, use constant (preferably 1989) values and indicate what adjustments have been made for inflation.

Capital expenses

Ideally, all participants will use the same approach to capital expenses. Analysts will then be able to make adjustments to reflect other assumptions. Participants should not substitute whatever is defined locally as "capital expenses", without documentation. This would invite distorted comparisons.

The approach to capital expenses follows that used by the subgroup of the ECMT Urban Transport Coordinating Group in the financial reporting model. As defined by the subgroup, capital expenses will consist of depreciation and interest calculations on the basis of real expense of replacement investments.

Unlike the model of the subgroup, this framework includes capital expense for infrastucture. It is assumed that differences in how infrastructure is owned, financed, and assigned usable lifetimes will make this item difficult to report. However, difficulty should be reduced somewhat because the case studies will be of recent new starts, where in most cases rights-of-way, tracks, and related assets were recently purchased. Because infrastructures are a major rail expense, it is important to estimate this information for any comparisons of productivity among LRT systems or other modes.

Capital expenses should be based on depreciation of assets. For example, if a transit undertaking owns some vehicles, receives others from a municipal agency, and operates over a right-of-way or using shelters owned by the Transport Ministry, capital expenses should include the depreciated value of all of these assets. An explanation should be included if the depreciated value of assets from another agency are listed, with an estimate of the depreciated annual value, translated into present worth using a discount rate defined at eight percent.

The annual expenses of leased or rented assets, and interest paid for loans to purchase assets can be combined, but should be separately identified, preferably as capital expenses assigned to rolling stock or other appropriate category. Depreciated capital expenses, leases, rents, or interest should not be incorporated into a single operating expense total unless it is unavoidable, and a clear explanation is provided.

To encourage consistency, the capital expenses listed in section 6.5 are specified using expected lifetimes and a fixed discount rate. Please identify any other assumptions that are used.

Basic data to include in analysis

Annual capital expenses used in the analysis should be taken from section 6.

288

Operating expenses

A key issue in providing LRT operating expenses is the appropriate level of detail to use. The objective is to provide enough information to explain the major aspects of a system's performance without requiring excessive detail. Analysts are interested in expenses in major categories, including labour, maintenance, management, and operations, and in productivity ratios that relate these expenses to service outputs and ridership.

All expenses incurred to provide LRT service should be identified, whether they are incurred by the transport undertaking or other agencies. For example, if a municipality provides police service, an attempt should be made to describe and identify these expenses. If services are contracted, whether for a "turn-key operator", for maintenance, management, or security, these expenses should also be identified and provided. Use of contracts for LRT will probably be minor relative to that for some bus operations.

Basic data to include in analysis

Data from section 6 should be used to analyze operating expenses.

Revenues

Revenue data should present a clear picture of the sources and amounts of funds consumed annually to operate the LRT system, and are vital to evaluation of economic performance. Analysts are interested in the extent to which expenses are recovered from fares, other "earnings", public agency subsidies, or other sources. For subsidies, it is important to identify the agencies providing funds and the annual amounts.

Although systems will typically be able to distinguish fares by mode, identification of subsidies by source and amount may be difficult for a multi-mode system. For example, U.S. operators typically receive federal, state, and local subsidies. A multi-mode operator should be able to identify LRT fares, but details on sources of subsidies may not be available or meaningful at modal levels. In this case, it would be appropriate to identify LRT fares and earnings, but provide total subsidies for all modes combined.

For international comparisons, it may be important to identify "indirect" or non-cash subsidies. For example, if an undertaking receives police services from a municipality or "free" vehicles from the Transport Ministry, these should be identified, and if possible, assigned a value as an indirect subsidy. Indirect subsidies should be distinguished from direct subsidies.

Direct or indirect assistance from private organizations should also be described.

Total revenues should generally be reconciled with total expenses, presenting a picture of the sources of annual income.

Basic data to include in analysis

Data for analysis of revenues should come from section 6, including:

a) farebox revenue, including proceeds from multi-ride and weekly/monthly/ annual passes;

b) other operating revenue related to provision of transit service, including contracts to carry students, postal or police employees; charter service; rentals; advertising, etc;

c) "concessionary" payments to carry elderly, handicapped, or school children at reduced fares;

d) sources of public subsidies, public assistance, or grants, including different levels of government;

e) revenues provided by the private sector (describe and measure);

f) subsidies for operating expenses and those identified for capital expenses.

Operations

This area should provide a picture of the annual output generated by operations of the LRT system, measured in units of service supplied by the undertaking.

The safety record of the system should be analyzed using injuries, fatalities, and damage to the property of the undertaking and of others, including pedestrians and automobile occupants.

Basic data to include in analysis

Data for this analysis area should come from section 6.

Patronage

The framework defines the three measures of patronage most commonly used internationally. **Passenger kilometres** are particularly useful for comparisons of ridership between systems or modes with different average trip lengths and as a measure of benefits to riders that is superior to boardings, which are the most accurate and easily collected measures of ridership. Passenger kilometres does not reflect circuity and is prone to inaccuracy. **Completed journeys** is a useful indicator of benefits, although it does not account for distance travelled. Considering advantages and disadvantages of individual ridership measures, it is recommended that participants provide as many of the three measures as possible.

Depending on the system studied, analysis of any of the following might contribute to an understanding of performance.

Shifts in ridership over-time, including changes in average trip length (Passenger kilometres over Passengers);

Ridership by time-of-day (peak or base periods);

The types of trips taken (work, shopping, recreation);

Socio-economic characteristics of riders;

Modes of travel prior to completion of the light rail system. Did riders previously travel by automobile or other public transport modes?

Basic data to include in analysis

Analysis of patronage should be based on the data from section 6.

Performance/productivity measures

To promote comparability, all case studies should use the following performance measures derived from ratios of the data items identified in section 6. These basic performance measures should provide the foundation for analysis of the productivity of each LRT system. The basic structure of performance measures used in this framework incorporates elements of the approaches in the ECMT subgroup's financial model, the UITP metro productivity study, and **Managing Public Transit Strategically**, by G.J. Fielding.

Participants are encouraged to provide additional analysis using other measures, data from other modes system-wide or within the LRT corridor, and historical data, as required to understand the performance of each system. For example, all ratios using Operating Expenses can be further refined into Operations, Labour, Maintenance, or Management expenses.

Basic data to include in analysis

Efficiency measures

Operating Expenses/Vehicle Kilometre
Operating Expenses/Vehicle Hour

Capital Expenses/Vehicle Kilometre
Capital Expenses/Vehicle Hour

Total (Operating plus capital) Expenses/Vehicle Kilometre
Total (Operating plus capital) Expenses/Vehicle Hour

Vehicle Kilometres/Peak Hour Vehicles

Cost effectiveness measures

Operating Expenses/Passenger (specify boarding or journey)
Operating Expenses/Passenger Kilometre

Capital Expenses/Passenger (specify boarding or journey)
Capital Expenses/Passenger Kilometre

Total (Operating plus capital) Expenses/Passenger (specify boarding or journey)
Total (Operating plus capital) Expenses/Passenger Kilometre

Operating Revenue -- Fares plus Other Operating Revenue/Operating Expense
Farebox Return Ratio -- Fares/Operating Expense

Service effectiveness measures

Load Factor -- Passenger Kilometres/Capacity Kilometres
Passenger Boardings/Revenue Vehicle Mile

Operational performance

Average Speed -- Vehicle Kilometres/Vehicle Hours

If available, provide any measures of reliability, including on-time performance, scheduled compared to actual revenue vehicle kilometres, or Mean Time Between Service Failures (vehicle hours divided by number of service interrupting equipment functional failures).

Safety performance

Analyze LRT safety using the following measures:

Injuries per Vehicle Kilometre
Injuries per Passenger Kilometre
Injuries per Passenger Kilometre
Repeat ratios for fatalities and property damage

If relevant, consider the safety record of the LRT system in comparison to other modes in the urban area.

Social policy

This section is designed to allow participants flexibility to analyze the performance of the LRT system in a broad urban context. The focus in any particular study will depend on the objectives for each system, and available information. Analysis should be based to the greatest degree possible on empirical evidence.

The following topics and issues are provided as suggestions.

Congestion:

What effects has the LRT system had on congestion?

- Consider public transport trip share before and after the LRT.

- Consider previous means of transport for LRT riders. How many formerly rode other public transport modes and how many were automobile riders/drivers? What is the cost per new public transport rider attracted to LRT?

- Consider trip patterns system-wide and in the LRT corridor before and after the LRT start.

Pollution:

Has there been a measurable reduction in air pollution that can be attributed to the LRT?

Urban revitalization:

Did the LRT stimulate economic development, either in the city centre or along the corridor?

- Consider development decisions affected by the LRT. Quantify in volume of housing or office space.

- Can a long-term increase in employment in the urban area be credited to the LRT?

- Did the LRT encourage any joint public-private sector initiatives, for example, LRT stations in new developments, or cooperative land use and public transport decision-making?

Other:

Include any other factors that would help analysts understand the overall performance of the LRT system.

Other considerations

In many cases the statistics suggested for analysis do not provide a complete picture of the operations of the LRT system. This section provides the opportunity to consider the effects on performance of any of the factors described in section 6 of the questionnaire. Factors might include major events or disruptions, including major fare increases, natural disasters, strikes, significant economic trends (economic growth, inflation, unemployment, or population growth), or unusual geographic conditions.

6. BASIC DATA TO BE COLLECTED

The data collected in this section should be incorporated into the case study, as explained in sections 4. and 5. In addition the Group can consider whether to produce a concise, standardized data base, in computer accessible form, possibly incorporating basic accuracy checks. Decisions will be required on the extent to which this information should be publicly available.

Background information

Name, address, telephone and fax number of undertaking.

Name and title of Chief Executive.

Contact person/person providing information.

Type of undertaking (place x)

Public   Private

Ownership

Operations

Management

Other -- describe

Scope of legal authority -- for example, operates or contracts for urban or regional service metro, commuter/urban rail, or bus.

Date Light Rail service began.

Operating environment

Population of service area

Land area of service area -- square kilometres.

Automobile ownership for service area.

Public transport mode split.

Public transport modes operated

	Vehicles	
	Operated in Peak	**Total Fleet**
Mode		
Light		
Rail/Streetcar		
Metro		
Motorbus		
Trolleybus		
Demand Response		
Commuter/suburban rail		

Note: all data items below pertain to light rail only

LRT Vehicle Fleet

Builder	Year of Manufacture	Car type or designation	Number of Cars
Physical network Line kilometres At grade, exclusive right-of-way			
			Kilometres
At grade, exlusive right-of-way			
At grade, with cross traffic			
At grade, mixed and cross traffic			
Elevated			
Open cut			
Subway-Tunnel/Tube			
TOTAL			

7. FINANCIAL INFORMATION

Capital expenses

Revenue vehicles and revenue vehicle equipment (fare collection, communications, lift equipment, etc.).

Assume 20 year lifetime.

Track, signals, catenary, buildings, and other equipment.

Assume 40 year lifetime.

Right-of-way -- value.

Assume an infinite lifetime (the depreciated value reflects only the value of interest, not an exhausted assets).

295

Right-of-way -- how acquired.

Describe when the right-of-way was acquired, whether it was abandoned, an existing right-of-way shared with another mode, or acquired through eminent domain, and at what expense.

Discount rate.

For uniformity, use an eight percent discount rate. If a different rate is used, please identify it.

Operating expenses

Expense of revenue vehicle operations, including scheduling.

Vehicle maintenance -- revenue and non-revenue vehicles.

Non-vehicle maintenance -- track, tunnels, stations, buildings, equipment, and other.

Labour expenses, preferably for above functions.

Contract expenses -- description of what is contracted for (management, maintenance, security, operations, and expenses.

Revenues

Source of revenues

Fares	Other Operating Revenues	Concessionary support	Required Operating Subsidies**	Other sources Identify	Total
Amount (identify currency)					
Percentage of Operating Expenses excluding annualized capital cost					100 %
Percentage of Operating Expenses including annualized capital cost					100 %

** Required level of subsidy as defined by the UTCG model

296

Source of subsidies

	Public Sector			
	National	Regional	Local	Other
Amount (Identify currency)				
For operating expenses				
For capital expenses				

8. OPERATING STATISTICS

Supply measures

Vehicle Kilometres

Revenue Vehicle Kilometres

Vehicle Hours

Capacity Kilometres

Safety measures

	Injuries	**Fatalities**	**Property Damage**
Passengers and System employees			
Others			

Ridership

Passenger boardings

Passenger journeys

Passenger kilometres

Supplemental information

Major events or disruptions

Describe any major events or disruptions that will assist analysts to understand the above data. Events could include major fare increases, natural disasters, or strikes.

Technological innovations

Describe any current or planned uses of innovative technology for light rail operations. Candidate actions include use of computerized fare cards ("chip or smart cards"); signal or traffic prioritization; automated operation; automated passenger counters; automated passenger information systems; real-time central control.

If possible, estimate the expenses of the technology (capital and operations) and describe the results of the application.

Other innovations

Describe any non-technical current or planned innovations. Candidate actions include:

Managerial -- use of part-time staff.

Financial -- contracting out some or all activities; private sector participation; joint development of facilities; passes subsididized by employers for employees; employer tax; innovative subsidy method.

Institutional/Organizational -- moves toward or away from regional control.

Marketing -- fare structures; monthly or annual passes; peak pricing.

Other

If possible, estimate the expenses of the application and describe the results.

Maps and other helpful information:

Please include a system map and any other information that might be helpful in understanding the LRT system, including fare structures, or innovative marketing brochures. This material may be included in appendices to the case studies.

9. DEFINITIONS

Operating environment

Service area -- actual area served is preferred, not necessarily political jurisdictions. Describe formal criteria defining area (for example, walking distance or 500 meters from fixed route service). If area is defined by political jurisdictions only, state this and provide these data.

Operated in peak period -- vehicles required to meet maximum service requirements, during maximum annual period. Excludes spare or standby vehicles, vehicles in or awaiting maintenance, and out-of-service vehicles. Ignore requirements for special events. For rail, provide count of passenger cars, not trains.

Total fleet -- Vehicles available for service, including those operated in peak period plus spares, out-of-service vehicles, vehicles in or awaiting maintenance.

Network description

Line kilometres -- total length of all lines. Two lines over the same right-of-way are counted once and separate directions are not counted separately.

At grade, exclusive right-of-way -- right-of-way from which all other traffic, mixed and cross is excluded. Median right-of-way is included if all crossings pass over or under.

At grade, with cross traffic -- right-of-way over which no other traffic may pass, except at grade-level crossings. Include median right-of-way with grade-level crossings at intersecting streets.

At grade, mixed and cross traffic -- right-of-way over which other traffic moving in the same direction or the cross directions may pass. City street right-of-way is included.

Elevated -- right-of-way above surface level on fill or structures.

Open cut -- below surface right-of-way in an excavated cut without covering.

Subway-Tunnel/Tube -- below surface right-of-way with a cover over the tunnel.

Financial information

All financial information should be reported for the undertaking's fiscal year. Unless otherwise stated, it will be assumed that annual expenses are those of the undertaking and revenues are those received by the undertaking. Any expenses to other public or private organizations, for example, if the municipality provides police at no expense to the undertaking, should be identified separately.

Sources of revenues

Farebox revenue -- includes proceeds from multi-ride and weekly/monthly/annual passes.

Other operating revenue -- revenues related to provision of transit service, including contracts to carry students, postal or police employees; charter service; rentals; advertising, etc.

"Concessionary" support -- to carry elderly, handicapped, and school children at reduced fares.

Sources of public subsidies -- public assistance, or grants, from different levels of government.

Other sources -- other sources of subsidies; include private sector (employers, developers) and other governmental agencies; identify source and amount.

Amount -- identify currency and for historical data, indicate whether any adjustments are made for inflation.

Operating statistics

Vehicle kilometres -- the movement of one vehicle for a distance of one kilometre, including revenue and non-revenue ("deadhead") kilometres; passenger cars count as vehicles;

Revenue vehicle kilometres -- Revenue service only; excludes travel to and from storage facilities and other deadhead travel.

Capacity kilometres -- Revenue vehicle kilometres multiplied by the average seated and standing capacity of vehicles in revenue service.

Passenger boardings -- boardings by passengers; also known as "unlinked trips".

Passenger journeys -- completed origins-to-destinations, which can include more than one public transport vehicle or mode. Also known as a "linked trip".

Passenger kilometres -- one passenger transported a distance of one kilometre. (Ten passengers travelling 2 kilometres equals 20 Passenger kilometres.

Injuries, Fatalities, Property Damage -- provide local definitions, specifically, what "threshold" is used to define an injury? "Others" injured include pedestrians and automobile occupants.

MAIN SALES OUTLETS OF OECD PUBLICATIONS
PRINCIPAUX POINTS DE VENTE DES PUBLICATIONS DE L'OCDE

ARGENTINA – ARGENTINE
Carlos Hirsch S.R.L.
Galería Güemes, Florida 165, 4° Piso
1333 Buenos Aires   Tel. (1) 331.1787 y 331.2391
                    Telefax: (1) 331.1787

AUSTRALIA – AUSTRALIE
D.A. Information Services
648 Whitehorse Road, P.O.B 163
Mitcham, Victoria 3132   Tel. (03) 873.4411
                         Telefax: (03) 873.5679

AUSTRIA – AUTRICHE
Gerold & Co.
Graben 31
Wien I   Tel. (0222) 533.50.14

BELGIUM – BELGIQUE
Jean De Lannoy
Avenue du Roi 202
B-1060 Bruxelles   Tel. (02) 538.51.69/538.08.41
                   Telefax: (02) 538.08.41

CANADA
Renouf Publishing Company Ltd.
1294 Algoma Road
Ottawa, ON K1B 3W8   Tel. (613) 741.4333
                     Telefax: (613) 741.5439
Stores:
61 Sparks Street
Ottawa, ON K1P 5R1   Tel. (613) 238.8985
211 Yonge Street
Toronto, ON M5B 1M4   Tel. (416) 363.3171
                      Telefax: (416)363.59.63

Les Éditions La Liberté Inc.
3020 Chemin Sainte-Foy
Sainte-Foy, PQ G1X 3V6   Tel. (418) 658.3763
                         Telefax: (418) 658.3763

Federal Publications Inc.
165 University Avenue, Suite 701
Toronto, ON M5H 3B8   Tel. (416) 860.1611
                      Telefax: (416) 860.1608

Les Publications Fédérales
1185 Université
Montréal, QC H3B 3A7   Tel. (514) 954.1633
                       Telefax : (514) 954.1635

CHINA – CHINE
China National Publications Import
Export Corporation (CNPIEC)
16 Gongti E. Road, Chaoyang District
P.O. Box 88 or 50
Beijing 100704 PR   Tel. (01) 506.6688
                    Telefax: (01) 506.3101

DENMARK – DANEMARK
Munksgaard Book and Subscription Service
35, Nørre Søgade, P.O. Box 2148
DK-1016 København K   Tel. (33) 12.85.70
                      Telefax: (33) 12.93.87

FINLAND – FINLANDE
Akateeminen Kirjakauppa
Keskuskatu 1, P.O. Box 128
00100 Helsinki
Subscription Services/Agence d'abonnements :
P.O. Box 23
00371 Helsinki   Tel. (358 0) 12141
                 Telefax: (358 0) 121.4450

FRANCE
OECD/OCDE
Mail Orders/Commandes par correspondance:
2, rue André-Pascal
75775 Paris Cedex 16   Tel. (33-1) 45.24.82.00
                       Telefax: (33-1) 49.10.42.76
                       Telex: 640048 OCDE

OECD Bookshop/Librairie de l'OCDE :
33, rue Octave-Feuillet
75016 Paris   Tel. (33-1) 45.24.81.67
                            (33-1) 45.24.81.81

Documentation Française
29, quai Voltaire
75007 Paris   Tel. 40.15.70.00

Gibert Jeune (Droit-Économie)
6, place Saint-Michel
75006 Paris   Tel. 43.25.91.19

Librairie du Commerce International
10, avenue d'Iéna
75016 Paris   Tel. 40.73.34.60

Librairie Dunod
Université Paris-Dauphine
Place du Maréchal de Lattre de Tassigny
75016 Paris   Tel. (1) 44.05.40.13

Librairie Lavoisier
11, rue Lavoisier
75008 Paris   Tel. 42.65.39.95

Librairie L.G.D.J. - Montchrestien
20, rue Soufflot
75005 Paris   Tel. 46.33.89.85

Librairie des Sciences Politiques
30, rue Saint-Guillaume
75007 Paris   Tel. 45.48.36.02

P.U.F.
49, boulevard Saint-Michel
75005 Paris   Tel. 43.25.83.40

Librairie de l'Université
12a, rue Nazareth
13100 Aix-en-Provence   Tel. (16) 42.26.18.08

Documentation Française
165, rue Garibaldi
69003 Lyon   Tel. (16) 78.63.32.23

Librairie Decitre
29, place Bellecour
69002 Lyon   Tel. (16) 72.40.54.54

GERMANY – ALLEMAGNE
OECD Publications and Information Centre
August-Bebel-Allee 6
D-53175 Bonn   Tel. (0228) 959.120
                       Telefax: (0228) 959.12.17

GREECE – GRÈCE
Librairie Kauffmann
Mavrokordatou 9
106 78 Athens   Tel. (01) 32.55.321
                       Telefax: (01) 36.33.967

HONG-KONG
Swindon Book Co. Ltd.
13–15 Lock Road
Kowloon, Hong Kong   Tel. 366.80.31
                       Telefax: 739.49.75

HUNGARY – HONGRIE
Euro Info Service
Margitsziget, Európa Ház
1138 Budapest   Tel. (1) 111.62.16
                       Telefax : (1) 111.60.61

ICELAND – ISLANDE
Mál Mog Menning
Laugavegi 18, Pósthólf 392
121 Reykjavik   Tel. 162.35.23

INDIA – INDE
Oxford Book and Stationery Co.
Scindia House
New Delhi 110001   Tel.(11) 331.5896/5308
                       Telefax: (11) 332.5993
17 Park Street
Calcutta 700016   Tel. 240832

INDONESIA – INDONÉSIE
Pdii-Lipi
P.O. Box 269/JKSMG/88
Jakarta 12790   Tel. 583467
                       Telex: 62 875

ISRAEL
Praedicta
5 Shatner Street
P.O. Box 34030
Jerusalem 91430   Tel. (2) 52.84.90/1/2
                       Telefax: (2) 52.84.93

R.O.Y.
P.O. Box 13056
Tel Aviv 61130   Tél. (3) 49.61.08
                       Telefax (3) 544.60.39

ITALY – ITALIE
Libreria Commissionaria Sansoni
Via Duca di Calabria 1/1
50125 Firenze   Tel. (055) 64.54.15
                       Telefax: (055) 64.12.57

Via Bartolini 29
20155 Milano   Tel. (02) 36.50.83

Editrice e Libreria Herder
Piazza Montecitorio 120
00186 Roma   Tel. 679.46.28
                       Telefax: 678.47.51

Libreria Hoepli
Via Hoepli 5
20121 Milano   Tel. (02) 86.54.46
                       Telefax: (02) 805.28.86

Libreria Scientifica
Dott. Lucio de Biasio 'Aeiou'
Via Coronelli, 6
20146 Milano   Tel. (02) 48.95.45.52
                       Telefax: (02) 48.95.45.48

JAPAN – JAPON
OECD Publications and Information Centre
Landic Akasaka Building
2-3-4 Akasaka, Minato-ku
Tokyo 107   Tel. (81.3) 3586.2016
                       Telefax: (81.3) 3584.7929

KOREA – CORÉE
Kyobo Book Centre Co. Ltd.
P.O. Box 1658, Kwang Hwa Moon
Seoul   Tel. 730.78.91
                       Telefax: 735.00.30

MALAYSIA – MALAISIE
Co-operative Bookshop Ltd.
University of Malaya
P.O. Box 1127, Jalan Pantai Baru
59700 Kuala Lumpur
Malaysia   Tel. 756.5000/756.5425
                       Telefax: 757.3661

MEXICO – MEXIQUE
Revistas y Periodicos Internacionales S.A. de C.V.
Florencia 57 - 1004
Mexico, D.F. 06600   Tel. 207.81.00
                       Telefax : 208.39.79

NETHERLANDS – PAYS-BAS
SDU Uitgeverij Plantijnstraat
Externe Fondsen
Postbus 20014
2500 EA's-Gravenhage   Tel. (070) 37.89.880
Voor bestellingen: Telefax: (070) 34.75.778

**NEW ZEALAND
NOUVELLE-ZÉLANDE**
Legislation Services
P.O. Box 12418
Thorndon, Wellington   Tel. (04) 496.5652
                       Telefax: (04) 496.5698

OECD PUBLICATIONS, 2 rue André-Pascal, 75775 PARIS CEDEX 16
PRINTED IN FRANCE
(75 94 12 1) ISBN 92-821-1197-2 - No. 47589 1994